HEAR US, EMMANUEL

ANOTHER CALL FOR RACIAL
RECONCILIATION, REPRESENTATION, AND
UNITY IN THE CHURCH

GENERAL EDITOR: DOUG SERVEN

For the Church

For the Presbyterian Church in America

For all those who have gone before us
For those who have eyes to see
For those who have not yet awakened, may they
For those who lend their voices
For those who have not yet spoken up, may they
For those who hear
For those who have not yet heard, may they
For our children and grandchildren
For our neighbors

May they inhabit a different church and world,
filled with more shalom and flourishing in all ways until
you return, Jesus, a day we long for

Love, patience, courage, wisdom, resolve, compassion, humility,
justice, mercy, truth, dignity, respect, liberty, hope

May these qualities transform us and by their fruit, may you be glorified,
God the Father, God the Son, God the Holy Spirit

May your Kingdom Come, Lord
May your will be done on earth as it is in heaven

Hear our prayers, cries, confession, grief, and longings,
O Emmanuel, God With Us

ALSO BY WHITE BLACKBIRD BOOKS

Follow whiteblackbirdbooks.pub for titles and releases.

IN PRAISE OF HEAR US, EMMANUEL

Ecclesia semper reformanda est is a Latin phrase that means the church must always be reformed. *Hear Us, Emmanuel,* just like *Heal Us, Emmanuel,* gracefully leads the church to always be reforming. The contributing voices in these pages will challenge and bless you. Listen to their voices. Learn from their voices. Lament with their voices. Love their voices.

Alexander Shipman
Pastor, The Village Church
Huntsville, Alabama
Director, African American Presbyterian Fellowship, African American Ministries (PCA)

Heal us, Emmanuel is one of the evidences I can point those to who ask me, "How can a black man remain in a white denomination like the PCA?" Its existence and complimenting endorsements alone speak volumes to the progress being made by our denomination. While our past is stained by the sins of *our* spiritual forefathers, our future is full of hope as long as we remain faithful to the Gospel and live out its implications, which is where this book directs us

Phillip Holmes
Vice President for Institutional Communications
Reformed Theological Seminary
Jackson, Mississippi

In our current cultural moment, sensitivities are high and wounds are fresh around the subject of race. Now more than ever, I am personally convinced that the only solution to our woes is a brown-skinned, Aramaic-speaking, Middle Eastern refugee who was born poor. Jesus Christ, who affectionately referred to us as "the ends of the earth," has marked us for welcome into his blood-bought family of faith. Having received such mercy and kindness, Christians of all people must lead the way in doing justly, loving mercy, and walking humbly in the multi-ethnic space. The many credible voices in *Hear Us, Emmanuel* (a sequel to the equally impactful *Heal Us, Emmanuel*) serve as a practical guide in this endeavor. Please read this book. Even more, please start doing everything in your power to live it.

Scott Sauls
Senior Pastor, Christ Presbyterian Church
Nashville, Tennessee
Author, *A Gentle Answer, Irresistible Faith*

Hear Us, Emmanuel is a beautiful tapestry of thoughts and perspectives that weave together authentic stories, deep Biblical reflection, and a challenge to live in a manner worthy of the calling we have in Jesus Christ. This book is an invitation to listen, lament, repent, and reflect on a way forward... a way to a more beautiful picture of the family of God here on earth as it is in heaven. I'm so grateful to be a part of an expression of the body of Christ, the PCA, that feels deeply, reflects Scripturally, and commits unwaveringly toward racial reconciliation to the glory of God!

Lloyd Kim
Coordinator, Mission to the World
Atlanta, Georgia

C. H. Spurgeon once said: "We need to be daily converted from some sin or other, which, perhaps, we have scarcely known to be sin." Ah, that's one challenge with racism isn't it? If we judge ourselves to be free of animus or contempt towards people of a different color, our hands and hearts are clean, right? Some of us are certain that it is not a sin of ours, and yet it is, but we are blind to it. One thing we can do is listen. And there are hard stories from good friends here to listen to, and learn from. And there's hope here too. Just listen to the hope in Randy Nabors' foreword and in the testimonies of sisters and brothers throughout the book. Just listen. Then pray: Hear us, Emmanuel. Lord, help us. Lord, heal us.

Ligon Duncan
Chancellor and CEO, Reformed Theological Seminary
Jackson, Mississippi

Listening to other voices tell us about their experiences in the church is a vital process to learn and grow as a church family. I don't know what it is like to exist as another person unless I pay attention to them. Honoring the words of others even when we disagree is a work of grace and empathy that enables us to love our neighbors and our enemies as Jesus commands. This book is an excellent opportunity to do so if we have the courage to try.

Brittany Smith
Campus Staff, RUF, University of Arizona
Tucson, Arizona
General Editor, *Co-Laborers Co-Heirs: A Family Conversation*

The strength of the first three chapters is strikingly forceful and unmatched by any book in this genre. These, combined with the eloquent chapter "Can a Man Love God and Hate His Neighbor," are worth buying this book for yourself and a few friends. This book demands that we hear one another and then love another.

Steven Gilchrist
Family Ministry Director, Renovation Church
Atlanta, Georgia

The adage from St. Augustine's conversion to "take up and read" applies to *Hear Us, Emmanuel*. Each page is uniquely sharpened by the history and experience of brothers and sisters in Christ to carve away the church's hardness of heart. The question remains for the church if we can endure the proverbial paper cuts on our path "to repent, to lament, and to listen."

Joshua Torrey
Computer Chip Designer/Engineer
Austin, Texas

I was honored to be included in the first *Heal Us Emmanuel* book, and I learned so much from my fellow contributors. But I still have a lot to learn, so I'm excited for this second volume. I love the wide variety of essays and stories and can't wait to dig in.

Kevin Twit
RUF Campus Minister, Belmont University
Nashville, Tennessee

My great concern is that we might once again fail our brothers and sisters who desire to pursue the biblical vision of a multi-racial, multi-cultural church. *Hear Us, Emmanuel* assembles a wonderful group of writers, thinkers, dreamers, and hopers who call on our denomination to "hear us" and, above all, to hear the Spirit's voice calling for racial justice and faithfulness. Mixing together personal reflection, theological exploration, and pastoral direction, *Hear Us, Emmanuel* brings us back to issues of supreme importance—whether we will be one new humanity in Christ or not. May God give us ears to hear!

Sean Michael Lucas
Pastor, Independent Presbyterian Church
Memphis, Tennessee
Chancellor's Professor of Church History, Reformed Theological Seminary
Author, *For a Continuing Church*

It feels surreal to hold a book like this. Can the PCA really be saying these things? It almost feels too good to be true! But that's the power of this book. *Hear Us, Emmanuel* tells story after story (with multiple voices!). It sings a chorus of lament and hope for a denomination that has struggled in its complicity in racism. The next generation needs this book as a reminder of where we can go. I'm grateful to the contributors and the stalwarts who have led the way for the rest of us.

Slim Thompson
Pastor, Mosaic Waco
Waco, Texas

The first volume of *Heal Us, Emmanuel* made an indelible mark on my life and ministry. This second volume carries the theme into new territory and continues to make its impact upon me. With insight and grace, the authors highlight opportunities for the church to grow in the often uncomfortable areas of race and identity. I wish both volumes had been available to me earlier in life as they would have undoubtedly shaped my identity and understanding of race for the better.

Jeremy Fair
Pastor, Christ Presbyterian Church
Tulsa, Oklahoma

I was profoundly blessed by the thoughtful, heart-felt experiences shared in *Heal Us, Emmanuel*. Once again, as I read *Hear Us, Emmanuel*, I experience both the pride that our denomination is continuing this dialogue, and the sorrow that the conversation must be had commingled with the lament that it has taken us so long. I'm am so thankful for each of these brave souls leading us in our resolve to continue repenting, conversing, and rectifying these realities that are so contrary to the heart of God. This is a must read for all Christians!

Sarah Viggiano Wright
Author, *A Living Hope: A Study of 1 Peter*
San Antonio, Texas

It is very important to decry injustice in one's culture, but it is quite another to ask God to remove its roots from one's own heart and to make us vessels of real change in our society as he changes us as well. *Heal Us Immanuel* is a volume that succeeds in opening eyes, hearts, and minds to that needed transformation. Its sequel, *Hear, Us Immanuel*, summons us to engage in ways that transform the Church from spectator to prophetic voice and center for healing mercy. The average Christian in the world today looks nothing like a White North American middle-class Protestant. No, she is dark-skinned or Asian, poor, frequently persecuted, and bears a striking resemblance to the man of sorrows we call Savior. She can teach us much, and one of those lessons is how very much we need one another here and now. This book shows us how to embrace that lesson. I hope we will heed its call.

David Cassidy
Pastor, Christ Community Church
Franklin, Tennessee
Author, *Indispensable: The Basics of Christian Belief*

As an Asian American who grew up believing and embracing the Model Minority Myth, I am realizing that I have so much to repent of and how much I need the Word of God to correct and reshape my thinking about race and racism. I am so grateful for this timely and necessary resource especially for the new chapters that directly address the Model Minority Myth. I long to see more Asian Americans educate themselves on racism and racial injustice and then to work for racial justice, and this resource will help us to do that.

Owen Lee
Pastor, Christ Central Presbyterian Church
Centreville, Virginia

Reconciliation is a long narrow road of healing through many mountainous obstacles. Tunneling through skin color and the rocks of cultural differences are huge difficulties often avoided but must be overcome if we ever expect to build the highway to heaven. This book calls us to take action with a righteous indignation and anger to stop those who are destroying souls that God created and saves regardless of their skin color. We are all part of the human race God loves, and we must adopt God's way—loving God above all and our neighbors as ourselves. This is a fabulous compilation of real-life stories exposing the devastating consequences of not being caring Christian's in action.

Arn Quakkelaar
Author, *Doing God's Work: With Brothers and Sisters in Christ Serving in Milwaukee*
Milwaukee, Wisconsin

The American Church so desperately needs this book. Reading the stories in *Hear Us, Emmanuel* further purifies us by removing the scales from our eyes so that we might better see reality and then be transformed. If we sit with these stories, and allow God to do a great work in us through them, then we will not so blindly submit to, or propagate, white supremacy. Instead, we will fight against it and the racism so many have called America's original sin. It is what we as the Church must do. Read it carefully, contemplate the contents, repent, and prepare for change. I am so deeply grateful for it!

Marlena Graves
Author, *The Way Up Is Down: Finding Yourself by Forgetting Yourself*

"Tell me your story" is a beautiful invitation to hear and a pastorally-loving one to utter. Herein are stories from twenty brothers and ten sisters in Christ, each unlike mine. I was raised in the suburban Northeast, and my public high school had over 3,000 students, only one of which was Black. I never heard my parents utter a racial slur, and my siblings and I would have been soundly disciplined if any of the six of us ever did. I didn't have the experiences that many describe in this book, but having been in the PCA now for the last thirty-eight years, I'm very glad to be able to read these.

Howie Donahoe
Elder, Redeemer Church
Moderator, 47th PCA General Assembly
Redmond, Washington

Hear Us, Emmanuel reminds us that the church is never about "me" but about "we." We are enlightened to make sense of our sufferings in hearing the stories of others. We are blessed by listening to lived experience, theological conviction, and wise orthopraxy of those who for far too long have been unheard. We grow in empathy as we hear how those within the church have often done the greatest harm. Sharing these stories comes with a great cost, a cost that the authors of *Hear Us, Emmanuel* have paid with their lives because of their love for Christ and His Church. The question before us as we read must be "Do we hear them?"

Jonathan Song
Assistant Pastor, Redeemer Presbyterian Church
Charleston, South Carolina

The more I read and the more I am learning to hear and to recognize the voices on these pages something of the mystery hidden from ages past is being worked out in me. Thank you everyone for speaking and, in some cases, for speaking again. I didn't know. I didn't see. I couldn't hear. I still don't at significant points. Thank you for helping me. Even this said, there would seem to be no arrival in these days of faith, only the task of learning to love. By grace, learning to love is part of the destination and part of the plan. May we arrive at the place we started with new friends and beauties, learning to hear Emmanuel's voice. Make us one Emmanuel, even as you are one. Hear us, we pray.

Brad A. Anderson
Pastor, Valley Springs Presbyterian Church
Roseville, California

Warm, thoughtful, and engaging, Al LaCour's remembrances of growing up in the Jim Crow south during the 1960s as a self-styled "Mississippi Progressive" sheds instructive light on how the state that has been my home for the last two decades has struggled to appropriate the principles of the Kingdom in daily life. Jesus was offensive to both conservative and liberal and called both to repentance and faith. Seeing the '60s through one man's journey to Christ is both enriching and encouraging to "Lift High The Cross" for the next generation.

Les Newsom
Pastor, Christ Presbyterian Church
Oxford, Mississippi

HEAR US HYMN

BY REV. MARK PREUS

Tune: Nun Bitten Wir

Hear us, O Lord, in mercy when we pray,
For we know not how or what to say;
Breathe through us the words which come down from heaven—
Make us ask and it shall be given!
Hear us, O Lord!

How can we call on You unless we've heard
From Your lips the mercy of Your Word?
So in faith which You only are supplying
We pray, "Abba!" on You relying.
Hear us, O Lord.

As now You plead at God the Father's right,
But are hidden from our mortal sight,
Give to us Your Spirit when doubts allure us,
That God loves to hear us assure us.
Hear us, O Lord.

Elijah prayed, and rain refused to fall;
Seven times God heard His servant call.
Then from out the sea came a heavy shower–

So we pray!—now show us Your power.
Hear us, O Lord.

Once when the armies hemmed Jerusalem,
Hezekiah prayed, and God helped them;
As He sent His angel to give salvation,
So save us from every temptation.
Hear us, O Lord.

Teach us to pray according to Your will,
And until Your promise You fulfill
Help us to be patient, in hope still waiting
With Your Spirit still advocating!
Hear us, O Lord.

Soon, soon the answer to our greatest prayer
In the light of heaven shall appear,
And we will with You in Your glory basking
See how You answered all our asking.
Hear us, O Lord

A NOTE ABOUT LANGUAGE

The editors of this book would like the reader to know:

We have chosen to capitalize the words Black and White when they refer to racial distinction rather than colors in a palette. Our reasoning comes from the capitalization of other distinctions like Asian or African American. These are proper nouns, and it follows that black and white are not proper nouns. However, these terms have become racial designations, and many of our authors prefer Black instead of African American. Dr. Carl Ellis wrote the forward in our first volume, *Heal Us Emmanuel*. During the editing phase, he convinced us that we should capitalize Black and White for these reasons. However, other works do not follow this convention. When works are quoted and cited, we have left their capitalization preference intact.

We have included a chapter that discusses one of Flannery O'Connor's essays. O'Connor wrote in the South in the 1950s. Her original work uses the N word. The chapter in our book looks at this work and makes an important point about it. If you look up her essay, you will find the offensive word printed. We have replaced it with n----- in our book.

When a local church is mentioned or discussed in this volume, the word is in lowercase. When the broader universal Church is meant, we have capitalized it.

CONTENTS

CONFESSION AND RECONCILIATION
ARE NECESSARY FOR OBEDIENCE

A WAY FORWARD

FOREWORD

RANDY NABORS

The dynamic is changing.

It is a wonderful, far-too-long-in-coming, confusing, exciting, a bit threatening, and yet promising change. I am speaking of the progress within the Presbyterian Church in America (PCA, the denomination I serve in) and the broader Christian church coming to grips with racism, racial hegemony, and ethnic avenues of power in evangelical institutions and life. The chapters in this volume give various personal views of and testimonies to this struggle.

There will always be those who dismiss the idea of progress, just as there will always be those who oppose that same progress. In the meantime, I hope the rest of us can give glory to God for his work of grace among us, for the reality of sincere repentance, for the confession of past wrongs, for the admission of present obstacles, and for the friendships, fellowship, and common efforts toward reconciliation.

We are not in heaven or on the new earth yet. We are not in the new city where the tree of life has leaves for the healing of the nations. This means the fight for truth and justice, against injustice and oppression, and for healing from the deep wounds of history and lingering present injustice must be recognized as legitimate and necessary.

I am sure there will be some who think what has been accomplished is quite enough, and we should stop speaking of these things.

At the same time, the more we venture into the specifics of racial and ethnic inclusion, and the expansion into the life and leadership of the church of those disciples of Christ who are people of color, the more opportunities for conflict, frustration, and sin will arise. Though we are the Church, we are sinners.

I remember when you didn't even need a full hand to count the African American pastors and leaders in the PCA. Today I meet African Americans that I had no idea were in the denomination, and it's wonderful. I look around and I see White pastors almost desperate to identify or make friends with various African American pastors.

These White pastors are eager and vigorous to make sure their names and public postures can be identified as "friend-to-a-Black-pastor." There is a temptation to ask these White pastors, "Where have you been?" But it is good to realize that the denomination has more champions for racial justice and reconciling love than it has ever had. Many of these White pastors are from a younger generation, and I am thankful for them. This is also true of younger or second generation Korean pastors. They are becoming strong advocates for a biblical life that has little patience for personal or institutional racism and ignorance.

Of course, we will continue to face challenges. There will continue to be those who are racist in their view of people of color. Some will never acknowledge this as wrong, or repent of it until they face the judgment. As when dealing with any sin in the lives of sinners who claim Christ, we must pastor folks as we find them. We must love the people in our churches even in those moments when sin must be confronted. We do so by preaching the Gospel which calls for repentance, faith, and a holy life empowered by grace.

Our position on sin has to be consistent, but that has always been hard for us. Our culture often chooses some sins as acceptable to struggle with but others we will not tolerate. Some of our churches are more understanding of same sex attraction than they are of racism. Some of our churches have allowed racism both in acts of commission and omission. Some are more incensed by abortion than they have ever been by racism. If you ask me my stand on any sin, I hope I'm consistent enough to say, "I'm against it!" I also hope I can consistently say God forgives and loves sinners.

As he does, so must we. In other words, if Jesus died for us while we were still sinners, and if God loved the world while it was unbelieving, then we too must love our enemies even while they remain enemies. I have known enemies of racial justice in the Church. I know that there were those in the Church who hated my interracial marriage.

When I was ordained, I intended to combat that racial justice sin —confront it, shame it, and preach against this hypocrisy. I would not let it intimidate me or keep me from preaching the Gospel. I would join in to help open the gates for more people of color to come to Jesus and invade this stereotypically Southern denomination.

I needed allies. I needed experience. And I needed to see God's work, because the whole counsel of God is for everybody, and Jesus has a lot of the elect among people of color.

At the same time, I know all too well I am no better than anyone else in the PCA. I suppose if there is a pecking order in heaven, I will be close to the bottom. Because of that I am willing to live out my ministry among those who might not always be consistent or obedient to the doctrine of love. I respect those who have labored in other denominations. I understand my friends who have left the PCA to work somewhere else. My doctrine of love is tested every day. I work on consistency and obedience in my own life, along with repentance.

We are moving from having almost no people of color to having some. We are moving from hardly hearing, and mostly ignoring, voices for change, to having some voices that sound like trumpets in our denomination. We are moving from a Western European and American Presbyterian denomination that refuses to speak about social sin, to one that demonstrates a prophetic call for inclusionary justice.

The people of color who come into our denomination are not all the same, and they will not all have the same opinions about race, ethnicity, culture, or participation. Some will crave an ethnic experience of worship and not a cross-cultural one. Some will give a missional and evangelistic apologetic for ethnic, linguistic, or cultural expressions of the church. Some people of color will find it frustrating to wait for elevation to places of leadership in the denomination. They will want to create alternative spaces and places so their voices, names, and writings can be respected. Some of them will not realize many White pastors (usually GenXers and Millennials who are still waiting for the Boomers to step aside) feel the same frustration.

It is important for older pastors to open the doors of opportunity for younger ones of all colors. As the denomination grows older it must intentionally recruit and champion—give scholarships, internships, pastoral and ministry positions—rising young leaders. At the same time, every young pastor needs to realize none of us are entitled. It will be healthier for them to think that none of us is owed anything, and we each must prove our own ministry, by the grace of God. There has been too much envy, jealousy, and competition among ambitious preachers. It is distasteful in any color. Humility and servanthood are profoundly attractive.

The rhetoric we use to discuss these issues will not simply be right or wrong. Some will be winsome, while others will be offensive, off-putting, and divisive. Some will attempt to make peace, and some will attempt to make peace without making justice. Some will attempt to make a point about justice, without making friends. Some will speak for the applause of friends and supporters, while others will attempt to build bridges.

I hope we can all pursue learning from each other and our various cultures with humility so that we can give a practical and physical testimony of love. None of us should pretend this will be easy, and none of us should be easily discouraged when things don't change as fast as we would like.

So, let me say it as Scripture does: *"And let us not be weary in well doing: for in due season we shall reap, if we faint not"* (Gal. 6:9, KJV). And as the hymn writer Albert A. Goodson put it, "We've come this far by faith, leaning on the Lord." We need to continue to do that in this quest for racial inclusion in the Presbyterian Church in America and for the Gospel witness of meaningful reconciliation.

As James Weldon Johnson put it in "Lift Every Voice and Sing," this has been a pilgrimage, a journey, and it's not over yet. It is hard for me to sing this second verse without weeping. I think of the long history of what Black folk have been through, of injustice, slavery, and racism in this country, and yet of the valiant march toward righteousness. Oh Lord, let us keep marching, together!

> Stony the road we trod,
> Bitter the chastening rod,
> Felt in the days when hope unborn had died;
> Yet with a steady beat,
> Have not our weary feet,
> Come to the place for which our fathers sighed?

We have come over a way that with tears has been watered,
We have come, treading our path through the blood of the slaughtered,
Out from the gloomy past,
Till now we stand at last
Where the white gleam of our bright star is cast

.

INTRODUCTION

DOUG SERVEN

You're holding the second volume of a work by members and pastors in the Presbyterian Church in America (PCA). To make it confusing, the first one was named *Heal Us, Emmanuel,* but this edition is completely different: *Hear Us, Emmanuel.*

Heal Us came about as an attempt to unify our voices to speak up for biblically based, Gospel-focused racial reconciliation. We debated a resolution at our denomination's General Assembly in 2015, and that was passed in 2016.

In that intervening year, we complied chapters by PCA pastors and elders to form *Heal Us, Emmanuel,* which was published before our denominational General Assembly in spring of 2016. These called for listening, taught theology and history, and asked for next steps. We stand by that book. But we knew we needed more.

This book (*Hear Us* or as we call it HUE2) adds important new voices to the discussion. Thankfully, we have ten women represented in this volume, and we are far better for their contributions.

As a White Presbyterian pastor in Oklahoma, I (Doug) have been profoundly changed over the past years. As I've entered into this discussion, I've been shocked at how passionate some are against it. I've been called: liberal, progressive, a sell-out, a Marxist, a social justice warrior (which I suppose is a specific derogatory term), and more. I've been told I'm making things worse, not better. I've been asked to leave it alone, to stop bringing up race in discussions, meetings, and policies. I've been accused of trying to be culturally relevant instead of committing to the spirituality of the church.

Eh. It's not about me. It's about Lee and Wanda, Dominique, Shreka, Uganda, Kat, Ana, George, Naviir, and a host of others in our church. Friends. Dear ones, whom I need desperately. I can't understand Jesus without them.

It's about 33 kids in a third-grade class who won't pass their reading test, the one required to move on to fourth grade. There are 36 kids in the class. Three might pass. It's about calling the doctor and getting an appointment. It's about public transportation and sidewalks, soiled uniforms, healthy eating, and parents who are home to read to their kids. It's about meetings regarding policing.

It's about our pulpit swaps, our in-town, and inter-denominational friendships and partnerships.

It's about George Floyd, and all of the other who have gone before him.

That means it's all about Jesus. We're called to be his hands and feet. We're told that loving orphans, widows, and the poor is close to the heart of God. We know we're to love our neighbors as ourselves. We're called to repent and believe, to expect the Good News to change us and our world.

We planned for *Hear Us* to come out the month before our denomination's General Assembly, which was set to be held in Birmingham, Alabama for June 2020. Unless you live on Mars, you know what happened next. Everything was cancelled.

Although everyone had time, no one had any capacity to read, certainly not about a deep, emotional subject. We waited.

Racial violence can happen any moment, and we have had many incidents even in 2020 alone. When George Floyd was murdered on May 25, 2020, our country erupted in protest. Rightly so. Like many others, I have spent time in marches, protests, meetings with police, prayer, and panel-discussions with other pastors.

In the back of my mind, I was thinking about Barbara Jones' chapter, the first in this volume. She writes about being a girl who grew up to be a woman, one with black skin, and how she's made it in our denomination. I thought of how Ryan Zhang discusses how assimilation made him a bad Christian. Of Emily Hubbard, and how she is a White mom with brown kids. Of the conversations she has with her children about these issues.

I thought of how many times (since I worked on editing the book these past years) I've read Rob Wootton's chapter about growing up in the South. And his wife, Robin, writing about growing up Korean adopted by loving White parents. And how their marriage has been redemptive for them, and how God has called them to plant a church in Billings, Montana.

I thought of Becky Carlozzi's chapter as she shares how she grew up, was trained to think, and how God had been shaking her to a new, deeper, better reality. This chapter is similar in nature to Tim LeCroy's in the first book.

Sherrene DeLong shares her pain, but she also shares her joy when she writes about Micro-Hospitality. Irwyn and Alexander allowed us to use their sermons from their time as moderators for our General Assembly, and I am so proud to be able to call them friends. Maria Garriott raised her family in the inner city, and she has few if any regrets. Mark Dalbey used the rubric of a prayer song for his chapter.

Do we have something to say? You bet we do! We may not say it exactly as you'd like, but please listen. Our words are first of all to Jesus, and then they're to the pastors and members of our churches. Hear us. After that, they go out a world wondering if the church will speak up, stand up, and wake up. If we're honest, we don't have the greatest track record. Repentance is necessary for many of us.

With God's help and by his grace, the church can do this. The PCA can do this. Join hands with those who have gone before, those who are already at work, and lend your voice however late it is in coming (like mine).

AN INVITATION TO LISTEN

DOUBLE JEOPARDY

BARBARA D. JONES

Barbara Jones served four years as a missionary with the Evangelical Covenant Church on a church plant team and was an Associate Staff member with Cru for two years. She began serving at Mission to the World (MTW) in 1998, left to serve at World Relief in refugee resettlement for two years, and then returned to MTW in 2001. She has served on a missionary assessment team, directed a short-term ministry program, and currently serves as a Senior National Mobilization consultant to help MTW and the broader church in efforts toward unity and diversity in missions. Barbara is currently pursuing an MDiv. She loves the arts, discipleship, and writing. She is married to Ernest, and they have adult twin sons, Sebastian and Julian.

———

My elementary school teachers were the source of some of my fondest memories as a young girl. They—and then I—looked forward to celebrating Black History Month every winter. We hung up the same posters above the chalkboard year after year. The teachers pulled out the same chronicles and autobiographies for us to read and reflect on for writing book reports. They arranged school ceremonies celebrating the inventors, pioneers, and heroes of our past, but not our present.

We never tired of these celebrations. This patchwork array included African American poetry and songs depicting men and women of worth. They were imprinted on our minds not only for a solid month but, inevitably, throughout the entire year.

I remember vivid discussions around our dinner table about the various individuals highlighted during class sessions. These memorable moments informed my younger brothers and me that, despite our circumstances, we could one day be as brilliant as any of these men and women.

During February, this shortest month of the year, I was given permission to believe Black men and women were, and are, an integral part of our nation's fabric. Because of February's annual emphasis, I privately told myself that my image as a dark-skinned girl was not that bad after all. I pondered the idea that even though my reflection was not often viewed as one of beauty or worth back then (on television or in the novels that I read to escape), I—as a Black girl—indeed had great value.

Although as young students, we were taught that these inventions, discoveries, and firsts made Blacks great people, I often wondered why these champions were not celebrated *beyond* the confines of my community. I quickly realized our Black history had a common theme: the successes of these great men and women were often neither credited to them or esteemed as valuable until long after their deaths, if ever. I learned that in most cases the credit for their accomplishments not only were largely unacknowledged, but the praise often was accorded to a White person. Once I realized this all-too-frequent pattern of discrepancy, it challenged my ability to celebrate who I was as a person of color.

Nevertheless, I needed to know that I mattered as a Black girl. Therefore I chose to celebrate alongside others who, at the time, realized this was our only option.

As I grew older, I also chose to believe that the color of my skin would not prevent me from becoming a woman of worth. I imagined that my identity as a young Black woman would one day mean something other than what Hollywood depicted as the ideal image of beauty.

I worked hard to represent the opposite. I was not promiscuous. I was married before I had children. I worked hard. I aimed to avoid coming across as a stereotypical "angry Black woman."

I quickly learned how to assimilate into the majority-White culture so that I could gain entry into this world that didn't easily welcome me. I sought to let my voice as a Black woman fade into the fabric of White culture and rhetoric. I learned that my genuine role as a Black woman was to be reserved for the family dining room table, a place where I safely gathered with like-minded friends and family of color to swap stories of survival and celebrate as we lived together in authenticity, with the hope of a future where we would be seen as worthy image bearers of God (Gen. 1:27).

As a Black woman entering the workplace, I understood clearly that I had to work harder than the White woman next to me. In many respects, I carried on my back and shoulders all the Black women who had not gained access to the same open door as I had. With honor and timidity, I carried the torch and sought to represent Black women well. I worked effectively and efficiently in order to show my White colleagues that Black women were able to work harmoniously along-side them and without drama. And, for the first time in my life, my sense of worth began to "fade to White" just so that I would fit in.

I learned to speak differently, and I laughed quietly at jokes I did not understand or even appreciate. I dressed differently during week-days, and I even read books that didn't interest me. These books were important because they informed me about the subject, or people, to which I had been called: the majority-White culture.

Over a period of time I had unknowingly begun the journey of losing a sense of my identity in order to fit in, and thus, survive. After a while, I also realized nothing I did as a Black woman in my own strength would allow the majority culture to see me as an equal.

Nonetheless, I felt compelled to keep trying. It dawned on me that my proven experience and knowledge did not really matter. I began to recognize that surviving meant I must conform to the standards set by the majority culture. Otherwise, I'd be regarded as a lower-class person or perhaps even an outcast. So I made some compromises and conformed for survival's sake. I survived by seeking to accomplish certain milestones in a professional setting. I earned a title, moved to the suburbs, and bought the house with the white picket fence. I had earned my ticket out of the 'hood. I came to trust in my own ability to survive the system that would have shut me out if not for these accomplishments.

However, the "accomplishment-bubble" burst after ten years of working my way into the role of a university system director. A newly hired general manager informed me that I no longer fit in with the department's future direction. When I questioned him about that new direction, I was informed that, "A Black woman did not represent the brand." Therefore, I had a choice to either resign or be fired and be shut out of the industry.

Devastated, I began thinking how naïvely I had bought into the narrative that I mattered. I refused to resign because I somehow thought I had rights. I knew I had a clean record and allowed myself to believe that "they" could not get away with tossing me out unjustly. I also thought all my White colleagues would acknowledge the injustice and fight for me, but they did not.

I was wrongfully fired from my position, and I was heart-broken. And while this blow caused many negative repercussions, thankfully, it was part of what God used to call me to himself, and it prepared me for what was to come.

So at the age of twenty-seven, I initially became angry with God, but soon enough I surrendered to him. God helped me to realize that, despite racism, I was indeed his child, his beloved daughter. In time I would also come to realize I mattered to him because he created me in his image. However, I was new to this journey and didn't realize the route I'd need to take in order to fully own this truth.

Therefore, the Lord rid me of many things I had spent years accomplishing on my own. He humbled me and started me on a completely new trajectory, one orchestrated solely by him. In this new space, I began an adventure of believing my Christian family would be the counterculture to what had been missing in my non-Christian life and corporate world.

Eventually, I answered God's call to enter vocational Christian service with a renewed sense of being. I welcomed the privilege of serving on an inner-city church plant team as a missionary for four years. During my term, I was invited to lead and serve on a variety of boards. We spoke to the idea of our identity in Christ as we sought to grow in the areas of diversity and inclusion of women's voices.

I knew a select few of us were pioneers in a strange land, so I counted it a privilege to be one of the few people of color invited to the table. With different motives this time around, I poured myself into working and serving. While I faced many challenges, it was a sweet time of watching God provide for me in miraculous ways and always reminding me I was enough in him. Because of his leading, my identity as an African American female was enough for the people in my sphere of influence. My calling and journey, though filled with ups and downs, was a beautiful reminder that nothing is wasted.

This truth of God's sovereignty was confirmed after my four-year term ended, and I explored serving in another new ministry capacity. During this next season, I had hoped, even expected, my White brothers and sisters to welcome me not based on the color of my skin but because of Christ and the content of my visionary heart. Sadly, that turned out not to be the case.

When I applied for a particular role at the first Christian organization, it was not until I showed up for the interview that I got that "look" of surprise. It was an expression I knew all too well. They had not realized I was a Black woman. After awkwardly shuffling me around from person to person, I was politely informed I would not be a good fit. I had been through several telephone interviews with them that indicated just the opposite. Code-switching my voice during the phone interviews got me in the door, but my in-person image quickly caused them to dismiss me. I was devastated by this rebuff. It seemed like another familiar disappointment, but this time it was occurring in a Christian setting. Nonetheless, I persevered, continued my job search, and prayed every step of the way.

After several attempts to return to a ministry setting, I concluded my only option would be to accept an entry-level position. I quickly learned the invitation to this next phase in my life would become the place where God would not only confirm my call as a woman of color, but it would also be the place where my faith would be greatly challenged as both a woman and a person of color.

Immediately, in this new administrative assistant role, the woman I reported to found it necessary to state bluntly that it was my responsibility to serve her in the same way that a slave serves his or her master. This woman smiled in my face and was at ease reminding me that she was my boss, and that I needed to be thankful for the privilege of answering to her.

In shock, I prayerfully refused to become the angry Black woman who verbally expressed what I secretly felt in my heart. At first I tried to summon up sermons I'd heard in church that might help me address this scenario, but none came to mind. I then prayerfully restrained myself before eventually taking my concerns to HR. After going to HR and receiving no support or resolution, I prayerfully stepped out in faith and gave my two weeks' notice.

Miraculously, God then opened the door for me to serve at another Christian agency, one wherein I did find solace. This was a diverse community serving an ethnic mosaic of immigrants and refugees, and it was also a space where community and prayer were foundational to our work and ministry. As the Lord developed me, it seemed he would appropriately provide me with an ebb and flow of struggle and rest. I always welcomed the periods of rest with open arms, but I did not readily welcome the struggle. It always caught me off guard.

During those seasons of rest, the Lord reassured me in my calling to serve him. He also used this time to remind me that my joy had to be completely in him and not in the people to whom he had called me. Although these were sweet times of beautiful community, he also allowed a continuous tug at my heart, prompting me to trust him as he constantly called me back to a more difficult people and into a deeper journey of faith.

As I trekked through these places, I often reflected on that little girl who sat in the classroom dreaming of a future beyond where she was. I thought of my voyage into the various workplaces and roles in which the Lord had allowed me to develop. I saw more and more that it was in him that I lived, moved and had my being (Acts 17:28). I found rest in the fact that my accomplishments, challenges, and seasons of emotional and spiritual restoration had happened only because of him. And though my belief in what God said about me was constantly under attack, I slowly grew to accept that I was a Black woman of worth in God's eyes.

While I found no space in the church to help me navigate through these struggles, I came to realize my worthiness was not because of who I was, but because of who he is. The truth was that to be an image bearer, I would have to lose myself. And while I did not understand what it meant to have assimilated, or realize that I had developed a cultural IQ, I longed for identity and acceptance as a woman who just happened to be an African American.

I could see small glimpses of progress within the cocoon of my classrooms and community, but as soon as I stepped out into the real world, the reality of my Blackness reminded me of the place to which I had been relegated. It was oftentimes unspoken, but as a young girl, I quickly learned to hear the subtle ways I was exhorted to remain within the parameters set for me. I learned that to step outside of these boundaries was like violating the laws or rules of a slaveholder.

I experienced seasons of uncertainty, faithlessness, insecurities, and questions.

Why hasn't the church addressed these issues of identity with truth?

Why are White people so afraid of me (and people like me) reaching the potential God created us for?

Why must I continue to die to self?

Where are you, Lord?

Had not we, as people of color, yielded so much already?

These and many others were the questions I pondered, and I still wrestle with today.

My lifelong battle for self-worth as a person of color and as a woman did not begin with me. It began in the wombs of our fore-mothers and the hearts and minds of our forefathers. For those forced to give up their children to those who took possession of them, a message was imprinted upon us which sprouted within us a deep-seated feeling of worthlessness and insignificance. For Black men and women in America, the word "worth" has a tainted definition that planted a seed which continues to germinate to this day. Such destruction is apparent in the institutional racism and sexism that developed before and after slavery, much of which is still intrinsically in place. As we have seen of late, the message or idea that Black and Brown lives have little value—and that women are insignificant individuals or sex objects to be subjugated to a lesser role—runs rampant throughout our culture today.

In many respects, the abuse endured by our forefathers continues. Once it was a slave master creating dysfunction in families and individuals as a means of control. Now, the system is the slave master: the system takes what it wants, no matter who watches. It dismembers bodies and divides families, leaving no room for a man or woman of color to expect any more than what the master doles out.

The current system of American government suppresses the voices of Blacks and others, precluding their ability to stand up and fight for themselves and their families. Should they do so, their efforts can result in grave consequences. This system, or worldly master, views the efforts of African Americans and other minorities as malevolent and dangerous, thus devaluing the worth of both the people and their culture. It screams out that African Americans and others are not welcome in the majority culture and should, in other words, stay in their place.

If men and women of color are relegated to a space of silence, where do we as persons of color stand? How do we fit into the church or the body of Christ? Despite biblical truths, the intractable nature of racism and sexism continues to exert itself on our society.

While I desired to remain in the communities that provided me a time of restoration, those seasons always came to an end. And without knowing it, I would find myself back in the belly of a large smelly fish or a community of people who devalued the woman God made me to be. In this place, I often found myself wallowing in self-pity and self-hatred, and equating dying to self as an attempt to blend-in while moving farther away from my real self. I was silenced, did not stand up for myself, and "Yes sir, boss" was my demeanor. I became a faithful laborer, even though my successes and contributions were overlooked. Oftentimes, my journey was even more painful because I identified with my Black and White sisters who experienced the pain of being a woman in a denomination where we were relegated to an outer space and a lesser role. Moreover, as one of the only females of color in leadership, I experienced "double jeopardy" and what appeared to be my reward once again banished me to a lonely space that even my White colleagues could not understand or identify with.

While I expected to be accosted by the world, I was constantly caught off guard when I learned this same attitude was prevalent in the heart of the Christian community of which I was a part. Because I believed God called me to this community, I welcomed the idea of being a pioneer, and this gave me a renewed sense of hope. The idea of being one of the few pioneers in a denomination that did not fully represent people of color felt somewhat naïve, even arrogant, and some may see it as such. However, this entry could be likened to a lynching rather than pride for those called to serve in a place that rejects people either overtly, or covertly, because of gender and race. It was that way for me. In fact, each time I found myself insulted, offended, or hurt, I would not only wrestle with God in prayer, but I would also cry out to him in anger for calling me to work and serve among White Christians, a people who seemed so far away from the love that he spoke of in his Word. I would ask God, "Why, oh Lord, do they not see you in me?" Each time I cried out or professed my anger against the Whites who marginalized people who did not look or act like them, he would graciously beckon me to hold up the mirror to my face.

As the Lord allowed me to develop my role in this organization, I often wondered if I were just a token Black woman who had made it into the "big house." In fact, one of my African American female co-workers remarked to me that I did not really understand what the rest of them were going through because I was in a higher position than any other person of color in our organization. Painfully, she told me I no longer understood because it was as if I had made it into the "masta's" house.

I was heart-broken by that statement. But instead of seeking to understand the hurt she was experiencing, I lashed out because she was right. I had found myself watching to make sure other people of color did not embarrass us by being too Black or too Asian or too Latino. Once again, I was angry with God because not only could I not be authentic and transparent as a Black woman, but I was also afraid the others would tear down the tower of respect I thought I was building for my people. Little did I know the burden I carried was not mine to carry, but my White colleagues had bred in me the innate belief that it was. They would say things like, "Oh, but you are so articulate," or "You're different," and my favorite is "Sooo, how did *you* get here (in this role)?"

While serving with this organization, I was taught to be silent during worship. It was impressed upon me that it wasn't acceptable to lift my hands as an act of praise to God. This was their way of saying my indigenous ways of worship weren't any more valid than my gender and race.

Over a period of time, I found myself no longer wearing the bright colors which looked great on my skin. Why? Because of the subtle, but demeaning comments made by my White brothers and sisters in Christ. I stopped allowing my natural hair to show because I despised being asked repeatedly if it was okay to touch my hair, which for me was a violation of my personal space. I felt like I was some type of spectacle. I have imagined my ancestors on the slave block being viewed from head to toe: teeth check, muscle check, skin check, feet check, hair check, all of which screamed questions of worth.

On many occasions, the overt and covert racist experiences caused me to cry on my way to and from my workplace, knowing that I hated it, but was called to it.

One day in particular stands out in my memory. While assessing missionaries as part of a team (myself and two White, male coworkers), I was questioned as if my job were on the line. I quickly realized that the older man was attempting to validate, justify, or measure my worth. I, therefore, responded to his questions by sharing a bit of my background and ministry experience in assessing and training missionaries. And it was at this point that this White "gentleman" tilted his head in order to view my name tag and then proceeded to inform me that his forefathers were my slave masters.

All this could be determined by looking at my name badge?! Where did this come from? Why was I always surprised at the depths to which people would stoop in an effort to exert power and authority over another race or person?

While serving in this capacity, I had not expected to be told over and over again, "I don't see color" or "Maybe it's time to move on." I didn't anticipate my White teammates and denominational leaders would treat me as if I were invisible in almost every meeting. As a woman of color, I didn't expect to be told the colors I wore were too "this or that" or my earrings were too big. I didn't expect to ache so much from the pain of rejection and violation in a Christian environment. As a woman of color, I didn't expect to grieve the lack of Black, Asian, or Latino males in leadership. However, for a time, grief seemed to be the ministry God had called me to.

It seemed things had changed. God no longer provided the sweet moments I had come to expect when I reached a breaking point. Now these moments were confined to individual interactions with a select few within the belly of the fish. I desired, like Jonah, to be rescued from this place, but God forced me to remain, wrestle, and grow. I developed the skill of holding up a mirror to see both who God says I am, and also the sins growing like weeds in my heart and mind (such as sins of intolerance and accusation toward God and man). This place of employment became a place of judgment and the place where I learned to find my rest in Christ alone.

When I found myself ready to be delivered, the Lord graciously gave me a glimpse of his Spirit at work. When I became bitter and ran away from the circumstances, God always drew me back in order to finish the work he had begun in me, that of pruning my broken heart. On occasion, he would point out idolatry in my desire and need to be seen as a Black woman who was worthy enough. And when I failed to see the beauty of my position in life and was angry with God for allowing it, he would sustain me and draw me to his bosom.

Throughout the years, God used my circumstances to help me realize that my identity in Christ, as well as the position he had allowed me to live in, was all a part of how God brings glory to himself. He used the same circumstances to help rid me of myself.

While there were many painful experiences I did not expect, I also did not expect to have a dear White brother ask me to forgive him for the many years he didn't take a stand against the racism which had been occurring in his church and family long before I knew him. I didn't expect another brother to come to me after three years to apologize for his racist slurs against me. In addition, I welcomed those who took the time to tell me the code language that the majority-Christian culture would use in my presence to demean me unknowingly. I became more appreciative of the White voices who thanked me for remaining in the belly of the fish. They empathized with my pain, and they knew they needed me there as their sister in Christ.

Some people say racism does not exist. They say we've made progress and we should move on. But have we really made progress? It saddens me how much effort I've had to put in to proving my legitimacy in a Christian culture that has systematically spurned me and others like me.

I serve in a denomination where I rarely see a man of color in a leadership role (though that has improved). I serve in a community of believers where people of color aren't always invited to the table. I minister alongside people who proudly profess they do not see color. I vacillate between trusting God and crying out to God because I experience some form of racism almost every day of my life. And every day I am given that opportunity to look in the mirror. And each time I come face to face with the truth that God is in control, and he will deal with sin, including mine. So where does this leave me? From racist slavery comments to my role as a leader being disregarded, I have come to learn I have a right to feel embittered. But daily I choose to place my painful experiences in a reservoir of forgiveness as the Lord does for me.

The acceptance of biblical truth constantly reminds me I am indeed an image bearer. My worth is found in Christ alone. I am who I am by the *grace* of *God*, whose image I bear, scars and all (1 Cor. 15:10). I have also learned that I do not have to be silent, and I can rejoice in the fact that I am an integral and vital part of the kingdom because of the way God designed me. Yes, men will continue to assert themselves, seek power, and diminish others, especially with women and people of color, in an effort, consciously or unconsciously, to feel good about themselves. But I choose to feel good about God's power and the fact that he created us all uniquely for his purposes. He is omniscient and has a purpose for every one of us. With this knowledge, I believe I am indeed a part of his sovereign plan, and it is comforting to accept that my mission field is to live among a people for his glory and by his sovereign grace "for such a time as this." I now count it a privilege to walk in this knowledge, showing love that can only come from him. Because of this, my joy is complete in him. I am no longer the little girl, but instead a woman of God, who just happens to be African American. God made me this way, and it is good. Indeed, very good.

ASSIMILATION MADE ME A BAD CHRISTIAN

RYAN ZHANG

Ryan Zhang serves as an assistant pastor at New City Presbyterian Church in Cincinnati, Ohio. He also works as the translation manager for China Partnership, an organization that connects Reformed house churches in China with churches in the West. He has a BA from Georgetown University and an MDiv from Gordon-Conwell Theological Seminary. He and his wife Abigail have one son and one daughter.

———

I recently had lunch with an African American church planter in Cincinnati. It was a few days after a second mistrial was declared in a case in which a local White police officer was charged with murdering an African American man at a traffic stop. When I asked my friend Sherman how this made him feel, he responded, "There is not one day when I don't feel different from other people."

His short reply caused me to pause and reflect on what a privileged life I have been living as an Asian in America. Although I am a Chinese immigrant who still speaks English with a noticeable accent, I can more or less choose whether or not to feel different. Here I was sitting across the table from a man who was born in the United States, has lived here all his life, and is in every sense more American than I will ever be. Yet he still feels marginalized in his own country every day.

As an immigrant, I often take pride in what I have achieved in this country through hard work and assimilation into the majority culture. Yet there is also a part of me that wants to identify with Sherman and say, "Yes, I am different too, and I should not be ashamed of that." It took me more than a decade to embrace this difference and acknowledge the sins behind my approach to assimilation, and to seek out a way forward through the Gospel.

Before I go further, I would like to define what I mean by "assimilation." Some churches use the word to describe the process of integrating a new Christian into the life of the church. This is an essential part of our sanctification.

But the assimilation I am speaking of is strictly cultural. It is the process by which a person's or group's culture comes to resemble that of another group. In the suburbs of Cincinnati, and many parts of the country, this means conformity to White middle-class culture. It is a pressure, at least what I assume to be a pressure, to abandon my own practices and preferences and adopt the White middle-class ones.

The False Promises of Cultural Assimilation

My family immigrated to America in March 1999 when I was twelve years old. We settled in a suburban town forty minutes north of Cincinnati. No one in my family spoke English when we arrived. I was the only China-born student out of the 750 people in my high school graduating class. During my first year in America, I sat alone in the cafeteria because I didn't know how to talk to anybody. When I went home after school, my mom would ask me what homework I had, and I could never answer her question because all day long I hadn't understood what my teachers were saying.

During that period I often wondered, "What do I have to do to fit in? What do I have to do to have a normal life in this country? Do I have to get rid of my Chinese accent, make White friends, study American history in an elite university, and marry a White woman?"

Nearly twenty years later, I have done most of these things; my accent still hangs around. Within two years of coming to America, I had learned enough English to become a straight A student. All my closest high school friends were White. I took pride in knowing more about US history and government than any of my American friends, which eventually motivated me to major in Government and American Studies at Georgetown University. After college, I worked in a large corporate law firm adjacent to the White House, in which more than 90 percent of the attorneys were White. I only dated White women, and I eventually married one who was born and raised in the Midwest. Even becoming a Christian was a way for me to gain acceptance and credibility in the Anglo-Protestant world I inhabited.

As I made inroads into what I considered normal American society, I would often look down on immigrants who did not learn English as quickly, have as many White friends, or have as much success in American society as I had.

A Self Divided

Outwardly I behaved normally, but privately I was still Chinese to the core. I only knew how to cook Chinese food. The only pop songs that I listened to were in Cantonese. I spoke to my parents on the phone everyday in Chinese (even calling my parents daily was a very Chinese thing to do). And I still preferred a bad Chinese restaurant over anything else. The secret to my success was to keep my Chinese life as private as possible unless it would help me get ahead in school or land a job. I *acted* normal in public.

This sharp divide between my private and public worlds was initially invisible to me. I had grown so used to straddling these two worlds that I hardly noticed any incongruity in myself. One day my best friend from college visited me at my parents' house in Cincinnati. He spent the night before we drove to Atlanta for a wedding. The next morning after my parents had fed him, among other things, octopus for breakfast, the first thing that came out of his mouth in the car was, "Oh my gosh, everything makes so much sense now!" Puzzled, I said, "What are you talking about?" He replied, "Now I know why you are who you are, because when you leave your house you are in America, but when you go home you are in China!"

Any trace of the illusion of a seamless transition between my two worlds was completely shattered when my future wife, Abigail, entered my life. During the first meeting between Abigail and my parents, my mom clearly told her, "Ryan is very Chinese. Do you think you can handle that? Think about it!"

The evening before we got engaged, my parents sat her down and spoke to her, through my translation, about what she should expect if she married into our family. The Chinese side of me became more apparent as I started to see my life through Abigail's experience. It showed up when my parents sent us home on the plane with a whole cooked chicken, when we fought over what types of food were acceptable for breakfast, when Abigail sat alone while my relatives and I conversed in Chinese over hot-pot (a Chinese dish served similarly to fondue)[1] and Abigail finally begged me to order some pizza for dinner.

Our cultural differences became even more obvious to me through the way strangers looked at us. TSA agents and restaurant hostesses often mistake us for two separate parties. Graduate school exam proctors suspected my wife was cheating because her last name and appearance didn't match. A common comment when Abigail was pregnant was, "I love biracial babies. Biracial babies are so cute!" Although these were often innocuous and well-intentioned mistakes, they reminded me that, as much as I wanted to believe otherwise, our marriage was still not considered normal. As recently as 1967, there were laws in the United States forbidding our union.[2]

I eventually began to see how these two cultures collided and competed for my attention. Easter Sunday 2015 was a perfect example of the chaos of this divided life. That Sunday also happened to be Qing Ming (pronounced Ching Ming), a Chinese holiday on which families honor their deceased loved ones by visiting their graves. My wife and I started the day early. I preached at our predominantly White church's sunrise service. We stayed for the annual Easter breakfast and the 10 a.m. worship service. After that we rushed out in our Easter attire to join my extended family at various cemetery visits. The irony of the day consisted not only of us intentionally visiting cemeteries on Easter Sunday, but also in highlighting how little my two worlds related to one another.

Almost none of my relatives knew that earlier that morning I had preached at a predominantly White church. If they did, they would assume my vocation as a pastor only reflected the extent of my assimilation into White Protestant culture.

On the other hand, most of our church friends had probably never even heard of a holiday called Qing Ming. While many of them were having Easter brunch with their extended families, I too was surrounded by my extended family, only we were eating Chinese pork buns, octopus from Chinatown, and homemade red bean pastries by my grandma's grave.

Miroslav Volf describes four ways we bolster ourselves through the exclusion of others. The first way is literally *killing or driving others out* of our living space, as we have seen in many genocides and ethnic cleansings through the last century. The second is *dominance*, where a minority group is accepted in society only if they are relegated to an inferior place. The third way is *abandonment*, where we exclude others by disdaining and ignoring them. Historically the African American communities have suffered under the second and third ways. The fourth, and no less oppressive form of exclusion, is *assimilation*, where a group of people is only accepted in society if they conform to a set of patterns and standards, which do not allow them to manifest differences.[3]

I have not personally experienced the first three forms of exclusion, but the more I learned to lean on the love of Christ for security and acceptance, the more I began to recognize all the damage assimilation had done to me. I began to look deeply into my whole life, both the normal public persona and the private Chinese side of me I so desperately wanted to hide from others. I saw a whirlpool of sin that manifests itself in my perpetual desire to succeed, to rise in elitism, and to prove myself more worthy than others. Two years ago I listened to two Korean American pastors reflecting on the idea of cultural assimilation, and one of them said something I will never forget: "You won somebody else's game. You were given the prize by someone else. The rules were written by someone else. The play was refereed by someone else. Even if you perceive yourself having won, you've lost!"[4] And I realized I had lost in so many different ways.

First, assimilation made me a bad son. I tried to impress women, professors, and even pastors by boasting about my Midwest upbringing and knowledge of American history and government. In the process of seeking acceptance in normal American society, I had consciously and unconsciously checked my Chinese heritage at the door, often by distancing myself from other Chinese immigrants, students, and even my parents. My one constant consternation was the Chinese accent that stubbornly stuck to my words, forever signaling to others that I am not quite normal.

Second, assimilation made me a bad citizen. By taking pride in the degree of my assimilation, I had perpetuated the oppressive idea of White normativity. I considered one set of cultural preferences to be superior and regarded all other cultures as abnormal and inferior, which included my own Chinese culture. Often East Asians are held up as the model minority because we have readily accepted that success in America means conforming to White middle-class norms. This sets us up as a foil against all other ethnic groups who have not so readily acquiesced, and those groups include my African American, Hispanic, and Southeast Asian friends, among others. We have been pegged as the good guys, and they are the noncompliant bad guys.[5] But by participating in this competition, we have all lost.

Third, assimilation made me a bad historian. As much as I liked to boast about my knowledge of American history and government, I had been blind to the thing that makes America truly beautiful. If there is any claim to exceptionalism in America, it is the sparkling light of the American mosaic that makes our society vibrant and beautiful. Progress in America is not just the prosperity of one culture, while all other cultures are pushed aside or trampled upon. I pray my own Chinese culture, along with African American, Arab, Latino, and many other cultures, will shine as brightly in this society as the array of Caucasian cultures.

Fourth, assimilation made me a bad ambassador of Christ. The Apostle Paul writes in 1 Corinthians 9:22: *"I have become all things to all people, that by all means I might save some."* God had given me this unique experience to serve as a bridge between two cultures, and I had rejected his calling. Not only had I failed to use my Chinese background and language skills to reach Chinese non-believers, I had often distanced myself from them. Like the Judaizers that Paul condemned in Galatians, I had associated Christianity with a particular culture and set up unnecessary barriers to the Gospel.

Ironically, my assimilation also made me a poor ambassador of Christ to White Americans. One of the most enriching discoveries in our marriage has been seeing how each of our cultures has positively affected the way we love God. I discovered that being an immigrant gave me a deeper understanding of Hebrews 11:13–16 because my family has lived as *"strangers and exiles"* in a foreign land. Knowing Chinese wedding traditions gave me deeper appreciation for Jesus' promise in John 14 that *"I will come again and will take you to myself, that where I am you may be also."* Watching shows about Chinese emperors leaving their thrones to live as commoners helped me visualize the humility of Christ as he left his throne to become one of us. These experiences provide me with a vast treasure trove for my writing and preaching, but it begins with a willingness to embrace my cultural heritage as my own.

Ultimately, assimilation made me a bad Christian because it gave me a distorted perception of what it meant to be a good Christian. When I relied on my own works and assimilation to gain acceptance and success in society, I confused being White with being secure and blessed by God. I used being a Christian as a means to become successful and accepted in America. God was at times just a little tool in my life to get to something else. I now tell people my conversion was first motivated by 80 percent peer pressure and 20 percent curiosity. By the grace of God, he made himself known to me despite my foolishness. I am no less a sinner because I have White friends and am married to a White woman, but I am also no less loved and accepted by God because I speak with a Chinese accent.

A Way Forward

How do I move forward as a Chinese American Christian caught between society's pressure to assimilate and the desire to be myself? One postmodern answer to this assimilation dilemma is to claim my right to create my own identity by digging deeper into my home culture. This approach does not work because I have inherited just as much sin from Chinese culture as from the White culture I have adopted. *"For there is no distinction: for all have sinned and fall short of the glory of God"* (Rom. 3:22–23). I am in no way a better Christian by living out my Chinese identity than by assimilating into the White culture. But another more practical reason why simply being myself would not work is because the world does not bend to my own will. However much I want to gain approval and worth by just being myself, people in the dominant culture still look at me with skepticism or even disdain. The prevalence of police violence against African Americans who are simply living their normal lives testifies to this cruel reality.

How do we as the Church welcome others without forcing them to assimilate but still challenging them to abandon their former sinful ways? We can gain great wisdom by observing what the Apostles did in their letter to the Gentiles in Acts 15. They refused to lay extra burdens on the Gentiles by requiring them to be circumcised into Judaism, which was the dominant culture within the Church at the time. Yet they challenged them to abstain from what has been sacrificed to idols and from sexual immorality, which were common practices in their former pagan way of life. What made their recommendation possible?

The cross points the way forward. Jesus' death gives us the humility to admit that no culture can save us. We are so sinful that nothing short of the death of God's Son can redeem us. This humility frees us from thinking of ourselves more highly than others, thus removing the pressure of assimilation that we place on others. Yet the cross also gives us the security we need as strangers and exiles on earth. We are so loved that even God's own Son was willing to die for us. This frees us from seeking worth either by assimilating into a dominant culture or by digging deeper into our own identities. We can give up our pitiful efforts to find worth in the world and lean into the dignity and security that God grants us as his children.

This means I should have the humility to admit that all my efforts to gain acceptance through assimilation or self-assertion are only forms of idolatry. My worth is in Christ. It should also give me the security to confront and repent of the sins I have inherited from both Chinese and White culture. God confronts and redeems all the cultures in the world and creates *"in himself one new man"* (Eph. 2:15). In this new humanity, the worst of our cultures will be redeemed and the best will be made even better. We begin to truly glorify God in a diversity that reflects all his fullness and creativity.

One of the best experiences I've ever had in Cincinnati was at a Christmas party in which Christians from India, China, the Caribbean, and Ghana shared the different ways they celebrate the birth of Christ at home. As different as those traditions are from Santa Claus and Christmas trees, it reminded me that Christ is truly a light for all the nations.

The Kingdom of God, even as it manifests itself in the suburbs of Ohio, is multi-dimensional; it is not tied to just one ethnic culture. Our shared life not only makes the Church stronger, it makes our witness authentic. It reflects a radical humility as we admit that all our cultures are fallen, and we need each other to point out our blind spots and sins. It also reflects a radical security in Christ as we welcome different people to the table and invite them to teach us how to glorify God better. Through this we learn to love one another, and all people will know we are Christ's disciples (John 13:35). When all nations, tribes, and tongues stand before the throne and before the Lamb, I hope we will not only sing, *"Salvation belongs to our God who sits on the throne"* (Rev. 7:9–10) but we will also greet each other and say, "Without you, there is no us. Our love for Christ is made infinitely more profound because of you."

---

1. Wikipedia, s.v., "Hot pot," https://en.wikipedia.org/wiki/Hot_pot
2. Loving v. Virginia, 388 U.S. 1 (1967).
3. Miroslav Volf, *Exclusion and Embrace: A Theological Exploration of Identity, Otherness, and Reconciliation* (Nashville, TN: Abingdon, 1996), 75.
4. Duke Kwon and Abraham Cho, "Beyond Black and White: Why Repentance for Racism Matters to Other Communities of Color" (lecture, Reconciliation and Justice Conference, St. Louis, MO, February 1, 2016).
5. Kwon and Cho, "Beyond Black and White"

WHITE GUILT AND BROWN KIDS

EMILY HUBBARD

Emily Hubbard is a White Mississippian now living in Missouri. She is a life-long member of the Presbyterian Church in America (PCA). Her husband is a pastor at a multiethnic church in St. Louis, and they have four children. She has degrees from Mississippi State University, including an MS in sociology. She is a public school advocate, loves to discuss birth, and in her spare time enjoys crocheting, gardening, and reading.

———

As soon as I could, I married the man who said, "I want to be involved in your mess." We are now over ten years into our marriage, and I'm thankful we continue to struggle through mess together (much of it probably more literal than he imagined).

And though I didn't realize it at the time, a large part of the non-literal mess has been owning and learning what it means to be a White person in intimate relationship with Black people.

My great-granddaddy was a policeman in Atlanta in the 1940s. It's a family belief that he was also a KKK member. I've never tried to confirm it, and I hope it's not true. But many of the Atlanta police were at that time. At the least, my great-grandfather enforced discriminatory Jim Crow laws. Atlanta police at the time were known for terrible racial brutality.

It's a gut punch every time I contemplate this. Is it *my* sin? I don't know. But I know the sins of the fathers go to the third and fourth generation.

I have my own sin: my childhood nostalgic loyalty to the Lost Cause[1], my embrace of it with only a shamefaced shrug for the impact White supremacy had on half the residents of my state of Mississippi, including those who share my Savior, if not my skin color.

I don't know if Jesus paid for my great-grandfather's sin, but I know he has paid for mine. Jesus' imputed righteousness frees me from my guilt, both personal and corporate. He gives me the grace to muddle through the fear, failure, and isolation I face in trying to be a good White woman in a culture that often unknowingly worships the idol of White supremacy (trust me, I'm a sociologist).

When a White person marries a Black person, everyone asks, "What about the kids?" It's a fun little micro-aggression ostensibly rooted in concern for the quality of life your children will have. In practice, though, it smudges the image of God, and it surrenders to the societal sin of racism instead of offering solidarity to the parents of brown children. Because let's be honest, if you want to worry about my no-longer-theoretical children losing out on a nice life because they won't be White, you should worry about *all* the brown kids—all those who lose out because of our society's embrace of White supremacy and our churches' failure to fight it.

My children? They are beloved children made in the image of God, and as such, they deserve everything you expect to come easily for your White children.

But that doesn't mean raising them doesn't come with its own set of particular fears for me. Our eldest child is eight years old. The three oldest attend public school so, at least in January and February, they are learning the aspects of American history that particularly affect the Black experience. We talk about it. I try to be wholly factual about the history of our country.

I say, "White people enslaved Black people and treated them as less than human. They used them as tools or animals so they didn't have to pay for labor."[2] I try not to minimize the impact of White supremacy's effects on brown people and even on our family. I explain, "Daddy's ancestors weren't paid for their work like mommy's were. Fifty years ago, it wasn't legal for a Black person like daddy to marry a White person like mommy. Many White people still see brown people as scary."

I still haven't broached the ways my own family, especially that policeman grandfather, and even I, has participated in White supremacy. I haven't been able to articulate all the ways that violence, rooted in and rationalized by White supremacy, has affected people of color now and in the past. I know I will have to one day. But I'm not ready yet.

They are still young children. I'm not ready. And yet I know that many children (of all ages) live with the evidence that their country does not grant them, or their parents, the humanity they deserve because they are made in the image of God.

I forecast this conversation: "Hi kids! Something awful happened in the world today, and guess what! I gave you the blood of the bad guys!"

My kids ask WHY about everything. So, they'll surely ask why when they learn about the world. "*Why* did White people do these things, mommy? *Why* don't they want to live with Brown people? *Why* did they kill Martin Luther King?"

I won't always know the answer. I might say, "They started to do it first for the money, I guess. Then it was a lie they got used to and had to hold on to, because if they were wrong, they were *dead wrong*."

I look at their beautiful brown faces. I see their clear intelligence. I wonder if they will come to hate me. I imagine their questions, as they learn more and more of our country's history. "Why would you give this heritage to your children? Why would you sully us with your generations of participation in oppression?" Is it enough that their dad was the best, truest man I'd ever seen, and I grabbed hold of him as hard and as fast as I could?

Anti-miscegenation screeds often talk about interracial marriage sullying pure White blood. Theodore Bilbo, a Mississippi governor and politician from the 1930s and '40s, wrote:

Personally, the writer of this book would rather see his race and his civilization blotted out with the atomic bomb than to see it slowly but surely destroyed in the maelstrom of miscegenation, interbreeding, intermarriage and mongrelization. The destruction in either case would be inevitable—one in a flash and the other by the slow but certain process of sin, degradation, and mongrelization.[3]

In his history of the PCA, Sean Lucas quotes G. T. Gillespie, a president of the then Belhaven College as saying, "The intelligent farmer doesn't allow his dairy and beef breeding stock to run in the same pasture, otherwise he would downgrade his herds, and have only a herd of scrubs or mongrels."[4]

Though most of these men say they are also concerned about Black racial integrity , it's clear their chief concern is White supremacy. The lynchings that occurred because of suspected interracial relationships demonstrate this concern.[5]

I confess my present concern is different. My path is already chosen, but I fear my children will one day realize the sins of acquiescing to and/or embracing the idol of White supremacy that has happened in my family and in myself—and they'll reject *me*, my large extended family, or my church.

I love the PCA so much. I love Reformed doctrine. I love the slow and steady ways things get worked out in committees. It will hurt me deeply if they chose a different path, but I would understand.

There are a lot of White Hubbards in Mississippi. It's a name I acquired through marriage. Some of these White Hubbards are Presbyterian. If I am without my family, people who meet me in Mississippi ask me if I'm related to a White Hubbard they know.

I mentally answer, "I sure hope not."

There were slave-holding Hubbards in Mississippi.[6] My husband's (Roy Hubbard) family is from Mississippi. If there were White slave-holding Hubbards who were Presbyterians who tithed,[7] and Roy's family name is connected to their original slave-owners, then the Presbyterian church in Mississippi has benefited from the unpaid and exploited labor of my children's ancestors. And if those White Hubbards continued to prosper and tithe while the formerly enslaved Black people were oppressed and were refused the opportunity to prosper through Reconstruction and Jim Crow, then the Presbyterian Church profited from the wealth they would have accumulated. Wealth stolen first by slavery and then by continued structural oppression such as sharecropping and school segregation. My children's inheritance has been robbed and plundered, and the Presbyterian Church has profited. I suppose I may never know. But I suspect it's true.

I hope my kids love me when I'm old. I hope they take care of me when I can't hear or see well. Will they love me if I love the PCA? Sometimes I don't know how I can ask them to be part of a church that profited from their family's oppression. Even if I can't draw a straight line from slaveholder to enslaved person to church, even if our denomination has apologized for slavery (in an overture in 2002) and for the civil rights abuses (in an overture in 2016)—what does it mean that we have profited from those things?

Have we truly made it right with an apology?[8] And if it's not my Brown kids who've been robbed, it's some other mother's kids. As a sociologist, I hate to get into economics, but we are raising four children with a non-profit job, and it's impossible for me to ignore the differences between my husband's family experiences and those of his White peers in ministry.

But while I wait for my children to understand the whole truth of their heritage and our country's and church's histories, and as I wrestle with this fear of their future rejection, I'm trying my best to be a good White mom.

As a biological mother of Black children, being a good White mom, a mom who is for the image of God in her children, has required dying to self in so many more ways than I could have imagined, far beyond sleep deprivation and endless laundry. For my children to exist, I have held blackness inside my body (which to be clear is not part of the sacrifice). They grew their hair that was already long and black by the time they were born, their skin brown, the blueprint already swelling and sprouting in their cells, their noses a little wide, their lips full. The image of God, the image of their father, nourished by my blood. And then the baby comes out, the cord disconnects, and there they are. I am the only pale member of our family. "White, mama. You white."

We talk about how we are all reflecting the image of God just as we are. We discuss that their dad, dark brown, is the image of God, and he's made with God's pleasure. We talk about how the same thing is true of me. And that they too, with their light brown skin and curly hair, are made in the image of God, just the way God wanted them to be made. And we love them so much.

All that is true. But the continuing racial hierarchies in our country, the not-so-hidden legacies of the one-drop rule,[9] separate me from my family. If I am out with my children alone, I'm consistently asked if they are adopted. It's easier for people to assume that I needed a judge, rather than an obstetrician, to have my children.

I was in our church the first time I was asked the question, "Where's that baby from?" My husband, an intern at the time, was in the pulpit. I had given birth weeks earlier. I stuttered out a response, "Uh, Mississippi?"

That first experience has been a stark reminder that even in the church, and maybe especially in our mostly White, conservative denomination, White ladies are not supposed to be joining their bodies with Black bodies.

I don't want to be crass, but the underlying supposition of the adoption question is this: "You didn't have sex with a Black man, did you?" My union with my family, from the most intimate one with my husband to my relationship with my children, all of whom I carried for nine months, fed from my own body, and slept close to during their earliest years, is constantly battered by our societal surrender to White supremacy.

The hardest thing is adjusting to a posture of insufficiency. In our family, I am the minority. I'm the only White person in my house. We've found communities that support our family and mirror those whom we can see our children growing up to be—of course I'm talking about people of color, who are out there loving Jesus and living with joy in the face of marginalization.

I've got a degree that focuses on race and religion, but I have not lived it like the Black and brown members of our communities have. In our country and our society, in our racist and White-supremacy-worshiping nation (and too often church), I cannot be the primary model for my children, especially my daughters. I can never know what it's like to be a Black woman. I can love my kids, point them to Jesus, change their diapers, and wash their clothes. But when it comes to a blueprint for how they can live in the skin God has blessed them with? I can't show them that. I've never done it. I've never been treated as less because of the color of my skin.

I can learn to take care of curly hair but I will never know what it feels like to have my place of employment or my school inform me that my hair, the way it grows out of my head, the way God gave it to me, isn't appropriate.[10] In a very particular way, I am not sufficient to nurture my children.

Accepting that truth has been one of the hardest things as a Christian parent. Asking women of color to love my children and model being Jesus-following, Black-girl-magic-bearing images of God has been one of the most humbling things I've done in my life. This is not the actual text of how I ask, but it boils down to this, "I married one of the best Black men in the world and kept him from marrying a sister, and I can't raise his kids right without you. Will you please help me?"

Praise God for the generous hearts of my Black sisters in Christ, none of whom have turned me or my daughters away. And what joy it has been to see the fruit, to see my oldest daughter blossom as her Black teacher, to whom, yes, I wrote an awkward email, has shepherded and nurtured her sense of self as a Black child, just the way God made her.

Living as a minority among minorities has taught me so much. Sometimes I feel left out, like when I covet the sweatshirt that says, "I love my Blackness and yours." I can never wear it, but I might buy one for my kids. I must consistently fight to remind myself, when those celebrating the image of God hurt my feelings and leave me feeling left out, that they have experienced actual measurable loss. They have been marginalized, oppressed, and discriminated against. People who claim to be brothers and sisters in Christ make instantaneous judgments about them. They've experienced so many losses through segregation and racist policies.

I've married into this burden that I can't fathom. I had a choice, and I took it. I am humbled by those who were born into this burden, and yet they continue in faith and joy. They are constantly forging paths toward justice and willingly bearing the traditional lot of prophets in their own country. Their union with Christ empowers them. And it does me too.

I write about my hopes for my children and for the necessity of these men and women of God to be here for my children, but as the protections of Whiteness are lost to me—as our family potentially brings down the property values of a neighborhood, as my husband faces increased police interaction, and as the statistics show that children of color are disciplined at disproportionately higher rates than White children. I ponder my White family's ability to accumulate and pass on wealth compared to Roy's different experience, considering that his enslaved ancestors received no compensation for their labor, and even legislation that helped my family was constructed to withhold benefit from his—I am forced to fly to Jesus, and cling to him.

The particular part of his earthly body that embraces me right back is Black women who already know this Jesus they cling to. They entrust their family to Jesus every day with a practical faith that runs far deeper than all the theology I learned as a proud Southern Presbyterian.[11]

Did I accidentally call for reparations in this essay?

Maybe?

Can we as a historically White church consider what our current generation's passivity and indifference, not to mention earlier generation's clear acts of racism (google "Mississippi Presbyterian citizens council" for some heartbreak), have done to our brothers and sisters in Christ—our truest family? It's easy and necessary for me to care about these things now that my flesh and blood are directly impacted. But we White Presbyterians have continued to act as if our actions and aspirations are free from the taint of our country's long guilty slog of racial injustice. We retreat into foxholes of doctrinal purity that allow us to ignore and dismiss the struggles and voices of our fellow Christians, as if Jesus never prayed John 17. And if you think fighting for racial justice is only a prophetic calling for a few weird radical White folks that you never liked anyway, you are wrong.

Too often in current discourse, it seems like being called a racist is just as bad as acts of racism. I'm here to tell you that racism, even passive assent, is a sin of which you can repent, turn to Jesus, and believe, and live a life far richer as you embrace the full cost and privilege of living in God's kingdom and with God's priorities. Until that day, with my children, I continue to ask "Why?" and with Habakkuk, I continue to ask God:

> O LORD, how long shall I cry for help,
> and you will not hear?
> Or cry to you "Violence!"
> and you will not save?
> Why do you make me see iniquity,
> and why do you idly look at wrong?
> Destruction and violence are before me;
> strife and contention arise.
> So the law is paralyzed,
> and justice never goes forth.
> For the wicked surround the righteous;
> so justice goes forth perverted. Hab. 1:1–4

---

1. An American pseudo-historical, negationist ideology that holds that the cause of the Confederacy during the American Civil War was a just and heroic one. Wikipedia, s.v., "Lost Cause of the Confederacy."
2. I would be remiss not to admit this is a direct echo from a line in the musical *Hamilton*.
3. Theodore Bilbo, *Take Your Choice: Separation or Mongrelization* (Poplarville, MS: Dream House Press, 1947), digital edition at: https://archive.org/stream/TakeYourChoice/TakeYourChoice_djvu.txt.

4. Sean Michael Lucas, *For a Continuing Church* (Phillipsburg, NJ: P&R Publishing, 2015), 118.

5. Jesse Daniels, "White Women and the Defense of Lynching," *Racism Review,* February 11, 2014, http://www.racismreview.com/blog/2014/02/11/white-women-defense-lynching/

6. "Slave Holders Census Schedules with Surname Matches for African Americans," *Rootsweb,*
   http://freepages.genealogy.rootsweb.ancestry.com/~ajac/msjefferson.htm.

7. "Presbyterianism in the Southwest," *Jefferson County MS,* http://jeffersoncountyms.org/reminiscences.htm;
   "The Story of Rodney Presbyterian Church," *Jefferson County MS,* http://jefferson-countyms.org/scrapbookRodney.htm.

8. There was a fund created at General Assembly 2017 for individual donations: https://pcamna.org/unity-fund/, but this does not entail a full corporate reckoning.

9. The one-drop rule is a social and legal principle of racial classification that was historically prominent in the United States in the twentieth century. It asserted that any person with even one ancestor of sub-Saharan African ancestry ("one drop" of Black blood) is considered Black. Wikipedia, s.v. "One-drop rule."

10. Karen Grigsby Bates, "Dreadlocks Decision Raises Another Question: What Is Race," *NPR's Codeswitch,* October 23, 2016, http://www.npr.org/sections/codeswitch/2016/10/23/498734157/dreadlocks-decision-raises-another-question-what-is-race.

11. This is not to say that Black women don't have a grasp of theology or that their suffering is solely for my sanctification, only that my spiritual formation, full of theology, as a White Christian was not sufficient.

ANALOGIES OF GRACE
ON MY ADOPTION AND INTERRACIAL MARRIAGE

ROBIN WOOTTON

Robin Wootton is a stay-at-home mom. She was formerly the Music Director at Grace Covenant Presbyterian Church in Williamsburg, Virginia. She has a Master of Arts degree in Organizational Management from University of Phoenix-Online, with graduate coursework in Adult Learning and Development from Regis University in Denver, Colorado. She is a Music Director at Rocky Mountain Community Church and the wife of Rob Wootton, Resident Church Planter, in Billings, Montana. They have four children.

―――

I want to believe the world is becoming more open-minded in a Gospel-centered way. I want to believe interracial marriages are widely accepted and accelerating the existence of biracial people on the planet. I also want to believe international adoption is so common that adoptees now will not struggle with the identity issues they have had for the past forty-plus years.

But I've been wrong before. I have my bouts of cynicism, even though I know the end of the story, and I have full confidence in the demographics of Jesus' throne room.

I've heard stories of couples walking down the street hand-in-hand while rocks were thrown at them. I've known people who have been threatened and beaten because they were a biracial couple.

I worry for my kids. I want to believe that by the time they are aware of their mixed-race identity, they will be surrounded by friends who fully accept and love them as-is. I want to believe their experience will be different from mine. I want to believe the past is in the past. I have a love-hate relationship with the past.

I have a habit of counting the number of people in a room who are not White. I've shared this with other people of color, and they admit they do it too. I am pretty sure my husband never did until he was dating me, and we talked about what it would feel like to be interracial.

I called ours a biracial marriage, and I mean that. I firmly believe in two becoming one. I firmly believe God has joined us together in real, tangible, physical ways. It was never clearer than on our wedding night, and we have that to remind us for all our days. My memory needs to go back to that moment for accountability when our marriage walks in the wrong direction. When we made the marriage covenant, we were bound for life. He took on my ethnicity, and I took on his. We are one.

In the 1970s when I was six months old, this little South Korean girl was adopted by a lower-middle-class White couple living in the suburbs of Long Island, New York. I had the added bonus of a school-teacher dad who could take a summer month off and drive across the country.

One summer we were driving through some part of Tennessee, and a woman at a restaurant made a comment about our family. It was something along the lines of, "I think your family is good, and I don't have a problem with it. But some people don't like that kind of thing, and you should be careful." It wasn't until hours later that my ten-year-old mind realized she was referring to me.

My parents have since forgotten this even happened. I don't think I ever will or could. I can picture the booth we sat in. I have a vague memory of her accent. Yet years later, I found myself wondering if it even happened at all. It was this kind of experience that made me question whether or not I was a trusted source. How much of my own interpretation and wounded heart clouds my mind? Can anyone really remember anything clearly?

As an adult, I've experienced the same feeling. Am I really understanding clearly what's going on here? Are my own prejudices and years of racial tension and bigotry contributing to conversations I've had, and particularly my recall of those conversations?

Throughout my single and dating years, I remember conversations

I think I had that made me feel as though my face was false advertising. I wasn't really that Asian. I distinctly remember a man telling me he was hoping to get some good Korean food from dating me. This was ironic on a few levels, the most important one being I was a terrible cook—of any food.

Another conversation I think I had was with a woman who asked me about my upbringing. Upon telling her, she determined that I wasn't really Korean, and all I could think of saying was, "I only am when I look in the mirror."

As an adoptee, I struggled with many things. I struggled with feeling like a fraud. Not quite Korean and not quite White, whatever those descriptors meant to other people. I struggled to accept the fact that I would never know my real birth date. The chances of finding that out are slim to none, and many have spent years and resources trying to find information to no avail. There are some success stories, but more often than not, the attempts are dead-ends and only bring bitterness.

It wasn't until I met Rob Wootton that I had the experience of someone I was dating cry about this. About my birthday—

When I told him I would never know my real birthday, I watched him closely. Seeing the tears in his eyes, him grappling with the reality of not knowing something so basic, I knew he was someone I had looked for all my life.

When we married, he took on my identity and I took on his. Two became one.

There are people who won't see us this way. There are still people in our culture who cannot fathom interracial *anything*, let alone marriage and children. Just recently, a friend relayed an incident at her daughter's school in which a boy teased her about being half-Chinese. These things still happen. I want to believe they will cease.

As my husband wrote in his chapter for this book, "No one *wants* to acknowledge their prejudices—racism, classism, or sexism. Yet if these tendencies were not part of our fallen human nature, why would the Apostle Paul need to address them? '*There is neither Jew nor Greek, there is neither slave nor free; there is neither male nor female, for you are all one in Christ Jesus*'" (Gal. 3:28).[1]

I now have a habit of noticing every interracial couple everywhere I go. We notice when others notice our children. Our children are beautiful to us. We know they are beautiful to God, who cheers his own good craftsmanship. We are grateful.

But we know the world is constantly at risk of losing sight of this type of beauty. We know the ugliness of sin, anger, pride, resentment, mistrust, and misunderstanding sometimes has an appeal—a warped, dark beauty that overshadows the light. Nothing is uglier than hate. Few things are more warped and deformed than a disregard for the sanctity and glory in every life.

As an adoptee, I have felt disregarded, thrown away, misrepresented, and incomplete. Even in writing this essay, I have felt like a fraud because I am not really being able to talk about interracial marriage in the same way as a couple bridging two more distinct cultures. My husband and I had nearly the same cultural upbringing and lifestyles. In fact, we took the same cross-country family trip, at just about the same age in life, and saw many of the same places and attractions.

Except for that one experience I had at a restaurant in Tennessee, it was almost the same. And maybe that's it. That's the difference I can write about—the expectations put on a person born out of appearances and prejudices. Someone looks at me and forms a notion about who I am, just like someone looks at us as a couple or a family and sizes us up according to whatever measuring methods they were raised with, experienced, or learned along the way. The notion is almost always wrong in some way. Until we as a society admit that it's wrong and are willing to recalculate the measurement systems in place, we will more often than not get people wrong. As Christians we are called to get people right.

According to my driver's license (since I don't really know my birth date) and naturalization certificate (I recently looked through my personal files to make sure I was indeed a US citizen), I gave birth to my first child five days before I turned forty. There was nothing quite like being pregnant and giving birth to remind me how connected we are through family. Flesh and blood; there she was... the first blood relative I had ever known. I had wondered for many years what my birth parents looked like, what they did for a living, or what made them laugh. I wondered if my baby looked like either of them. Whose nose did she have? Did she have her maternal grandmother's smile?

She had blue eyes for the first nine months of her life. Stunning, blue eyes. People were taken aback by them. God did that, I'm convinced, to remind me of the deep, complex wonder of genetics. She was her daddy's girl, through and through. Still is. My husband has beautiful grayish-blue eyes. Her eyes have settled into some shade of greenish-brown these days, but that period of time served to remind me of God's design in which he takes broad strokes and refined strokes across the world and fills it, and us, with wondrous sights. We miss the artistry of God when our eyes are shut. Indeed she is wonderfully and beautifully made (Ps. 139:14). We all are.

There is a "mystic sweet communion"[2] of those bonded together in Christ. The blood of Christ has united us as relatives, but in some ways, for better or worse, there is a strong bond in marriage and in family. I have two blood relatives now, my own two children. I hold such wonder in my heart at the sight of them. God has been so gracious to me. It's more than I deserve.

I know my adoptive family understands much of my experience. They have been a wealth of grace and kindness even in my darkest times. They know it's a struggle. They know I have visited dark, heavy places in my heart. And they know that they sometimes had to bear the brunt of my misdirected anger—often too complex for words. But just as the family of God mourns together and rejoices together, my family, the ones not even of my flesh and blood, have come alongside me as their own. It is indeed sweet and mystic. And I know I am blessed beyond measure.

But I also know not everyone is. I also know the very real, deep hurt many have experienced through their adoptive families. I have heard the pain in broken voices and resentment against those who claim the name of Jesus as Savior, but abuse the very real spiritual power they hold over an impressionable young person's heart and mind. Too many parents—some with the best of intentions and some with undeveloped, unchecked intentions—have abused the concept of adoption throughout Scripture by putting their children into no-win positions. How many times have I heard someone say to me that I must be very grateful that God rescued me when so many others never find a home? Or that God must have great things for me to do because he saved me like Moses from Egypt? People don't realize this puts a burden on adoptees to not only try to achieve great things, but also to choose to vilify our biological families and heritages as things to be saved from.

Adoption theology is its own book, but for my purposes here, I will briefly address it. My understanding of adoption has increased my knowledge of the grace and love of Jesus, and been indispensable in relating the Gospel to believers and unbelievers alike. Adoption speaks to people of many backgrounds and experiences.

I have started to use three questions that adoptees have to answer for themselves.

From what have I been adopted? *To* what have I been adopted? And what have I been adopted *as* ?

These questions help to outline the struggles of adoptees, and help non-adoptees understand the subtle and overt parts race and ethnicity play in an adoptee's struggle.

People sometimes carelessly talk about being adopted *out of* sin and disgrace. Without making clear that an adoptee's past and family are unknown, that language can be confusing to adoptees. It can sound like even the existence of an adoptee's heritage and blood line is sinful and disgraceful. Add ethnic differences to this, and you have a complex layer of privilege and superiority—being raised (statistically speaking) White, middle class, suburban, and Protestant is the ideal. Answering the question, what makes these things ideal or, at least better than an adoptee's other options, begins to get at the conflict an adoptee struggles against her whole life.

I have struggled with not feeling White enough to enjoy privilege, even though others are quick to point out that I have been a recipient of these privileges by being adopted into them. I have also been told on a regular basis that if I am anything but grateful, I must not really understand the sacrifices made for my life. Though not told specifics about what gratitude looks like, I suspect it includes not wanting to learn about my ethnic heritage or family whereabouts or ever questioning whether or not I am actually better off now than I might have been.

Wanting to learn about family heritage has been an exercise in futility for some, but a necessary process for others. I've had to parse out what I've been told about my past—all the conjecture about my birth mother, my culture, and my race—with how I have come to know and experience the ways God works and how he alone directs our paths. I've had to think about race as someone who was not born into a dominant culture, but who is consistently told it is better than wherever I would have been. Even writing that will strike many as being less than grateful.

I *am* grateful. I am eternally grateful to God for giving me pictures, stories to tell, of his real grace poured out on me, my adoption and my marriage. Sometimes, I think I understand God's grace better because of these circumstances in my life; the real stories I have to tell about what he has done in and for me. And my experiences must empower and equip me to point people to Jesus. Like the words of Sally Lloyd-Jones in the *Jesus Storybook Bible*, "Every story whispers his name."[3] I don't think of my life as the Bible, but all history continues to be Jesus' story. Every person's story is part of God's story, and as such we tell our stories, and we study them, and we make sense of them as best we can through the lens of the Gospel and the counsel of the Holy Spirit.

And my story must include the journey of sorting out the truths of the Gospel, the lies of the enemy, and the well-intentioned but misguided directions of others. My theology has been developed through years of hurt and sorrow. It has been born out of longing for meaning and heritage. I have had to dig out from under years of feeling inferior, undervalued, and misunderstood, by people of all cultures and ethnicities.

Other adoptees get it. We are a subset of a subset in many ways. We are uniquely defined and re-categorized. But my theology has come to rest in this "blessed thought" as written in the hymn by Joseph Gilmore, "He leadeth me by his own hand."[4] I can see God's hand. I see his hand before time was time. I see his hand creating and naming me. I see him write my name on his hand. I see him enter my name in his book. I see him walking the shores throughout my lifetime, calling my name, calling me to drop my nets and follow him.

My theologian-pastor husband introduced me to the *ordo salutis* (the order of salvation), a way to understand the different parts of our salvation in Christ. The events of the *ordo salutis* have been logically ordered, one leading to the next. For example, Calvinists believe God predestines before anything else, before calling, regeneration, sanctification, etc. So those who have been chosen and called have right standing with God through the work of Jesus on our behalf and are adopted as joint-heirs with immediate access to the throne room of grace.

I was raised in Arminian theology, though my parents have since become Reformed. The Arminian understanding offers a different order of salvation. Jesus first calls for all to believe in some general way, and I had to respond to him in faith and repentance. Then I was adopted, though it was now up to me to both prove it and improve it, meaning working hard to cast off sin and take on the characteristics of

Christ. In that order, the marks of salvation got tied up into who among us were God's children, and who weren't.

I mistakenly thought adopted was something *some* people had to be. As if to say, some of us were born into God's family and others weren't. But if you believe with all your heart and work hard, you can also be part of God's family by adoption.

Decades later I was given the grace to see God's plan of salvation. I can rest in knowing he chose me before time began and there is "nothing that my hands can do to save my guilty soul" but "his only Son has bought me with his blood."[5]

I look forward to the day when it will all come together in Jesus' throne room, that mystic sweet communion with all of his children. Until then, let's get to work. Let's tell and listen to stories. Let's fight battles. Some battles will be lost. Some won with dubious outcomes. But we move forward in Gospel confidence because we know this truth—Christ's bride will prevail. His children will prevail. When we see our identity ultimately in our relationship to Jesus Christ our Groom and God our Father, it will all come together.

---

1. Rob Wootton, "People Like Us," in *Hear Us, Emmanuel: A Call for Reconciliation, Representation, and Unity in the Church*, ed. Doug Serven (Oklahoma City: White Blackbird).
2. S. J. Stone's "The Church's One Foundation," (1866), https://hymnary.org/text/the_churchs_one_foundation.
3. Sally Lloyd-Jones, *The Jesus Storybook Bible* (Grand Rapids: Zondervan, 2007).
4. Joseph Gilmore, "He Leadeth Me," (1862), http://library.timelesstruths.org/music/He_Leadeth_Me/
5. Original words by Horatius Bonar (1861), music and alt. words Matt Richley, "Nothing That My Hands Can Do" (Sovereign Grace Worship, 2012).

AWAKENING TO PRIVILEGE

THE PROBLEM WITH PRIVILEGE

MARK PEACH

Mark Peach is pastor of City Presbyterian Church, a downtown Salt Lake City, Utah, church he planted in 2012. He has degrees from the University of Nebraska (BA) and Covenant Theological Seminary (MDiv). He and his wife, Melissa, have four children.

––––––

It was a typical hectic Chicago evening rush hour, and I was heading home from a long exhausting day of work and running tedious errands. My bus commute home was a straight shot west on Roosevelt Road. I got off at my usual stop, but this time I was followed off of the bus by two police officers. I was several feet ahead of them when I heard one of them shout, "Hey, stop!" Because I knew that the voice that I heard was from one of the officers, I stopped and turned around.

"What are you doing in this neighborhood?" asked the officer.

"I'm just heading home" I said.

"You live in this neighborhood?"

"Yes, officer, I live on Spaulding Avenue."

I thought for a moment, "Am I causing a problem?" I didn't think that I was. The officers continued their questioning. "You live on Spaulding? What do you do? Do you work here?" I had not lived in Chicago's North Lawndale neighborhood long, but at this point I realized what was happening. I was not causing a problem, but I'm White, and I was living in a neighborhood in which the only White people who would visit the neighborhood were those who were either looking to buy drugs or looking to sell drugs. I quickly responded, "Oh, I work downtown, but I volunteer with a Christian ministry in this neighborhood. I'm a volunteer youth worker here."

"Oh, so you are a social worker?"

"Yeah, I am a social worker of sorts," I said.

"Ok. Just watch your back around here," said the other officer.

I was annoyed and a bit startled that the police officers would stop me for no reason other than the fact that I had gotten off of the bus at the corner of Roosevelt and Kedzie Avenue, the stop closest to my apartment. I responded to their questions, turned, and walked away confident that I would be just fine. No harm done.

I tell that story because while I was annoyed and a little startled that the officers would question me, I knew deep down inside, throughout the whole conversation with the officers that I was safe, not in any danger, and not in need. I knew something even before I moved to my neighborhood with its high homicide rate.

I knew that I was protected by the system because of the color of my skin.

It had not yet been a year since I'd moved to Chicago's west side after living in mostly White middle-class neighborhoods for most of my life. So how could I feel safe? I knew I didn't have to watch my back because the system had my back. I know and those in my neighborhood know that the legal system protects White people more than it protects people of color. Even the encounter with the police officers produced little if any anxiety. After all, I was not causing a problem, and I am White.

We live in a world where the color of your skin has something to do with how safe or unsafe you are. Not only that, but the color of your skin also has something to do with how those who are in a position to serve and protect respond to you. Even though North Lawndale had one of the highest crime rates in the country, I never encountered any situation in which I felt like I would be harmed, whether I was walking to get a bite to eat, to the "L" station, or the grocery store.

I now live in a Salt Lake City neighborhood where police officers on bicycles will often ride down our street, patrolling our neighborhood. On more than one occasion, while my kids and I were playing in the front yard, they have kindly waved, stopped to say hello and given stickers to my kids. My kids love it when they stop by!

Being White in America comes with many privileges. One of those is automatically having a positive relationship with police. However for many, an encounter with the police is a terrifying experience even if there is no problem, and the police are just saying hello. For many of the African American youth I knew in Chicago, the presence of police would bring fear. For some, fear even to the point of tears. Why are many afraid? After all, not all encounters with the police involve an abusive use of power or an unjust use of power.

However, because of injustices in our civil and criminal system, stereotypes, and cultural conditioning, many people with privilege and power have had a tendency to see people of color as suspicious and a problem. Police officers are not exempt from the influence of injustice that is prevalent in American culture.

I began to see how unjust systems in American culture affected African Americans. When I moved into my predominately African American Chicago neighborhood, I began to hear stories from my neighbors about how they were so tired of seeing drugs being sold all around them, and how they would cry out to the police for help only to have the police not respond.

In many cases, my African American neighbors got tired of having the police ignore their cry, and they would find a White friend to call the police on their behalf. The police would respond more quickly to a call from a White person. I began to hear stories from my neighbors about being afraid of police officers and not being able to trust them because they didn't feel like the police had either served or protected them.

After hearing story after story, I was reminded of something I had read as a sociology student at the University of Nebraska prior to moving to Chicago. While at Nebraska, I remember reading *The Souls of Black Folk* by W. E. B. Du Bois. While in North Lawndale, I began to observe a little of what Du Bois was writing about.

Du Bois writes:

Between me and the other world there is ever an unasked question: unasked by some through a feeling of delicacy; by others through the difficulty of framing it. All, nevertheless, flutter around it. They approach me in a half hesitant sort of way, eye me curiously or compassionately and then, instead of saying directly, How does it feel to be a problem? they say, I know an excellent colored man in my town; or I fought at Mechanicsville; or Do not these Southern Outrages make your blood boil? At these, I smile or am interested, or reduce the boil to a simmer, or as the occasion may require. To the real question, How does it feel to be a problem? I answer seldom a word.[1]

I have never felt like a problem. But having never felt like I was a problem *is* the problem for many of us who are White.

What do I mean? A system that produced and upholds White privilege has made it possible for me to not feel like a problem. It makes it possible for me to easily avoid anxiety as I encounter a police officer, any other person in a position of authority, and even a store clerk. While I worked as a family teacher with youth in group homes in Chicago, I made numerous trips to various stores with African American youth to shop for school clothes, groceries, and other necessities.

A visit to a clothing store or grocery store with two or three African American youths would often mean being closely watched or even followed by the store clerks. On a couple of occasions, I remember the youths just turning to the clerk and calling out, "Quit following me!" As their guardian, I felt uncomfortable with their angry responses, but I knew their frustration and knew they were in the right. My experience growing up was different. I can only remember being watched or followed by a store clerk once, and that was the time I was with a friend who actually was shoplifting!

White privilege allows me to be free from fear and frustration that results from being viewed with suspicion or being viewed as a problem. The fact that African Americans are viewed as a problem and I am not—is a problem, and it is a problem that must be addressed.

Even more of a problem, however, is that privilege allows me to not feel needy. Many African Americans know what it means to be in need. Internalized oppression, the feeling of being a problem, often results from marginalization. Countless experiences of being marginalized and a victim of injustice lead many to see themselves as a problem and to experience anxiety that comes with victimization. I certainly don't pretend to know what it's like to be Black in America and to know the kind of fear my African American neighbors feel. However, I do know this—because of the color of my skin, I am protected. I am not considered a problem in society, and I don't regularly experience being looked at with suspicion. I feel safe most of the time.

Canadian writer and game designer David Gaider once said, "Privilege is when you think that something's not a problem because it's not a problem to you personally."[2] My understanding of White privilege began with my experience in North Lawndale. We live in a world where the color of your skin has something to do with how the powerful and privileged either see you as a problem or not. We also live in a world where the color of your skin has something to do with how powerful or powerless you are and how safe or unsafe you are.

Take for example the encounter Aaron Layton had with police officers in St. Louis. Layton was a fellow student in graduate school and the author of *Dear White Christian: What Every Christian Needs to Know About How Black Christians See, Think, and Experience Racism in America*. He describes a common encounter with the police for African Americans in the United States, and yet quite different from any encounter I have ever had. In reflecting upon Michael Brown's death in the predominately African American city of Ferguson, Layton states:

> Michael Brown's death reopened wounds from my childhood, reminding me that I was still black and powerless within a white society.... It reminded me of the time when I was sixteen and was pulled over for speeding. I was going 42 mph in a 35 mph zone. The white police officer approached the car and said, "Get out of the car and stand right over there on the sidewalk and don't move." I did what I was told while the police officer called for backup. Once his backup arrived, another white police officer came and stood right next to me, while the first officer began to search my car.
>
> With a flashlight in his hand, he checked under the driver and passenger seats. He then checked the glove box, the back seat, and under the car. As a sixteen-year-old, African American teenager, I felt helpless and scared. I wondered to myself, "Did he have the right to search my car? Did he follow police protocol when he pulled me over? Why was he treating me this way? I am a good kid! As these questions and many others filled my mind, I ultimately realized that he could do to me whatever he wanted, and that saddened me. Just as the situation of Michael Brown's death did.[3]

I have been pulled over at least a few times for greater speeding violations than Layton's, and I have never even been asked to step out of my vehicle. For Layton, an encounter with the police was both anxiety producing and humiliating as he felt violated, helpless, and powerless, to the point that when another African American experienced injustice it had a profound impact on him.

Overt and obvious incidences of racism like the incident that Layton experienced are tragic. Justice demands we condemn this kind of racism and all other accounts of racism. Many of us who are White have not experienced overt and obvious racism, so it doesn't affect us to the point of actually speaking out against it or doing anything else about it. Furthermore, those of us who have not experienced overt and obvious racism often are not willing to give the benefit of the doubt to those who have.

Perhaps you might be thinking, "These incidents of overt and obvious racism like the one that Layton experienced don't happen to every African American." While this may be true, many more African Americans do regularly experience incidents of racism that are less obvious to White people. If we are not willing to give the benefit of the doubt to those who experience obvious and overt racism, then we are probably even less likely to acknowledge and validate the experiences of those who experience micro-aggressions, which African Americans experience regularly.

Micro-aggressions are commonplace. These are verbal or behavioral, sometimes unintended derogatory racial insults. For African Americans, these include comments directed toward them such as, "You don't act like a normal Black person" or "You're not like those other Black people." Another example of a micro-aggression is when an African American is in a group where they are the minority, and they are asked to speak for all African Americans about any given topic. For hundreds of years, both overt racism and micro-aggressive racism have continued to be prevalent in American society. Many would acknowledge this to be true, and yet the problem continues. Part of that problem is the problem of privilege. With privilege comes a great deal of skepticism toward African Americans, skepticism toward them even as they vulnerably communicate their experiences of racism, and especially when they call for racial justice.

I continue to be troubled by the lack of willingness of many of us who are White to acknowledge and affirm the validity of the experiences that lead African Americans and other people of color to feel unsafe and to feel as though they are a problem. In order to make any progress to alleviate the real problem, White people must acknowledge what's underneath our skepticism toward and our unwillingness to acknowledge and affirm the validity of the experiences of African Americans and other people of color. We must acknowledge our own self-justifying of this injustice.

Self-Justifying Injustice

A few months after my encounter with the police in North Lawndale, another significant incident occurred. This time I was working as a family teacher in the group home. Most of the youth who were living in the group home were from Chicago's west side or south side neighborhoods, and all but two of the dozens of youth I worked with were African American. I remember on one occasion taking a few of the youth to a nearby convenience store in a mostly White neighborhood.

After we went into the store to buy snacks, we got back in the van. I was in the driver's seat and could see that Nedra was upset. When we got back to the group home, I asked Nedra what the problem was. With tears streaming down her face, she cried out, "You don't know why I'm upset?! The man working at the convenience store called me the N word!"

Immediately, in my White mind, I thought, "Are you sure he said that to you?" I was quite naïve and thought grown men don't just call someone the N word. I thought back to the incident at the store. I remembered I had walked into the store behind Nedra and two of the other youths. Upon entering, all of them were happy and laughing. Then I heard the man say something that I assumed was a greeting. I didn't hear what he said, but I did remember that from that moment on, Nedra was angry. Nedra cried out, "You have to believe me! That White man really did say that to me!"

I turned to Nedra and said, "I am so sorry. Will you please forgive me for not taking you at your word?"

My first instinct as a privileged White male is to deny the widespread racism that exists in our society. I also immediately want to justify the actions of the one who is most similar to me culturally, even when his actions are unjust. I immediately wanted to give the White guy working at the convenience store the benefit of the doubt, even before Nedra.

Why is this? I contend that those of us with privilege are naturally on a quest for self-justification. And why do we seek self-justification? I believe we want to ease our guilt from the sin of our own racism, and in seeking to do this, we work hard to try to justify our own actions. We will even work hard to justify the actions of others with whom we are connected culturally.

What does the self-justification of racism in America look like? African Americans have been affected by unjust systems and many have often encountered White people who see them as a problem. At the same time, individuals and groups with power and privilege within the system have sought to justify their actions against African Americans.

For example, following the death of Michael Brown in Ferguson, many White people came to the defense of Officer Darren Wilson and tried to justify his actions by pointing to the allegation that Brown had stolen a box of cigars, and that if he had obeyed the law in the first place then he would have not been shot by an officer. Brown was unarmed. Wilson, who shot and killed Brown, was not indicted on any charges following the shooting.

As a people with privilege, what is our problem? Our problem is that all too often we seek to self-justify injustice. We do it by saying, "Well, he shouldn't have stolen the cigars."

Or take for example, the killing of Philando Castile. After being pulled over with his girlfriend Diamond Reynolds, Officer Jeronimo Yanez fired seven shots at Castile, killing him. Yanez was found not guilty in the death of Castile. For Yanez, the justification was that the officer's life was threatened. Castile did have a firearm in the car, but he also had a license to carry it. Furthermore, he informed the officers as he was reaching for his ID that he was not reaching for his firearm. And yet, a not guilty verdict for Yanez communicates to the public that Castile is somehow responsible for his own death.

In an article entitled, "If Philando Castile Was a Threat, Then Black People Are Never Safe," Jemar Tisby writes:

> Black people have been sold the lie of respectability. The white power structure has always told us that if we conduct ourselves responsibly, then we'll be fine: Pull up those sagging pants, speak "standard" English, work hard, don't blame the system. This endless list of boxes to check makes it easy to blame black people for their own deaths. If any marker of respectability is absent, then the victims deserve what they get.... White supremacy has always found a way to make black people culpable for their own persecution.[4]

When will we who are privileged begin to see that just because something is not a problem for me, does not mean is not a problem at all? When will we see that our privilege is a problem? When will we see that our privilege makes us susceptible to self-justifying injustice? The responses of many White people in trying to justify police shootings and tragic deaths of many African Americans like Michael Brown, and Philando Castile is troubling, to say the least.

Jemar Tisby continues:

> The recent not guilty verdict of the officer who killed Philando Castile has added to the pain of being black in America. As I've pondered the events, as well as the dashcam footage that authorities released after the decision, I thought, "If Philando Castile was a threat, then black people are never safe."[5]

Why is it that those of us with privilege seek to self-justify our injustice against African Americans? I believe we are driven by the dreadful feeling of our own guilt. It seems that individuals and groups of people with power and privilege are on a quest to ease their guilt, to remain confident and not needy, and they do so by justifying their own racist actions against people of color. How do I know this is true? Because I do it too. I've tried to justify my own racism against African Americans and other people of color. I've done it by driving my own suspicious heels into the ground and refusing to take African Americans at their word. I've done this to the point of defending a person that I don't know personally but who is culturally similar to me, like with my initial reaction to Nedra following the convenience store incident. I've done this when I've heard that an African American was shot by police and immediately the question in my mind is, "I wonder what he did to deserve being shot?" Privilege is a problem. I know this because it is my problem.

Is There a Way Forward Toward Justice?

Perhaps a way forward for those of us who are White is to acknowledge our tendency to self-justify, resist our natural tendency to react with suspicion, and instead listen to African Americans. To truly listen to someone means to give that person the benefit of the doubt. This comes first by acknowledging that our self-justification is often wrong.

Thankfully, for those of us who profess faith in Jesus Christ, there is a tangible way to turn from self-justification. Ultimately for Christians, our justification has been provided through Christ's death upon the cross. This means we have no need to self-justify, but instead ought to respond to God and others with humility. Jesus Christ is the justifier. He is the one who took upon himself the sins of the world and displayed justice for the world to see. Furthermore, the response of the Christian is to give up power and to use power for the sake of the powerless. After all, Jesus himself gave up power and used power for the sake of powerless sinners before almighty God. Jesus became weak and powerless crying out, *"Father, forgive them, for they know not what they do"* as he died a criminal's death upon the cross (Luke 23:34). He did this in order that in his resurrection many who are powerless would be raised to life and indeed justified. He justifies the powerless and needy and leads the powerless and needy into the world to do justly, love kindness, and walk humbly with God.

What steps can White people take to begin to address the problem?

Last night, my eight-year-old daughter, Noelle, asked me, "Dad, does God love poor people more than others?" I answered, "God has a special place for the poor and powerless—those who know their need; those who cry out in need."

Sometimes that cry is like the cry of Diamond Reynolds, "You just killed my boyfriend.... Please don't tell me that he is dead.... He was just getting his license and registration, sir." Sometimes the cry is like the cry of Eric Garner, "I can't breathe." Sometimes that cry is like the literal cry of Patrick Harmon as Salt Lake City police tried handcuffing him after pulling him over for failing to have a rear light on his bicycle. He broke away and ran from the police. The police shot him three times as he ran away from them. He cried more as he lay dying on the street.

Sometimes the cry is "Hands up, don't shoot!" Sometimes the cry is "Black lives matter." Do we not hear the cries? Will we not respond to the cries with mercy and justice? What if the cry is from a person of another color, another ethnicity, another language? Will we not respond to those in need who know their need?

As a White man, if I cry the system listens. Will those of us who the justice system favors listen to the cries of those whom the justice system doesn't favor? Will those of us who when pulled over, show our license and go on our way, listen to the cries of those who are searched and interrogated? Will those of us who wave and say hello to the police on bicycles listen to the cries of those who run from the police? Ecclesiastes 4:1 states:

> *Again I saw all the oppressions that are done under the sun. And behold, the tears of the oppressed, and they had no one to comfort them! On the side of their oppressors there was power, and there was no one to comfort them.*

Will those who have power and the privilege not only cry out, *"Let justice roll down"* (Amos 5:24) but also stand with, march with, and know their own need for grace and mercy—and their need to give up power and privilege for the sake of those who truly know they are powerless in a society where privilege is a problem?

---

1. W. E. B. Du Bois, *The Souls of Black Folk* (Oxford: Oxford University Press, 2007 [1903]), 7.
2. David Gaider, "Privilege is when you think something is not a problem because it's not a problem to you personally," Facebook, October 1, 2013, https://www.facebook.com/guerrillafeminism/posts/541422665928366
3. Aaron J. Layton, *Dear White Christian: What Every Christian Needs to Know About How Black Christians See, Think, and Experience Racism in America* (Lawrenceville, GA: Christian Education and Publications, 2017), 16–17.
4. Jemar Tisby, "If Philando Castile Was a Threat, Then Black People are Never Safe," *Reformed African American Network*, https://thewitnessbcc.com/philando-castile-threat-black-people-never-safe/.
5. Tisby, "If Philando Castile Was a Threat."

SITTING WITH MY WHITE PRIVILEGE
WHERE WHITE PEOPLE START

ASHLEY HALES

Ashley Hales is a writer, speaker, and host of the Finding Holy podcast. She is married to Bryce Hales, a pastor in the PCA, and they have four children. She is author of Finding Holy in the Suburbs *and writes at aahales.com.*

———

When I was eight years old, my family and I travelled to New York City. We toured the sites, but I most enjoyed the magic otherworld of Broadway theater. I sat enthralled with the set design and mirrors in *A Chorus Line,* and I swooned over seeing Bernadette Peters on stage.

After the show, I delighted in how my new pink, silky nightgown felt as I looked down on the big city from my hotel room. I was on the edge of something, the next adventure, the next life stage.

One morning, I smelled a noxious odor. My parents hugged my body close as a Black woman wearing a trash bag as a poncho pushed her shopping cart past us. I grew up in a pristine suburb on the West coast. That woman was my first brush with real homelessness. I'm sure my parents did the best they could, but all I remember is, when I heard the term "bag lady," my tender heart broke. How could the world be like this—where people wandered streets? Where all they had was in a shopping cart?

While I sat enamored by the lights of Broadway in New York City, others dug through trash. At the time, I didn't know what to do, so I wrote pencil lines of poetry. I still have those poems, and when I look through them I see the beginnings of childlike empathy. All these years later, I still ask the same question. What's one White girl from the suburbs supposed to do in the face of so much?

I grew up on the golden sands and golden promises of sunrise in southern California. A world of racism seemed in the historic past—stories of a broken humanity in another, more evil time. Surely we were past all that. I had a few friends of color, even if my neighborhood and my private school were largely White. I hadn't been involved in racist slurs or actions. My parents hadn't. It wasn't a part of my blood, I reckoned.

Oh but it was.

During my childhood I heard that our distant family members in Arkansas had owned slaves. Their names were recorded in the family Bible. When I was told about this history, it was quickly added that we weren't like those slave owners in *Uncle Tom's Cabin*.[1] Instead, the slaves our relatives owned generations ago were treated well. Our people were benevolent slave masters (as if there was such a thing), somehow better than all those other slave holders.

I was glad we'd all moved past those awful days.

Yet those words still ring in my ears: *They. We. Ours.* My family members owned humans—made full of worth and dignity. Each person created by God with their own particularities to glorify him and enjoy him forever. My family treated fellow human beings as *things* to be bought and sold. They were considered property. My family was shackled to the way things were, or economic success, or other polite sins that were easy not to call sin because they were acceptable. My family was built on the backs of oppression which allowed them to prosper because of White privilege. I am a part of the legacy of a family that owned people.

My knee-jerk reaction was to swallow this pill of my family's benevolent slavery—that we were the good ones at least, even when the world was so very broken by injustice and racism. It was easy to excuse as a young child because I didn't know any better. In childlike innocence, multiplied by my White privilege, I dismissed it.

I had dance classes to attend and homework to do. I travelled half an hour to my White, Christian, private school and forgot about any sort of slave-owning past. I gazed out the window of my mom's car, watching my world speed by at 65 mph, not knowing my hobbies, my education, and this very car ride were built on a foundation of systemic racism.

The Holy Spirit has more recently brought those early stories home to roost in my heart, however uneasily. I can't move past them at highway speed any longer. I can't excuse my beloved grandmother's reticence to meet the Black boyfriend of a relative with the convenient excuse, "She's from another time and another place." And I can't excuse the racism in my own heart which prefers Christian woman-hood in the church that only looks like me: blonde, blue-eyed, skinny jeans, and lattes.

I'm still learning how to own those stories of our past generations. I'm weary of passing racism like a hot potato to someone I can argue is more culpable. It's easy to hide in a cloak of abstractions like "justice for all," and "all men are created equal" and excuse oneself, excuse one's past, excuse the countless little ways we are culpable as individuals and as churches. I'm still trying to learn what it means to own my part in systemic sin. I'm still learning how to not simply be ashamed of my White privilege, but to sit with it, study it, and use it for good when the Lord leads me to.

That, too, is the call for my denomination, the Presbyterian Church in America (PCA). We are to glorify God and enjoy him forever in the Gospel proclamation to all peoples, tongues, and races. And when we have treated other believers as less than fully clothed in the righteousness of Christ (by our sins of commission or omission), we are called to repent, to lament, and to listen. Maybe that's how the church, and particularly how this one White woman from the suburbs, starts a journey toward racial reconciliation.

Where Does a White Person Start?

Therefore be it resolved, that the 44th General Assembly of the Presbyterian Church in America does recognize, confess, condemn and repent of corporate and historical sins, including those committed during the Civil Rights era, and continuing racial sins of ourselves and our fathers....[2]

We move toward reconciliation in small ways. We confess, we use words like "privilege," and we begin to listen.

Because most of us don't consider ourselves outright racists, we easily dismiss the "continuing racial sins of ourselves and our fathers." We think of ourselves as autonomous individuals, and the blessings we enjoy are the rewards we've worked hard to earn for ourselves. We de-personalize racism by putting it in the past (back then, before Civil Rights) or in another place (an urban core in another city). In doing so, we escape the idea that we are racists.

We then baptize a White, Protestant, boot-strapism faith as Christianity and think that with enough hard work anyone can succeed just like we have. But the problem is we have lost the ability to think about this as a collective problem. We think in terms of I, me, and mine, rather than in terms of we. And when we lose the ability to be "we" before "me," then we cannot move toward reconciliation.

This meritocracy of individualism is perhaps the most insidious part of owning up to our White privilege. John Metta wrote in the *Huffington Post*, "White people do not think in terms of we. White people have the privilege to interact with the social and political structures of our society as individuals."[3] Privilege means that for those in the majority culture, we have both advantages and access to systems of power and authority, but we're often completely unaware of all we have access to. It's simply the water we swim in.

I was born into a family of privilege. I grew up with two White parents who had jobs based on their accomplishments (and perhaps the color of their skin). It meant I had a private school education, and, being White, I didn't have to feel like I didn't belong. Systems, ways of doing things, how I wore my hair, what clothes my parents could afford, my education—these were all gifts of privilege. I never feared for my safety or worried about looking dangerous. I could be anything I wanted to be, do great things for God (a catchphrase in the heyday of evangelicalism in the '90s), and if things went terribly wrong, my parents could bail me out. This safety net was assumed, unarticulated in the fabric of my privilege. For middle-class Whites, racism was "back then," and our mostly White congregation was just our particular brand of Christianity. Or so I thought.

But as Christians—no matter our race—our primary allegiance is not to a race, a society, or a nation, but to the Kingdom of God. The story of salvation does not start with "I," it starts with God. We love and serve a God who models power through weakness to save his bride, the Church.

In Jesus' Church, we start with confession. We're called to rethink the very privilege that might construct our stories from any individualist perspective, that we can do anything, be anyone, work hard, and end up successful. In order for us to move toward reconciliation, we must start with owning up to the privilege that we have because of our race.

The Church must lead the way in both repentance and lament. We must allow space for those of us who are White to grieve our generational silences and all the ways our lives are made easier because of our racial and socio-economic advantages. We must allow people of color the space to offer Gospel-centered critique of the ways we've been infected with a version of Christianity that has more to do with our skin color and the advantages that it affords us than the Gospel of Jesus. Because, if God is making all things new through his Gospel, then in God's Kingdom even here and now there will be a foretaste of tearing down walls and division. If we are one in Christ (Gal. 3:28), then the church must be ethnically, racially, and socioeconomically diverse. We must welcome critique and differing cultural experiences.

We always move toward reconciliation through confession. When Jesus wanted to tell us about the character of God, he told a story of a father who runs to meet his child who has come home after disowning the father and squandering the father's resources and love (Luke 15). When we experience a love like that, we can have the courage to take a flying leap and cast ourselves on the mercy of our Father in heaven. We can learn to sit uncomfortably in our places of privilege.

We Start by Listening

Our first gesture toward reconciliation must always be confession. We repent when we see we've fallen into blame-shifting and self-justification. We must repeatedly place ourselves firmly within the grace and mercy of Jesus' redemption. Then we begin conversations not by talking but by listening.

But how do we do this? It's easy to get overwhelmed by the insidious ways racism infects our own hearts, let alone our neighborhoods, cities, and systems. Where do we even start?

Just like starting a new habit, we stay put and start small. When we want to eat healthy, we start with the next meal and the meal after that. When we want to begin a workout routine, we plan it out and get accountability. When we work at growing our imagination beyond the confines of privilege, we pray for God to move and we begin to listen to other voices, day by day. Diversity isn't just a seat at a White table where we include racially-other people who have bought into the ways, means, and beliefs of White culture. Diversity means our own tables are up for deconstruction and reconstruction by a Gospel that embraces all peoples.

I've had to start small. I've listened in on conversations between women of color on Twitter and been a part of more intimate conversations through a voice-messaging app. I ask questions about what's one White woman to do in the suburbs, and I listen. I've consciously followed the writing of Christian men and women of color to see what they love, what they read, and what they're concerned with. I've invited women of color to tell me how my writing rubs them the wrong way because of the inevitable blind spots of privilege. I listen to podcasts from Christian men and women who share from their experience as racially-other in a White America. As we take in information online about an experience that is not our own, we learn to call a spade a spade, to name our privilege, and ask good questions.

Then we move out into our real-world, lived experiences. In her book on hospitality Christine Pohl writes that because "many of us are situated so centrally... we have to make conscious decisions to experience marginality in our lives."[4] We say hello to someone who doesn't look like us. We start conversations with the other soccer moms who aren't White. We show up to the town meeting and hear from people who don't hide behind their picket fences because they can't; they don't have the privilege to do so. We meet our neighbors and invite them into our home. We read books. We always move toward bearing the burden of someone who does not have the same access we do. After all, Christ entered into our vulnerability and limitations, not to lecture us out of it or even as a good example, but to show us the way home in God's Kingdom.

Our conversations feel small. Our listening feels inconsequential, because it is. It's inconvenient. We might never start a movement, but by God's grace we show up in laying down our privilege for others— even in small ways. As Dr. King acknowledged in Montgomery, Alabama, after they'd marched from Selma: "There are no broad highways that lead us easily and inevitably to quick solutions."[5] There is only our firm commitment to de-center ourselves, to recognize the ways in which we are complicit in a legacy of racism, repent, and pray for healing—for us, our neighborhoods, cities, nation, and world.

Dear White people, let us learn to sit in our privilege, repent, and begin the long road of listening.

1. *Uncle Tom's Cabin*; or, *Life Among the Lowly*, is an anti-slavery novel by American author Harriet Beecher Stowe. Published in 1852, the novel had a profound effect on attitudes toward African Americans and slavery in the US and is said to have "helped lay the groundwork for the Civil War." Wikipedia, s.v., "Uncle Tom's Cabin."

2. https://byfaithonline.com/wp-content/uploads/2016/06/Overture-43-clean.pdf

3. John Metta, "I, Racist," Huffington Post, July 10, 2015, http://www.huffingtonpost.com/john-metta/i-racist_b_7770652.html.

4. Christine D. Pohl, *Making Room: Recovering Hospitality as a Christian Tradition* (Grand Rapids: Eerdmans, 1999), 123.

5. Martin Luther King Jr., "Address at the Conclusion of the Selma to Montgomery March," March 25, 1965, http://kingencyclopedia.stanford.edu/encyclopedia/documentsentry/doc_address_at_the_conclusion_of_selma_march.1.html.

PEOPLE LIKE US

ROBERT LEE WOOTTON, JR.

Rob Wootton is a church planter in Billings, Montana. He has a BFA in Art Education from Virginia Commonwealth University and an MDiv from Covenant Theological Seminary. Rob is married to Robin (who has also contributed to this book); they have four children.

———

Driving on the rural backroads of Suffolk, Virginia, I had no idea where I was. I had no map (this was before GPS on the phone) so I pulled into an unusually busy country fuel mart. Two women stood behind the counter—a middle-aged Black woman and a younger White woman. Without thinking, I approached the White woman and asked if she could give me directions to the junk yard I was trying to find. She looked at me as if I were speaking another language and after an awkward pause the Black woman started to give me clear concise directions. She wasn't angry, but I could feel the tension in her voice. And when I looked into her eyes I saw what was in my heart: racism.

You may protest and say something like, "Rob, you're being too hard on yourself. We all gravitate toward people who are more like us." Yes, but that's the beginning of perceiving those who are like us (racially, economically, socially) as the ones to be trusted over and above those who are different. Add to that entrenched positions of power and privilege I've enjoyed as a White male and, inevitably, you have the makings of a racist.

If you're like me, you learn most by stories. So here's another one from my life.

I lost a silly bet with my wife. Since she won, I had to cut my hair into a mohawk and dye it blue. I liked the look of it, but since it wasn't a look I could keep for work, I only kept it a couple of days. One of those days we went to a museum, and as soon as we walked in, a security guard started to follow us. I am not a small guy (broad shoulders, nearly six feet tall). I often have a big beard, can wear a scowl across my brow if I'm not careful, have a few tattoos, usually wear a t-shirt, jeans, and boots. I have been told I can be intimidating. Add a blue mohawk and, if you're a security guard at a museum, that is a guy you want to make sure doesn't do anything stupid. We were followed.

Robin and I laughed about it and still do at times.

Then, not too long ago, I was sitting with a congregant (a recently retired blue-collar worker who had grown up poor). The issue of White Privilege had come up, and he protested that he had enjoyed little privilege growing up as an impoverished White man in rural, central Virginia. I tried explaining the privilege he enjoys. For example, when he walks into a convenience store, the clerk typically won't closely watch him, wondering if he'll try to steal something or do something even worse. I told him about being followed by that security guard because of my stupid haircut. And then I asked him, "What if I was followed every time I went into a museum... every time I walked into a department store... every time I went into a gas station... not because of a stupid haircut (a decision I did make) but because of the color of my skin (a decision I didn't make)?"

We all prejudge people every day based on appearance. We prejudge people based on what they wear, their jewelry, their hair, their height, their weight, and the color of their skin. Then we, often subconsciously, make decisions about that person's intelligence, significance, and importance. That's what I did in that Suffolk fuel mart all those years ago. I assumed the middle-aged Black woman was not as knowledgeable as the White woman. I assumed the White women would be more articulate and would know where I needed to go.

I assumed these things in the blink of an eye because I have been raised in a culture that had impressed those judgments into my heart and mind without my ever being aware of their racist implications. In James 2:4, the Apostle James says that because I make these distinctions, I have become a judge with evil thoughts. Evil!

It's stunning to consider that making those distinctions between two female employees places me in the category of *evil*. And that's where the conversation turns. Are our subtle, often subconscious, pre-judgments (based on race) really *evil*?

No one *wants* to acknowledge their prejudices—racism, classism or sexism. Yet if these tendencies were not part of our fallen human nature, why would the Apostle Paul need to address them? *"There is neither Jew nor Greek, there is neither slave nor free; there is no male and female, for you are all one in Christ Jesus"* (Gal. 3:28). Paul is talking to Christians, so we should assume that these racist tendencies don't automatically go away upon our conversion.

We White Christians may have Black friends. And we may have never used the N word. But the evil of racism can still be prevalent.

That's been true for me. I remember using the N word—in anger, fear, and frustration— because I wanted to blame *them* for all the difficulties I had encountered during my middle school years. I was in seventh grade and, after getting into a fight, had just gotten off the school bus. I went into our house crying. My mother asked me what was wrong, and I blurted out something like, "It was because of all those stupid n-----s." What would lead to such prejudiced blame-shifting?

My family had moved to Southampton County, Virginia, during the summer before my sixth grade year. My father worked for the Virginia Department of Corrections (VADOC), and he had been transferred to the Southampton Correctional Center to serve as the Assistant Warden. There had previously been a rule in the VADOC that the Warden had to live on the grounds of the facility where he served (not inside the fence but on the property). As the story goes, a former Warden had his own property in the area, and he circumvented this rule by having a large six-bedroom mansion not too far from the fence built slowly by one inmate. It reportedly took twenty years to complete! By the time we arrived in Southampton, the rule had changed, and the current Warden lived elsewhere.

We moved into this mansion on a three-acre yard, manicured each week by inmates, with a white fence surrounding it. The immaculate residence sat up on a little hill and looked down upon several hundred yards of green grass and neatly trimmed bushes adjacent to a rural Virginia backroad. It looked much like a southern plantation home from the days of slavery.

Yet this occurred *after* the Civil Rights movement. So did my enrollment in Virginia's public schools: the summer of 1984 (in a district historically run by majority-White Southampton County). But by now, the student population was more than 70 percent African American. The county demographics had never previously shown blacks to be in the majority. Just fifteen years prior (1969) desegregation was mandated by the Commonwealth of Virginia and, as was the case across most southern states, private schools (majority-White) opened within the same year. For us it was Southampton Academy.

Though it is rarely stated plainly, it was clearly in response to desegregation. My father was born in California and moved regularly all over the world as the son of a career Air Force officer. He was politically liberal and would have nothing to do with sending me and my sister to the all-White private school. So I was picked up each morning in front of our inherited warden residence, the mansion. And when that chubby twelve-year-old White kid stepped onto the bus and looked up at all those Black faces, he had no idea about the troubled racial history he was entering.

Southampton County had been the site of the largest and deadliest slave uprising in US history. It's where Nat Turner (1831)[1] led more than seventy enslaved and free blacks in a revolt that killed as many as sixty-five White southerners. In retaliation, nearly two hundred Blacks were executed or murdered.

One hundred fifty years later the racial tension in the county was still palpable. Our family was attending Capron United Methodist Church, founded thirty years after the Civil War (1895). In the mid-1980s when we were there, it was still all White. I do recall one occasion when a Black man came into the service late and sat near the back. The small church gathering, with fewer than fifty attendees, noticed this man (some staring), and the tension this created for the rest of the service was evident. At the end of the worship service, this man stood and politely thanked us for allowing him to worship with us and left. As a preteen and then teenager, I never heard any more about his visit.

I did hear rumors of a family in the church whose home was the site of one of the Nat Turner killings, that even the hardwood floors were still stained with blood. There was also a rumor that another family from our church kept, as an heirloom, a change-purse made from Nat Turner's skin after his brutal execution.[2]

Does this give you pause? Can you begin to enter into the emotional horror of these rumors, and what these stories (plus the attitudes behind them) mean for Blacks in America?

Did the thirty-or-so Black children on that bus know anything of the history that surrounded me when I walked into their lives? Probably not. They knew what they saw: a chubby White kid who lived in a mansion.

It didn't matter that we were squarely middle class, my father being a mid-level state employee. It didn't matter that the reason we were able to live in such a nice, big house was because of my dad's job. Yet, I must admit, our family income was higher by far than most of the Black families in the county, which ranked nationally among the lowest income levels. What mattered is the White kid getting on the bus that day had what they did not, and what most of them would never have.

So I was bullied. This word doesn't seem sufficient. I'll use *abused*.

I kept getting abused in sixth, seventh, and part of eighth grade. By whom? One hundred percent by Black kids, and it became a significant part of my counseling later in life.

In eighth grade, I wrote a three-page suicide note and put a gun to my head, feeling the pressure on the trigger as it moved a millimeter before firing. I didn't pull any farther. I didn't understand at the time all the forces that were working against me. There were issues other than the history of racism in Southampton County that moved me into that chair with a gun in my hand. But this issue of racism should not be discounted as a main factor. I didn't understand the effects racial prejudice had on the kids who abused me, on their parents who grew up in segregated schools, on their grandparents whose country's armed forces were segregated, or on their great-grandparents who grew up with actual eyewitness accounts of southern slavery's horrors.

Was I singled out because of my skin-color? Yes, but the racism I experienced was not born out of a sense of superiority, or even that I should be made aware of those distinctions. What I suffered was just the opposite. My abuse was born out of the frustration, pain, and suffering of my county's Blacks who had been made to feel inferior, and were themselves abused because White men thought their African American ancestors were less than human.

Does this excuse the actions of those kids who bullied and abused me? There had been a significant system of oppression at work in Southampton County, a system going back to Nat Turner's generation. That system had continuing implications.

But that doesn't excuse sin leading to more sin. Were they using race or the abuse their fore-bearers suffered as an excuse for why they attacked me? No. But it helps me now to understand why those kids did what they did to me.

It helps me to forgive. It helps me to extend grace. It helps me listen patiently when minorities share the difficulties their families have faced because they never had the positions of privilege and power Whites have enjoyed.

Privilege. It has become a hot-button word laced with political implications. Can we set aside those implications and consider what the word actually means? Dictonary.com defines it as, "a special right, advantage, or immunity granted (or available) only to a particular person or group of people."[3]

I recently went to court with my sixteen-year-old so he could receive his driver's license. It is the type of event meant to impress upon parents and their newly empowered children the great responsibility of driving. As the county's Commonwealth Attorney, a State Police Officer, the County Sheriff, and the Juvenile & Domestic Relations District Court Presiding Judge lectured us all on the dangers of driving and the importance of wearing your seatbelt. The point hammered home above all others was that your driver's license is a *privilege* not a right.

I was privileged to grow up in a home with both my parents. I was privileged to grow up never wondering where my next meal would come from. I was privileged that both my parents had college degrees and expected the same for me. I was privileged to travel our country, and even a few others, as a kid. I was privileged to receive a college education. And I received many other privileges of which I wasn't aware, ones which relatively few in the history of the world have ever had.

When I was born Robert Lee Wootton, Jr. at Saint Mary's Hospital in Richmond, Virginia, it was less than four miles away from Monument Avenue and the memorial to slave-owner Robert E. Lee, the famed and celebrated General of the Confederate States of America. If you've never seen this street, it is impressive. The statues are grand, towering above the equally grand homes. Other Confederate heroes memorialized besides Lee are: J. E. B. Stuart, Jefferson Davis, Thomas "Stonewall" Jackson, and Matthew Fontaine Maury.

Over the years this Monument Avenue area was developed and became a highly favored neighborhood for Richmond's upper-middle and upper-class residents, many of whom named their sons Robert or Lee (as did my middle-class parents). Robert and Lee are both names that have been and are still widely used in our Southern culture. Robert was also a family name, and it was not at all unusual that my paternal grandparents, both Virginians, named their first-born Robert Lee Wootton. Born in Richmond and growing up in Virginia, I heard many glowing tributes to my namesake's brilliance as a general, his kindness as a man, and his respectability as an outstanding member of society.

Contrast this with the Black baby born in the same city, in the same hospital, even on the same day, born to a single mom in the projects. What did his mother say to him when they later walked down Monument Avenue together? How did she explain why this former slave owner who fought for the right to continue owning people of a different skin-color was memorialized and celebrated more than one hundred years after the Civil War?

When faced with White privilege, did she keep her head down as many before her did? I looked up, and most of the time I wondered if I could climb that statue. But I also thought, "That is an impressive work of art." I looked up to Robert E. Lee. I kept my head high. I walked around without any thought to the suffering that was a direct result of why that statue was created in the first place. I have always looked up, without fear, without worry, without wondering if I would be able to obtain any of the goals my privileged upbringing had set for me.

I'm smart but not brilliant. I work hard when I have the right motivation. If I had been that Black boy born to a single mom in the urban projects, would that same level of average intelligence and motivation be enough to escape the systemic poverty and injustice into which many Black children are born in this country?

Maybe. But I'm not convinced of it. For example, in high school, I got caught up in drugs and alcohol. Without the privileges of my race and upbringing, would I have been able to break free from those shackles? Not all my White friends with similar privileges escaped.

What if there were other shackles like poverty, substandard government housing, failing schools, broken families, domestic violence, and the ghetto violence of a community that has been left behind?

Maybe it wouldn't have been surprising if I had ended up in a group like those young White supremacists who marched in Charlottesville, Virginia, during that horrible August day in 2017. I remember seeing the media images of those men and experiencing something peculiar. They looked like me, or at least like I did before my hair turned gray.

Racially, these were my people. But theologically, their message was different from mine—indeed, directly in opposition to mine. My message is the Gospel of Jesus Christ which unites all peoples of every hue under his banner. Without God's amazing grace intervening, I could have been one of them.

I had been born in the "cradle of the Confederacy" at a time when parents of school-age kids were grappling with the angst caused by court-ordered segregation in the White community. Then there was the bullying and abuse I received at the hands of Black kids when I was in middle school. These factors could have led me to the place where I joined with people like me to protect, and even fight for, the place of privilege into which I was born. When my son and I were lectured about the privilege of driving, the judge made it clear it was a privilege that could be taken away. Is that fear of losing a privilege what's behind the angst of those who rise to defend their White heritage? Why had I not become a White supremacist, standing up to fight for my threatened privilege? "There but for the grace of God go I...."

What does the Bible say about privilege? How does the Word of God speak into our prejudiced culture? Well, if you do a quick search in your English translations for the word "privilege" you come up almost empty. There are two exceptions: 2 Corinthians 8:4 and Philippians 1:29. Searches for privilege's English synonyms, "advantage" and "benefit," take us far afield. We can better understand a word's meaning when we take a word from the original languages in the Bible (Hebrew, Aramaic, or Greek) and then see how it and its cognates are used throughout Scripture. We can also consider how the word is used outside the Bible during the same time period. But here and now, in this time period, we have a word that is arguably absent from the Bible and yet is widely used and its meaning debated. So how do we apply the Bible's wisdom in seeking to understand privilege, particularly the issue at hand—White privilege?

In the New International Version (NIV), we read in 2 Corinthians 8:1–4:

And now, brothers and sisters, we want you to know about the grace that God has given the Macedonian churches. In the midst of a very severe trial, their overflowing joy and their extreme poverty welled up in rich generosity. For I testify that they gave as much as they were able, and even beyond their ability. Entirely on their own, they urgently pleaded with us for the privilege *of* sharing *in this service to the Lord's people.* [emphasis mine]

In this context, the Apostle Paul reports how the churches of Macedonia view it as their χάριν (*charin*) to give generously to those in need. In the NIV and New Revised Standard Version (NRSV) χάριν is translated as "privilege." Interestingly, here we see that the Christians in Macedonia were not the so-called "people of privilege" in their day. Not only were they poor, but they had little power and influence in their culture. What they did have, it was their privilege to give, to share.

In the NRSV Philippians 1:29 says: *"For he has graciously granted you the* privilege *not only of believing in Christ, but of suffering for him as well"* [emphasis mine].

Here the Apostle Paul encourages the members of the church in Philippi that God ἐχαρίσθη (*echaristhē*) privileges them to believe in Jesus and then suffer for him. In the NRSV ἐχαρίσθη is translated, *graciously granted you the privilege*. It is the Christian's *privilege* to believe. It is the Christian's *privilege* to suffer in Jesus' name. This is different from the way we usually consider *privilege!*

Those of you who are students of biblical languages will have noticed these two words and their cognates are not usually translated "privilege." They point to our understanding of who God is and how he responds to us by grace. Even the beginning Greek student will be familiar with χάρις (*charis*), the root of both χάριν (*charin*) and ἐχαρίσθη (*echaristhē*). It's one of the first vocabulary words in your stack of flash cards as you begin to study the language of the New Testament. It's one of the most important words in our understanding of who God is and how he responds to us. It's grace.

What if, instead of calling it privilege, we understand grace to be all that we have in our lives? We know grace is not deserved. It's given. We know grace is not a right. It's a gift. And grace demands humility. The privilege and the grace I've received in my life should give me more reasons to extend grace toward those who, without such privileges, have suffered.

This isn't likely to change the way our culture thinks and discusses White privilege, but it should change the way White Christians consider their responsibility in this generation. It makes clear that the fear of losing a privilege is in direct opposition to what the Bible teaches about the grace that we have received—and that whatever benefit we have, whatever advantage in life that has been graced to us, must be used to serve others. A goal of mine is to help the White community see they have privileges that, by and large, minorities do not have. Of course the goal shouldn't be that the minorities also have those privileges (or to take away the privileges inherent to growing up White in our country). The goal of pointing out White community privilege to fellow Whites is to challenge them to think how their privilege is used or abused.

Some then respond with White guilt or patronization that sends White Christians into poor minority communities to try and help, or assuage their guilt—trying to feel better about themselves in a misguided altruism. A better response from a clearer understanding of White privilege is twofold. We must listen, and we must remain quiet as people of color speak of how they have suffered. Have you listened and remained quiet amidst shared stories of marginalization, or of how people of color have been made to feel like second-class citizens? Every person of color has these stories. Every one.

We've seen that the Bible turns this idea of privilege on its head, pointing to *grace*. We're told as Christians (even middle-class White believers) that we're privileged to suffer, and that we are privileged to give despite maybe having little.

But beware. Many of the privileges I've had as a White male can become stumbling blocks. That's why Jesus tells us it's a huge challenge for the wealthy, those with worldly privileges, to enter the kingdom of heaven (Matt. 19:24). When we do enter his kingdom through the Gospel, it's our privilege to give of ourselves. It's our privilege to become less, so others can become more. It's our privilege to sit quietly in humility. It's our privilege to receive grace when we don't deserve it. It is God's grace to us. Therefore, it is our privilege to take a lesser place. It's our privilege to become more like Jesus.

So if there is any encouragement in Christ, any comfort from love, any participation in the Spirit, any affection and sympathy, complete my joy by being of the same mind, having the same love, being in full accord and of one mind. Do nothing from selfish ambition or conceit, but in humility count others more significant than yourselves. Let each of you look not only to his own interests, but also to the interests of others. Have this mind among yourselves, which is yours in Christ Jesus, who, though he was in the form of God, did not count equality with God a thing to be grasped, but emptied himself, by taking the form of a servant, being born in the likeness of men. And being found in human form, he humbled himself by becoming obedient to the point of death, even death on a cross. (Phil. 2:1–8)

In our sin we want to use whatever privilege we have to serve ourselves, to make our place in society exalted, to secure our rights. The Christian uses the grace received, no matter how small, to serve others, to give to those in need, to extend more grace—not to protect, not to preserve.

I don't need to preserve or protect my heritage. I don't need to preserve or fight for my history. I'm called to empty myself and serve. That is my privilege.

This painting was made by Abi Wootton, one of Rob's daughters. It depicts different hair color, textures, and styles. They're mixing together, not all the same, wonderful as each individually, but creating a picture of how we're better and beautiful together.

---

1. See Wikipedia, s.v. "Nat Turner," https://en.wikipedia.org/wiki/Nat_Turner

2. Christopher Klein, "10 Things You May Not Know About Nat Turner's Rebellion," history.com, May 24, 2016, http://www.history.com/news/history-lists/10-things-you-may-not-know-about-nat-turners-rebellion.

3. "privilege," *Random House Unabridged Dictionary*, Random House, 2018. *Dictionary.com* http://www.dictionary.com/browse/privilege

SINS OF OMISSION AND COMMISSION

CAN A MAN LOVE GOD AND HATE HIS NEIGHBOR?

BECKY CARLOZZI

Becky Carlozzi lives in Oklahoma City, Oklahoma, with her husband and two boys. Becky is part of a multiethnic team that created a job-training program designed to provide community and full-time employment with a living-wage salary for single moms caught in the cycle of poverty and social injustice. She received her undergraduate degree from Oklahoma State University and her post-graduate degree as a Physician Associate (PA-C) from the University of Oklahoma. She maintains clinic hours at Good Shepherd Clinic in downtown Oklahoma City.

I stood in the antebellum St. James Hotel in Selma, Alabama on a Friday evening. I was the only White person in the hotel. It was my first ever trip to the Southeastern United States. I'm a New Mexico native who eventually settled in a predominantly White urban core neighborhood in Oklahoma City. I had no significant experience with Black culture.

As I arrived in Selma in my oversized SUV with my Patagonia bag strapped on my back, I started to recognize the various White culture stereotypes that were strikingly true of me. I was accustomed to blending in with those around me and had rarely been in situations where I noticed that I belonged to a particular culture. As I sat in the St. James Hotel restaurant and looked at the faces of those around me, my mind swirled with questions. My heart was unsettled and apprehensive as I anticipated all the lessons I knew I had yet to learn about myself, others, and God through the lens of race and culture in the US.

Having toured the National Civil Rights Museum in Memphis that same morning, I arrived in Selma unsettled about what my skin color represented. The weight of this reality only increased after I saw from my hotel room the historic Edmund Pettus Bridge stretched across the Alabama River. I recalled how a protest was organized in 1965 to raise awareness of the unjust policies that prevented Black men and women from registering to vote.

The march was intended to conclude in the state capital of Montgomery, over fifty miles from Selma. Early on in the journey, on the opposite side of the river, armed Alabama state troopers, flanked by a crowd of angry civilians, blocked passage across the bridge. In a frenzy of unprovoked brutality, the state troopers attacked and pursued the protesters, dispersing the march to Montgomery. Members of the press captured the chaos on film, which raised national awareness and sympathy for the need for legislation for Civil Rights, including voting access for everyone.

Images from that day scrolled through my mind: White police officers on horseback with clubs outstretched in pursuit of unarmed Black men and women fleeing toward Selma. Tear gas filled the air, punctuating brutal displays of unnecessary force by Alabama state troopers. Recalling these scenes from Bloody Sunday stirred in me a mixture of anger, sadness, and solemnity. As my gaze fixed on the bridge in the distance, I felt like I was watching the events occur in real time.

Fatigued both mentally and physically, I decided to head to the hotel restaurant with plans to have a quiet dinner before retiring early. A staff member had informed me that I was the only overnight guest, but I soon discovered the hotel restaurant was a popular gathering place for locals on Friday nights. As I made my way downstairs, I started to feel hyper-aware as I naïvely felt like every step and body movement was being watched. Apart from visiting Johannesburg, South Africa as a teen, I had never felt as self-conscious about the color of my skin. Being "colorblind," I quickly discovered, was much easier to accomplish when I blended in. Taking my seat, I was ashamed and frustrated with myself for feeling unsettled in a room full of Black people.

A few minutes into my meal, a man named Frank, with a boldness I couldn't help but respect, said what everyone else must have been thinking: "I just have to ask," he said in a direct yet non-threatening way, "what in the world are you doing in Selma?"

I fumbled around with an answer about my church talking through issues regarding racial reconciliation. I tried to describe my hopes of knowing more about the history of race in the United States and mentioned my scheduled tour of the National Voting Rights Museum in the morning. Immediately, I was disappointed with the inadequacy of my answer. I knew my trip was motivated by a deficiency more profound than a better grasp of historical data and an orderly timeline of Civil Rights events. In a deeper place within my heart, I sensed a desire to be connected to my brothers and sisters of color, but I simultaneously recognized my unworthiness in seeking out this connection.

I knew I represented centuries of oppression because of my skin color and because of my faith. The more I learned about chattel slavery[1] and Jim Crow laws[2] in the United States, the more I wondered why the White Church didn't do more to fight against the injustices unleashed against the African American community. This unease echoed through my mind as I recalled an exhibit I had seen the same morning from the National Civil Rights Museum in Memphis. In one particular picture, an African American woman stood on a crowded sidewalk holding a sign with the poignant question: "Can a man love God and hate his brother?"

This image moved me to tears as I opened my heart to feel the sting of the accurate portrayal and condemnation of the White Church in America. From what I was learning, White Christians were often complicit in the suffering of their brothers and sisters of color. For example, in the early 1960s it took an entire campaign of "kneel-ins" to desegregate the all-White Second Presbyterian Church in Memphis. Elders of the church blocked the doors to the sanctuary and would not allow Black men and women to enter for worship services.

I wondered if instances like this went through Frank's mind as I sat with him and talked about my predominantly White church starting to wrestle through issues of racial reconciliation in 2016. The reality of segregated worship services just now starting to light a fire in my soul had been an unavoidable reality for Frank his entire life because his skin color was different than mine. The vast majority of churches in America remain mono-ethnic today, and I wondered how this ongoing reality affected Frank's view of Christ and his church. Segregation was not merely a sin of my ancestors but also a sin of my generation. It was and is my sin.

Over the preceding year leading up to that Friday evening in Selma, God had convicted me of prejudice inside my heart as well as my general lack of intentional love for my brothers and sisters of color. He also revealed my blindness to the ripple effect of past and current acts of racism. Like a surfer using an incoming wave to propel himself to the shore, I saw how I enjoyed riding the momentum of deep-rooted systems of injustice. My pride had cunningly camouflaged this truth for far too long. Thus, my journey to learn more about the history of race in the United States was becoming increasingly personal and less historical in nature.

Through the journey, I began to see myself more clearly. I wondered how much of knowing myself better was wrapped up into the very question of race I erroneously and ignorantly thought applied only to people of color. Thoughts like these swirled through my head, but I couldn't seem to corral any of them that evening, nor did I feel confident enough in myself to articulate to Frank my journey thus far. Uncomfortable in my own skin and stumped by a simple question, my first reaction was to shrink away and disappear back up the stairs.

But Frank was persistent, "What do you do for a living?" he asked inquisitively. "A reporter?"

"No, I am a stay-at-home mom of two young boys," I replied.

I also added how I enjoyed writing and had led a few women's Bible studies at my church. Frank leaned in slightly from his seat with a perplexed look on his face that revealed he was still curious about my solo journey that brought me through Memphis and Selma and with plans to head to Jackson, Mississippi. I knew that my replies to his questions were inadequate and disjointed, but I wasn't sure how else to explain my motivation for being there. I didn't possess a vocabulary that matched what was going on inside my heart. Perceptive enough to sense my squirming, Frank didn't press any further.

Instead of dismissing me as the novice I was, he treated me with respect by welcoming me into the ongoing political discussion with his friends. I was excited to be a part of this conversation and even felt a bit of relief that the topic was shifting away from race and my reason for being in Selma. Throughout my life, I have felt out of place because of my desire to bring up unsafe topics like politics and religion. I long for these types of conversations and felt more comfortable with my ability to contribute in a more articulate way.

Straightening up in my seat and trying to downplay my nerdy anticipation, I listened carefully to Frank and his friends as they discussed the upcoming election between Donald Trump and Hillary Clinton. The intensity increased as one gentleman, who had taken his seat to my left and appeared to be about my age, passionately made a point about the only difference he saw between subsidy and welfare.

"Subsidy is the word used when the government bails out White people and welfare is what they call it when Blacks are given money," he said with clear conviction in his voice. I wondered if he remembered I was sitting beside him.

"Surely this isn't true," I thought, but I didn't want to speak the words out loud.

The man didn't pause long enough for my brain to think of an argument to challenge his claim. Before I knew it, he began to rant about a recent local election in Selma. Evidently voter turnout had been very low, even among this man's family, and he was outraged by the apathy.

"Not voting!" he exclaimed in disgust, shaking his head while he spoke.

I recalled the local election in my home community in Oklahoma City. I didn't show up to vote. His anger seemed a little intense for a local election, and I was feeling uncomfortable again.

Sheepishly I asked, "Why does this upset you so much?"

"My parents were foot soldiers in the march of 1965," he replied in a raised voice as he pointed in the direction of the Edmund Pettus Bridge. "They risked their lives so we could have the right to vote," he added with a firmness and resolution I immediately admired.

At that instant, I began to recognize how vastly different our experiences of America were. His outright distaste for poor voter turnout was justified. Furthermore, what I initially interpreted as misplaced and overblown emotion in communicating his political views started to make more sense. How often had I misinterpreted emotion when it came to minorities discussing race relations in the United States?

No longer did the Civil Rights Movement feel like a distant historical event remembered through black-and-white photos in my high school history book. Sitting around me were individuals with countless personal experiences of bigotry and hatred unlike anything I had ever known. At this point I started to understand how deeply race and culture shape worldview. Undoubtedly, I was the last person in the room to make this connection.

Sitting there in mind-blown silence, I concluded race intertwines with every aspect of life because race matters. I'd always believed skin color didn't matter anymore in the United States. Perhaps because I didn't want to deal with the implications if it did. Within my myopic sphere of homogeneity, I'd been able to neatly relegate the color of my skin and its meaning to a box inside my brain, a box I ignorantly believed I could open and close at will. I didn't allow my boxes for politics and race to overlap much because I didn't see any benefit if they did. After so many years of viewing my life experiences in White culture as normal, I had not fully comprehended the complexities and enormity of my blind spots.

Imagining America as post-racial, my political views were woefully uniform. I remembered how pride accompanies poor lighting. My husband and I joke about how conscious we become of our skin blemishes when staying in a hotel that has a magnified mirror in a well-lit bathroom. Wrinkles, deep skin pores and hair in unwanted places all become undeniable with an extreme close-up view. Seeing my face in this light tends to foster humility in the same way that I was humbled by the exposure of my ignorance and hidden prejudice that Friday evening at the St. James Hotel.

What else had I been missing? How could confronting the reality of race—not only the history of race but the current reality of race in America—enhance not only my self-understanding but also my comprehension of my brothers and sisters in Christ?

Frank seemed to read the thoughts churning through my brain. He looked at me and said, "Things aren't all that much different even now, you know." He went on to describe a segregated current-day Selma where it was clearly understood that he was not welcome to join a local country club because of the color of his skin.

"I love playing golf. I came back to Selma to retire and play golf," he said, shaking his head. "A few White deacons in my church retracted their club membership when this happened to me," he said with some pride in his voice. "Relationship," he told me, "it makes all the difference. I joined a White Church so that people would get to know me for who I am. I love to greet families coming into church. I get down at face level with the kids as they walk in, and I see the fear in their eyes at first. After a while, they start to see me and feel more comfortable with me. Relationship," he said again, "that's the only way things are going to change."

I closed my eyes momentarily and rubbed my temples. I could hardly believe what I had just heard. A man who couldn't even play golf at the local country club because he was Black chose to attend a White Church so his White brothers and sisters would see the need for cross-racial relationships. I thought of the kneel-ins at the Second Presbyterian church in Memphis and felt undiluted admiration for Frank's persistent intentionality to desegregate worship services in 2016. This was a type of love that surpassed my comprehension and completely upended my concept of racial reconciliation.

Prior to this encounter, I equated racial reconciliation with exhortations to get along and play fair. After my experience in Selma, I began redefining a term I had often equated with a limited view of social justice. Hearing Frank's story of intentional pursuit of relationship within a predominantly White church felt like hearing a parable Jesus would tell if his incarnation happened in the United States today. Can a man love God and hate his neighbor? This rabbinic-style question was being fleshed out in an upside-down, inside-out, completely unexpected, and paradoxical way. The man who had been shown hate was exuding the love of God toward his enemies.

In his book *Strength to Love,* Martin Luther King, Jr. addressed the practical answer to the question, How do we love our enemies? His answer reminded me of Frank and the tougher road toward racial reconciliation for my Black brothers and sisters:

> First, we must develop and maintain the capacity to forgive. He who is devoid of the power to forgive is devoid of the power to love.... It is also necessary to realize that the forgiving must always be initiated by the person who has been wronged, the victim of some great hurt, the recipient of some tortuous injustice, the absorber of some terrible act of oppression. The wrongdoer may request forgiveness. He may come to himself, and, like the prodigal son, move up some dusty road, his heart palpitating with desire for forgiveness. But only the injured neighbor, the loving father back home, can really pour out the warm waters of forgiveness. Forgiveness does not mean ignoring what has been done or putting a false label on an evil act. It means, rather, that the evil act no longer remains as a barrier to the relationship. Forgiveness is a catalyst creating the atmosphere necessary for a fresh

start and a new beginning.... Forgiveness means reconciliation, a coming together again.[3]

Why was I so gripped by Frank's story? Core elements of what Frank shared reflect the story of redemption told in the Bible. It is a story of me longing for love and connection but simultaneously knowing I am unworthy because of my sin. It is the story of the incarnation, a stepping across the aisle when I wouldn't, to grab my hand and pursue relationship with me. Racial reconciliation is anchored by a deep and radical love that leads with forgiveness and expresses itself in intentional relationships. It is a reflection of the Father's love reminding me I am forgiven in Christ. I was reminded in Selma that Christ's promise to make all things right again is true.

My deep longing for connection with my brothers and sisters of color was starting to make more sense. Having been created in the image of the triune God, I was hardwired for community and relationship. My promised future involves perfect communion not only with my God but also with my neighbor. My current state, however, is fractured and divided with a strong proclivity toward the comfort of homogeneity. Sin not only separates me from God but also from my brothers and sisters. Racial reconciliation is a clear expression of God making us whole again. His redeeming work has always excelled at tearing down dividing walls of hostility:

> But now in Christ Jesus you who once were far off have been brought near by the blood of Christ. For he himself is our peace, who has made us both one and has broken down in his flesh the dividing wall of hostility by abolishing the law of commandments expressed in ordinances, that he might create in himself one new man in place of the two, so making peace, and might reconcile us both to God in one body through the cross, thereby killing the hostility. (Eph. 2:13–16)

---

1. Chattel slavery, also called traditional slavery, is so named because people are treated as the chattel (personal property) of the owner and are bought and sold as commodities. Wikipedia, s.v. "Slavery," https://en.wikipedia.org/wiki/Slavery#Chattel_slavery
2. Jim Crow laws were state and local laws that enforced racial segregation in the Southern United States. All were enacted in the late 19th and early 20th centuries. Wikipedia, s.v. "Jim Crow Laws," https://en.wikipedia.org/wiki/Jim_Crow_laws
3. King, Jr.

A REDEEMED MISSISSIPPIAN

AL LACOUR

———

Al LaCour lives in Atlanta. He is a retired coordinator of RUF International, a ministry for international students on American campuses. He graduated from Georgia Tech and Westminster Theological Seminary. After thirty years as a church planter and the senior pastor of four churches, Al now invests his time in his family, younger leaders, and occasionally teaches in local churches on Christian hospitality. Al and his wife, Elaine, have been married since 1974. They have two married children and three grandchildren.

———

The Presbyterian Church in America (PCA) is engaged in important and sometimes painful discussions about repenting from past racism. These issues are deeper for me than self-examination, church politics, or Bible interpretation. Truthful conversations, with brothers and sisters from different racial backgrounds, are personal and biographical for me.

Here is my story.

I am a child of mid-twentieth century Mississippi, the grandson and namesake of a successful business owner and bank president. My family thought of ourselves as progressive, well-educated, socially tolerant Southern Presbyterians (Presbyterian Church in the United

States or PCUS). As an eldest son, I was full of ambition,—a proverbial big fish in a small pond. And apart from God's redeeming grace and guidance, I would not recognize my racism. But I have lived and worked outside of Mississippi. I have traveled in Europe, Africa, Jamaica, and China. I have grown through truth-in-love relationships with friends who were not born a privileged, White Southerner like me.

My great aunt Elizabeth was a beloved, unmarried, liberal influence in my formative years. Her father, my maternal great-grandfather, was descended from New England Puritans, but he grew up near Jackson during Reconstruction.[1] A devout Methodist, he confronted the state's White supremacist governor and senator, Theodore Bilbo.[2] My great-grandfather sponsored the noted Methodist missionary to India, E. Stanley Jones,[3] and welcomed him in his Meridian home. A strict parent, he taught a Sunday afternoon weekly Bible class for his ten children in the family's "Old Home."

Aunt Elizabeth, my maternal grandmother, Sarah, and most of their siblings moved away from the piety of my great grandfather. "Big Beth," as the town knew her, was a Renaissance woman in my town. She respected Eleanor Roosevelt, knew Eudora Welty,[4] and she was a fan of *Harper's Magazine* editor Willie Morris.[5]

Although I was a progressive White Presbyterian, I was embedded in Southern social structure. We lived near the country club. Two fairways across from our home on Country Club Drive was Tenth Avenue, where caddies, domestics, and their families lived. Aunt Elizabeth took my brother and me collecting on many Saturday mornings. She had inherited rental properties from her father, and lived on weekly income from the African American tenants. I think being a landlady for Black families troubled her conscience, but she carefully maintained each rental frame house. I would ride shotgun in Big Beth's car while Timmy, a Black boy from the neighborhood, ran alongside her car and collected cash rents. After the collections were over, Timmy and I sat together on a curbside enjoying orange sherbet push-ups and bottled RC Cola topped off with salted peanuts.

We were typical Mississippi childhood Black and White friends. We were separate and definitely *not* equal.

I also remember Sunday lunches at my father's childhood house. Meals were prepared by Mattie, who had been the LaCours' "help" since my father was a child. In the summer of 1961, while watching black-and-white TV coverage of the Freedom Rides, I was shocked to hear Mattie say, "I don't know why those n----- come down here to cause us trouble."

My family also had "help" throughout my childhood. Bernice taught us to play checkers. During my high school years, Lucy cooked our family meals and was the one who explained the "facts of life" to my younger brother. After school I drove Lucy home from work. A quiet lady, Lucy always sat in the back seat of our car as was proper social convention. I waved to her husband sitting on their front porch. Years later after I had come to vital faith in Christ, I left the car and went to the front porch to greet her husband. I think both he and I were shocked when I broke a social taboo. Once home from college, I lingered after a family lunch, insisting that Lucy join me at the table. Typically Southern domestics only ate after the family. Another time, Lucy admired my modern translation Bible, so I purchased her a copy. She treasured the gift from a young "Mr. Al."

Throughout my teen years, I stayed active in our PCUS church, but I did not know God offered me a personal relationship with Christ. My home church received mention in Morton Smith's *How is the Gold Become Dim*, one notable example of the PCUS departure from biblical truth. My father was a church elder and once served on a pastoral search committee that invited a well-known denominational liberal to become our new pastor. That pastor was never approved by the presbytery or by the synod of Mississippi. My father described many of the founders of Reformed Theological Seminary in Jackson, later founders of the PCA, as the "opposition." In the mid-1960s, my perception of things was conservative theology and conservative politics were inseparable. Ironically years before the PCA's 1973 founding, the only Bible-believing Christian I knew on a daily basis who was clearly not a racist, was our Black domestic, Lucy.

In June 1964, as I prepared to enter eleventh grade, three Civil Rights activists were murdered in nearby Neshoba County, including James Chaney, a twenty-one-year-old Black man from my town. The following spring, in March 1965, some of my classmates (I disdained them as "poor White trash") skipped classes to do mischief during the Selma to Montgomery marches. In the fall, I was elected senior class president of the first public school to be integrated in my hometown. Sadly, perhaps unavoidably, our class cheer became, "We're the first, the first to mix, we're the Class of '66." As class president (and a self-styled White progressive), I tried to be an example of civility and to discourage unrest. But I did not speak to or offer hospitality to five brave young women who desegregated Meridian High School: Sadie Clark, Sandra Falconer, Faye Inge, Patricia Stennis, and Loreace Hopkins.

The fall of 1966 was personally and spiritually momentous. I entered Georgia Tech in Atlanta, and it was my first time to live outside of Mississippi. Racial tensions boiled across the South. My first evening in Atlanta, I viewed newscasts of officials who contested the seating of Julian Bond, a Black man who had been elected to the Georgia House of Representatives. But Atlanta marketed itself as a "city too busy to hate." Progressive politicians and pragmatic corporate leaders were determined not to repeat Birmingham-style civil unrest.

Most important for me, in the fall of 1966, I began a personal relationship with Jesus Christ. For the first time, I met vibrant Christians who believed the Bible but were not politically conservative. Through a campus ministry, this liberal Presbyterian became an evangelical Christian in spite of himself. I repented of my self-righteousness, all my self-efforts to make a reputation for myself, and I entrusted my life to Jesus Christ alone.

During college I met African American Christians like the Rev. William Holmes Borders, a Civil Rights activist and the pastor of Wheat Street Baptist. Some Christian friends became involved with scouting in the Techwood housing projects. I was in Atlanta in 1968 for the funeral of Dr. Martin Luther King, Jr. Through a friend, I met the Rev. Andrew Young, later mayor of Atlanta and UN Ambassador, during his first campaign for US Congress.

The greatest life changes came from the inside out. The Holy Spirit began to expose my inherent self-righteousness. By God's Word and providence, I became more self-aware of my own racism. In June 1970, from wrong motives (to show a friend I was missions-minded), I went on a PCUS summer missions project to West Africa. I worked alongside a missionary who was a university chaplain for college students at the University College off Cape Coast, Ghana. That summer, three incidents exposed my lingering racism.

First, a student invited me to walk with her on campus. As a "progressive Mississippian," I found myself awkwardly walking and holding hands, the expected local custom, with a pretty African co-ed. And I thought, "I am glad that my parents cannot see me now."

The next incident happened near Cape Coast at Elmina Castle, the oldest European structure in sub-Saharan Africa. Like a reverse statue of liberty, now a monument to bondage, Elmina was an important stop on the Atlantic slave trade route. Dutch and British slave trading took place just below the floor of the Christian chapel. Young children from nearby African villages played on castle turrets, but African American tourists were also at Elmina to retrace enslaved ancestral journeys. They visibly scorned my presence as a White American.

Finally, eager to return home with West African souvenirs, I went to a tailor's shop to buy a tie-dyed shirt. Entering the shop after me was a couple from New Jersey. After I invited them to fill their large order before my own, they left. The African tailor looked at me and asked, "African Americans?" Slavery's deep scars estrange not only Black from White, but even African Americans from Africans.

In the fall of 1971, I accepted a full fellowship to a mainline seminary, nominated by the PCUS missionary I had worked for in Ghana. Traumatically but relentlessly, the Holy Spirit compelled me to accept closer theological affinity with Evangelical and Reformed believers as a member of a Reformed Presbyterian Church, Evangelical Synod (RPC-ES) congregation.

During three years on staff with InterVarsity in Virginia, I learned the Bible, worked in campus ministry, served as a deacon in the RPC-ES congregation, and knew African American Christian students and staff with Tom Skinner Associates[6] at historically Black colleges. These included Carl Ellis[7] (later a classmate at Westminster Seminary). I was moved to tears when an African American brother played drums and portrayed Jesus as "the Blues Man," a reference to our Lord, the prophet Isaiah's Man of Sorrows.

I began to realize that I was a perpetually recovering racist, a man who looked down on social conservatives like a modern day Pharisee. I trusted in myself that I was right, while I treated both poor White trash and xenophobic conservatives with contempt. I remain a debtor to Christians from diverse racial and cultural backgrounds. I need God's Word and Spirit to dissect and extract conservative theology from conservative politics. I need life transformation from remaining sins in my embodied nature and attitudes from my privileged White Southern culture.

My journey has moved in the opposite direction from many of the other White men in this PCA conversation. I was not a social conservative who struggled to confront and repent of my racism. Rather, I am a Southern social progressive who has struggled to love my Christian brothers and sisters who embrace orthodoxy in cultural segregation or isolation.

Has there been any fruit of repentance in my life? I pray that some fruit will last. In the early 1990s, while on a road trip to Mississippi to visit my parents, I awakened my two napping middle-school-aged children as we drove through Selma, Alabama. Over their sleepy objections, I insisted we go to the Edmund Pettus Bridge. Years later, in an African American Studies course at the University of Missouri, my daughter told her Black classmates (she was the only White student) about her childhood experience.

During the late 1980s, I pastored a PCA church in Miami that took small steps toward multicultural fellowship. The catalyst was our receiving a Jamaican OPC (Orthodox Presbyterian Church) church—its members, deacons, and elders—as our equals in an expanded church. New members included descendants of African slaves, descendants of the indentured Chinese who emigrated after abolition of the British slave trade, and members who descended from Jews who came to Jamaica to escape persecution. A rich cultural tapestry reflected the presence of Christ. It was a pleasing aroma of God's coming kingdom of glory.

The PCUS missionary I worked with in Africa later founded Villa International House in Atlanta to welcome foreign scholars at Emory and the CDC. He had observed in me (before I did) gifts to minister cross-culturally.

2016 marked the fiftieth anniversary of my high school graduation. On behalf of the Reunion Committee, acting as the class president, I wrote a letter of invitation to each of the four living African American classmates to join us for the reunion. As I wrote, "Your classmates would say with me, I would never have had the courage to do what you five ladies did in the fall of 1965." Encouraged by the Reunion Committee, I opened the reunion weekend with a prayer of welcome and thanksgiving, in which I recognized each of "The First Five of '65" by name. In conversations with my African American sisters, we discussed our fears from the 1960s. Unknown to me, many of their family homes were targeted in drive-by shootings, and, although reported to the city police, no police records were kept of the incidents and no arrests were made. One African American sister said to me, "Al, I am writing a book, and you are in it! You and other White student leaders were what I call the Silent Majority. If you had spoken out, our homes might not have been targeted." And that gave me an opportunity to remember my own fears and do some repenting. My fiftieth reunion gave me an opportunity to repent of my self-righteous progressivism, my failure to love, and to conquer my own fears.

So following Christ together, we pray, struggle, and seek to be knit together in love so that we may more fully experience and embody God's plan for Christ's Church: to reflect his glory in all human cultures and races, in all the earth.

---

1. The Reconstruction era was the period in American history which lasted from 1863 to 1877. It was a significant chapter in the history of American civil rights. Wikipedia, s.v. "Reconstruction Era," https://en.wikipedia.org/wiki/Reconstruction_era
2. Wikipedia, s.v. "Theodore G. Bilbo," https://en.wikipedia.org/wiki/Theodore_G._Bilbo
3. Eli Stanley Jones (1884–1973) was an American 20th-century Methodist Christian missionary and theologian. He is remembered chiefly for his interreligious lectures to the educated classes in India. Wikipedia, s.v. "E. Stanley Jones," https://en.wikipedia.org/wiki/E._Stanley_Jones
4. Eudora Alice Welty (April 13, 1909—July 23, 2001) was an American short story writer and novelist who wrote about the American South. Wikipedia, s.v. "Eudora Welty," https://en.wikipedia.org/wiki/Eudora_Welty
5. https://en.wikipedia.org/wiki/Willie_Morris
6. Tom Skinner Associates is a ministry that furnishes leadership training, strives to dissolve racial and other boundaries and focuses on both young people and adults. Macon Church, "Tom Skinner Associates," https://maconchurch.weebly.com/tom-skinner-associates.html
7. Now a professor at Reformed Theological Seminary. https://rts.edu/people/dr-carl-ellis-jr/

THE NECESSITY OF PROXIMITY

HACE CARGO

Hace Cargo serves as a pastor at Brookhaven Presbyterian Church in his hometown of Atlanta. He has degrees from The University of Georgia (BA) and Covenant Theological Seminary (MDiv). Hace and his wife, Sally, have two boys.

——

[Editorial Note: This chapter contains language that may be offensive to some readers. O'Connor's word has been taken out and replaced. This chapter makes an important point about this very word and its use.]

Flannery O'Connor's short story, "The Artificial N-----" caught my attention not only for its provocative title, but also for the fact that it is set in the city in which I was raised, I live, and I pastor—Atlanta. Because of O'Connor's ability to see the brokenness hiding under the shiny veneer of Southern culture, I was fascinated to see how she, a native Georgian herself, would portray the city and its racial dynamics. I found her disarming prose exposed truths too easily overlooked. She shakes the conscience of any reader hoping to romanticize or escape unwelcome realities.

"The Artificial N-----" is about a boy named Nelson and his grandfather, Mr. Head. Their most notable shared trait is their outrageous racial prejudice. The two travel from their all-White county in rural Georgia to the big city of Atlanta so Mr. Head can convince his ignorant grandson that Atlanta is not as wonderful as he envisions. Mr. Head explains Atlanta has many flaws, the greatest of which is it is "full of n-----s."

Full of allusions to Dante's *Inferno*, O'Connor casts Mr. Head's trek through Atlanta as his personal journey through humiliation and hell. Within a matter of hours they wind up lost in an all-Black neighborhood, forcing Nelson to ask a Black woman for directions when his grandfather will not endure the disgrace of doing so himself.

Later events separate Mr. Head and Nelson in the busy city. In a panic to find his grandfather, the boy collides with a woman and injures her. Angry and afraid of the crowds that witnessed the event, Mr. Head disowns the boy, claiming not to know him. By the day's end, Mr. Head and Nelson are entirely lost, unable to find the train station that will deliver them back to the safety of their home. They end the day emotionally distant from one another.

As they wander through Atlanta humiliated, they eventually get so far from their starting point that they roam into a wealthy, all-White suburban neighborhood far from the city core. There they stumble upon some kind of baffling lawn statuary: a plaster figurine of a Black boy with "a wild look of misery," set atop a yellow-brick fence that separated the road from a private lawn and wealthy home.[1] They stand before it entirely perplexed, and O'Connor portrays their shared bewilderment as an epiphanic moment.

In the "artificial n-----" (as Mr. Head ignorantly calls the statue), they see a depiction of their own misery that humbles their pride and reunites them to one another. O'Connor explains in later correspondence: "What I had in mind to suggest with the artificial n----- was the redemptive quality of the Negro's suffering for us all."[2] The experience not only confronts their obvious prejudice, but also addresses their own sense of inferiority:

They stood gazing at the artificial Negro[3] as if they were faced with some great mystery, some monument to another's victory that brought them together in their common defeat. They could both feel it dissolving their differences like an action of mercy. Mr. Head had never known what mercy felt like because he had been too good to deserve any, but he felt he knew now.[4]

The power of this picture gripped me for days after my first reading. While O'Connor's depiction of Atlanta was familiar in ways I will return to momentarily, it was the picture of prejudice passed down and shared between generations that I first struggled to untangle.

In particular, I was burdened by the intersection between the exposure to Black life and the corresponding prejudice depicted in Mr. Head and Nelson. Nelson's prejudice is especially comical and grievous because it is so obviously inherited and unsubstantiated. In fact, on the train ride to Atlanta early in the story, Nelson sees a Black man for the first time in his life (and fails to recognize that he is Black given that his skin is not actually black, but brown). After he learns this is a Black man, Nelson "felt that the Negro had deliberately walked down the aisle in order to make a fool of him and he hated him with a fierce raw fresh hate; and also, he understood now why his grandfather disliked them."[5]

Somewhat like Nelson, I grew up with limited exposure to Black life. The places I was most familiar with were not segregated in the sense that Mr. Head and Nelson's home county was. But the effects of socio-economic division, private schooling, and other factors unintentionally left me with a naïveté of the Black community not unlike what is depicted in Nelson. Without Black neighbors, classmates, or church friends, much like Nelson, basically all I knew of what it meant to be Black came transitively through the generations before me. I learned from my parents, who grew up in more integrated worlds than I did. Coincidentally, I also gained information from my grandfather, a man who lived in the rural South in the era O'Connor captures with such devastating clarity.

I am grateful I never saw in my grandfather the most egregious bigotry depicted in Mr. Head. However, given the time and place in which he lived, my grandfather was a significant source of my exposure to racial prejudice. Though this prejudice presented itself in far less overt ways than Mr. Head's, there were still many things about his interactions with the Black community in his small town that confused me, like my distinct memory of him calling a particular Black man with grey hair a boy.

These dynamics of shared and inherited prejudice troubled me deeply and left me wondering how subtle prejudice in my own heart might still be identified and rooted out. But in subsequent readings of

O'Connor's work, I came to see that Nelson might not be the character I resemble most in this enthralling story, or at least the context of his home is not the setting most familiar to me. Shockingly, that realization was no less worrisome.

The Dangers of Caricature and Isolation

I don't know how I missed it in my first reading, but O'Connor clearly describes the world that I know as home, and it is certainly not the context of rural ignorance that Mr. Head and Nelson come from. It is the world where "artificial n-----s" exist.

By the time I was being raised in suburban Atlanta, no one still had figurines of Black children decorating their lawns. Yet caricature and token representation devoid of any real relationship remained the primary modes of my exposure to the Black community. During my childhood, the city known as the "Black Mecca" remained highly segregated (and is so today). But the presence of the Black community and relative lack of conflict in "The City too Busy to Hate" made it far too easy to assume prejudice was not our problem.

Throughout their humiliation in Atlanta, Mr. Head and Nelson were surrounded and overwhelmed by crowds of people, heightening the intensity of every event in their hellish journey. But by the time they wander into the suburbs, lost and defeated, O'Connor highlights the isolating nature of their surroundings—"here everything was entirely deserted."[6] The houses are far apart, there are no sidewalks, and they pass no one on the road. In this setting, just moments before their encounter with the confusing statuary sitting on the fence, Mr. Head and Nelson finally encounter another human being: a fat, bald man wearing golf pants out walking his two dogs, polite enough to point them toward the "suburb stop" for the train just three blocks away.[7]

Fast forward half a century and this could have easily been the father of half of my childhood friends. Give it a few more years for my friends to keep balding and gaining weight, and this could be any of them. If O'Connor had been envisioning any real neighborhood in Atlanta when she wrote this story in the 1950s, she very well could have been referring to Historic Brookhaven, the first country club community in Georgia and part of the community I now pastor.[8]

At a glance, such a setting might seem less prone to ignorance and prejudice. But O'Connor's depiction shows the seclusion of suburban wealth faces its own set of dangers. Here Black life is known, but only from a safe distance and in caricatured form. Unlike Nelson's ignorance that prevents him from even recognizing a Black man on his train car, this more dangerous naïveté allows a community to turn a Black boy into a landscaping accent, sitting atop a fence, "meant to look happy because his mouth was stretched up at the corners."[9] It is far too easy to look paternalistically at the caricatured Black boy sitting on the fence, failing to realize what a caricature he is, and to look condemningly at the ignorant bumpkins just outside the fence.

The Necessity of Mercy

Even more disturbing, I fear this false sense of familiarity leaves a community far less prone to experience the "action of mercy," as O'Connor calls it, that dissolves the differences between people "in their common defeat." From the comfort of "big White houses" so far down driveways that they look like "partially submerged icebergs in the distance,"[10] little feels like defeat. It is far too easy to be like Mr. Head, never having known what mercy felt like, "because he had been too good to deserve any."

And while such smug contentment is all too familiar to me, it was not to my grandfather. In the final days of his life, a number of people came through my grandparents' home to say their goodbyes. One of those visits stands out in my memory above the rest.

The grey-headed Black man whom I had once heard my grandfather call a boy came as soon as he heard my grandfather was dying. He spent some time by my grandfather's bedside, thanking him profusely for his help in all sorts of circumstances I knew nothing about. And when he was done, he went into my grandparents living room, laid on their couch and wept like I had never heard an adult man weep before. And all he could say between heaving sobs, over and over again, was, "No one ever loved me like Missa Guy."

In the days following my grandfather's death, as many Black folks came by the house as White folks. They told stories about my grandfather dating all the way back to their shared childhood when their families survived the Great Depression together, farming the same land. His funeral drew together multiple generations of both White and Black families. A thoroughly integrated affair in the least contrived way possible.[11]

Though I doubt he would have ever articulated it as such, I believe my grandfather experienced a "common defeat" with the potential to dissolve differences "like an action of mercy." For White men and women throughout the rural South whose lives were inexplicably intertwined with the Black community as they struggled together through many (though clearly not all) of life's challenges, this common defeat does not excuse or explain away real prejudice. But it should also give us pause when we might look back with any sense of progressive superiority. In that sense, even personally, O'Connor's work has been a blessed "action of mercy," bringing humility and reconciliation where generational pride and condemnation flourish too easily.

The Humanizing Effect of Proximity

Living in the very world O'Connor cuttingly critiques (only several generations removed), this question grips me most as I wrestle to understand the dynamics of race and prejudice in myself and in the community in which I live and pastor: Is there any willingness to acknowledge, much less personally engage, the suffering of the Black community that has a "redemptive quality" for us all? Or will we keep the suffering caricature at a safe distance, sitting on the fence in the yard, and "meant to look happy because his mouth was stretched up at the corners"?

I fear our strategies for doing the latter may be more deceiving than we want to believe. Is it possible we could know the lingo of social justice activism, use all the right hashtags on social media, be troubled by moving documentaries, show up for marches and vigils, and in the end still never have even one marginalized *individual* that could testify to a "common defeat" that dissolved our differences?

I'm still learning how that mercy is experienced, but if "The Artificial N-----" suggests any necessary condition, it would have to be *proximity*. Total lack of exposure to the suffering of the Black community cannot produce any more than ignorant prejudice. And, unfortunately, such prejudice does not always ensure the hellish humiliation Mr. Head and Nelson endure as preparation for their experience of grace. Exposure to the artificial is clearly no better. It denies those at a safe distance the possibility of seeing the redemptive quality of suffering in either its real or caricatured forms. Only in real physical and relational proximity can this redemptive suffering be a mercy to us all.

Throughout the whole story, the only *direct* interaction Mr. Head or Nelson have with a Black man or woman takes place when Nelson musters the courage to ask a Black woman for directions back to the train. In this brief but direct interaction Nelson is entranced by the woman, particularly in her definitive humanity—her bodily existence from "her great knees to her forehead." He is drawn to her, even wishing she would pick him up and draw him close to "feel her breath on his face." As O'Connor explains in later correspondence, the woman's presence is intended to "give him the required shock to start those Black forms moving up from his conscious."[12]

As simple as it may seem, perhaps such encounters are what we need most in the segregated worlds of Nelson's home county and the communities in which I have lived and now pastor. Though we might find these initial encounters just as paralyzing as young Nelson did, such proximity might also have the redemptive power that O'Connor suggests.

Sources of Redemptive Suffering

For O'Connor, this redemptive "action of mercy" is, of course, the result of more than just human interaction. The brilliance of her short story is capturing unexpected moments of grace. The central symbol of the story, the plaster Black boy sitting on the fence, is a Christ-like symbol whose suffering and humiliation reconciles, humbles, and offers forgiveness. This effect is sensed specifically between Mr. Head and Nelson, but is effectual in a much broader sense as well. As John D. Sykes, a scholar of O'Connor's work, explains, in this symbol the reader is "being shown an utterly unexpected way in which a human being is joined to Christ through redemptive suffering."[13]

The story simultaneously focuses the reader on both the grand and specific implications of our sinfulness: "For O'Connor the same sinfulness that generates social injustice has, more fundamentally, cut us off from God, so that God has had to take drastic action to rescue us from ourselves."[14]

But it is vital to note that in doing so, O'Connor is not using the Black boy on the fence, or the Black community as a whole, as a prop for White absolution or salvation. Her depiction of the Black community throughout the story is not patronizing in the slightest. Just the opposite. While Nelson and Mr. Head are seen as ignorant and helpless, Black characters are figures of knowledge and power.[15] Precisely because this is the case, the symbol of "the artificial n-----" works so poignantly. The "combination of power and humiliation" makes the statue a perfect picture of "self-emptying in which power is forsaken as an act of sacrifice." Not only is O'Connor capturing a picture of cosmic redemptive suffering in the segregated South, she is also making specific application *to* the segregated South, both in her day and in ours. Namely, "that blacks in the South, as a group, have served a Christ function, bearing the weight of sin on behalf of the region."[16]

And so while this short story shows us both the blatant danger of inherited prejudice and the more subtle threat of caricatured presence, perhaps what it depicts most clearly is the necessity of proximity—to one another, and, more importantly, to a redemptive figure whose presence is an "action of mercy." History and personal experience have taught us that proximity *alone* is not a solution. In fact, as O'Connor shows in Nelson's hateful response to the Black man on his train car, proximity has as much potential to cause strife and violence as it does healing if there is no reconciling force to mercifully humble us.

But if we claim to have experienced such an action of mercy in Christ, if we have eyes to recognize the power of self-emptying sacrifice, then the collective suffering of the Black community should leave us dissatisfied with segregation, prejudice, and demeaning caricatured presence. What a waste to remain content with distanced, paternalistic representation and miss the Christ-likeness of redemptive suffering when mercy, healing, and forgiveness sit on the fence by the street.

Daunting though it might be to see all our complicity, would we not desire to have such an experience of grace and arrive where Mr. Head ends the story?

He stood appalled, judging himself with the thoroughness of God, while the action of mercy covered his pride like a flame and consumed it. He had never thought of himself a great sinner before but he saw now that his true depravity had been hidden from him lest it cause him to despair. He realized that he was forgiven for his sins from the beginning of time.... He saw that no sin was too monstrous for him to claim his own, and since God loved in proportion as He forgave, he felt ready at that instant to enter Paradise.[17]

1. Such statuary, often called a "lawn jockey," was not uncommon in the era, but was foreign to such uncultured characters as Mr. Head and Nelson. It is clear in the story itself that O'Connor finds it comical and objectionable. In later writing she says, "there is nothing that screams out the tragedy of the South like what my uncle calls n----- statuary" Flannery O'Connor, Habit of Being (New York, NY: Farrar, Straus & Giroux, 1999), 101.

2. O'Connor, Habit, 78.

3. Note O'Connor's change in verbiage when she is narrating as opposed to Mr. Head's description, proof that the connotation of "n-----" was less offensive in the era in which O'Connor was writing. She was quite intentionally using the slur in a uniquely provocative and condemning way.

4. Flannery O'Connor, A Good Man is Hard to Find and Other Stories (San Diego: Harcourt Brace & Co., 1976), 103–132.

5. O'Connor, A Good Man , 112.

6. Flannery O'Connor, The Complete Stories (New York: Farrar, Straus and Giroux, 1971), 267.

7. O'Connor, A Good Man , 129.

8. Built in the late 1800s and early 1900s, Historic Brookhaven is about six miles from downtown Atlanta and continues to be a hub of Atlanta's blue-blood wealth.

9. O'Connor, A Good Man , 130.

10. O'Connor, A Good Man , 128.

11. I have since noticed that every funeral I have ever attended in the rural South has been thoroughly integrated. This is far different from the funerals I attend in suburban metro Atlanta, which tend to be even more homogeneous than church services that take place in the same sanctuaries on Sunday mornings.

12. O'Connor, Habit, 78.

13. John D. Skyes, "How the Symbol Means: Deferral vs. Confrontation in 'The Sound and the Fury' and 'The Artificial N-----,'" in Flannery O'Connor in the Age of Terrorism: Essays on Violence and Grace, eds. Avis Hewitt and Robert Donahoo (Knoxville: U Tennessee Press, 2010), 134.

14. Skyes, "How the Symbol Means," 137.

15. Skyes, "How the Symbol Means," 135.

16. Skyes, "How the Symbol Means," 136.

17. Skyes, "How the Symbol Means," 136.

HISTORICAL AND
THEOLOGICAL
PERSPECTIVE

NOT HERE BY ACCIDENT

IRWYN INCE

Irwyn Ince serves as the executive director of the Grace DC Institute for Cross-Cultural Mission in Washington, DC. He is a graduate of Reformed Theological Seminary (MDiv) and Covenant Seminary (DMin). He serves on the PCA Unity Fund board. He was the moderator for the 46th PCA General Assembly —the first African American with this honor. Irwyn and his wife, Kim, have four children. Irwyn is the author of The Beautiful Community.

———

[This chapter is adapted from Irwyn's acceptance speech upon being unanimously elected as the first African American moderator for The Presbyterian Church in America at its 46th General Assembly in Atlanta Georgia, June 2018.]

———

I will bless the Lord at all times; his praise shall continually be in my mouth. My soul makes its boast in the Lord; let the humble hear and be glad. Oh, magnify the Lord with me, and let us exalt his name together! I sought the Lord, and he answered me and delivered me from all my fears. Those who look to him are radiant, and their faces shall never be ashamed. This poor man cried, and the Lord heard him and saved him out of all his troubles. The angel of the Lord encamps around those who fear him, and delivers them. Oh, taste and see that the Lord is good! Blessed is the man who takes refuge in him! (Psalm 34:1–8)

I have a confession to make. I've been in the PCA since 2002. I first came under care as an intern in Potomac Presbytery and Mt. Zion Covenant Church under the pastorate of Rev. Kevin Smith. I was ordained in 2007 by Chesapeake Presbytery when we planted City of Hope Presbyterian Church. And for most of my years in this church I have struggled to greet any court of this church with the phrase, "fathers and brothers." "Brothers," yes, but, "fathers," no. That began to change for me only over the past few years as I became aware of Black Presbyterian fathers in American Presbyterianism.

One of those fathers, Rev. Matthew Anderson, took charge of the Glouster Presbyterian Mission in Philadelphia in 1879. He was wrestling over the decision to plant a Presbyterian Church for "the colored people" in that city. The year before he arrived he said he had a pressing invitation from the American Missionary Association to lecture in England and Europe on their behalf along with the Fisk Jubilee Singers. He wrote, "But we refused, choosing rather to labor humbly but independently at home than conspicuously but servilely abroad." He continued,

As we thought of these opportunities which we let slip and looked at the little dingy place of meeting in the second story back room in Milton Hall, and the little poor and almost childish audience we asked ourselves over and over again, "Were we not silly for coming to Philadelphia, to take charge of a mission, which could present no better outlook than this?" "Is this the ideal church which had been pictured to our imagination when preparing for the ministry?" "Is this the vast audience which we were to address?" "and are these the intelligent, industrious, and enterprising people which we had seen in imagination?" "Have we not been exceedingly silly to let so many golden opportunities slip of [sic] the fields which were commensurate with our ambition and ability for this poor sterile field, the Gloucester Mission?"[1]

How many church planters over the years have gone into the mission field and asked, "Is this it?" "Is this what we get to do with all of our seminary training?"

He would indeed decide to plant what would become Berean Presbyterian Church in Philadelphia in 1880. Rev. Anderson drew some conclusions along the way as to the hindrances and opportunities in planting this church. He mentioned two things I want to highlight.

First:

The apathy of the Presbytery had to be overcome by arousing them to the importance of the work. Mission work had so long been neglected among the colored people that the Presbyteries had almost lost sight of them, and they were ignorant as to their real wants. and condition.[2]

Second:

The apathy of the colored people also had to be overcome. In saying that we saw a demand for the establishment of a Presbyterian Church among the colored people, we do not for a moment mean to imply that they were anxious and eager to have a church planted among them and were standing ready to do all in their power to sustain it. There was a demand for the church, but it was demanded by the condition and wants of the colored people. They themselves, were for the most part indifferent, not so much toward the establishment of this particular church, but toward the Presbyterian Church generally, and this prejudice was inherited, being associated in their minds with the church which encouraged slavery, also as being cold, aristocratic, pharisaical, and which had no use for the Negro more than to use him as a servant. This spirit would have to be overcome before there would be any marked success. This spirit would have to be overcome.[3]

Rev. Anderson said this reticence and apathy toward the Presbyterian Church would have to be overcome

Last week I was sitting with Dr. Lloyd Kim in his office at Mission to the World (MTW)[4]. And as he prayed to open our meeting time, he confessed at least two times in that prayer that there are no accidents. God is on the throne. He rules and he reigns according to his good pleasure. He is sovereign over the affairs of this world. It has often felt to me as though I was Presbyterian by accident.

I have experienced that reticence and apathy Rev. Anderson wrote about in the early 1900s. But there are no accidents! As I look back over my life growing up in a Christian home, rejecting the faith during my teen years, becoming a radical Black nationalist during my college years, being changed by the Gospel of Jesus Christ as a young husband and father at NBBC (New Bethel Baptist Church) in Washington, DC, developing a divine discontent with the racial and ethnic polarization in the churches in America, to being called to the ministry in an overwhelmingly White denomination, there are no accidents! Twenty-one-year-old Irwyn would look at forty-nine-year-old Irwyn with disdain. If twenty-one-year-old Irwyn could conceive of being a Christian it would only be in an all Black Church. But there are no accidents. So, I can say with the saints of old, "I may not be what I wanna be, but thank God I'm not what I used to be!" God has always had a witness that the Presbyterian Church was his church.

Rev. Anderson talked about the apathy of the colored people toward the Presbyterian Church because they were living in the midst of intense racial separation supported and encouraged by Presbyterians. I've felt the reticence as I learned that history and experienced its aftermath, the fact that only 1 percent of our pastors are Black. But fathers and mothers, brothers and sisters, there are no accidents! I'm delighted to serve as a pastor in this branch of Zion because it's where God has called me. It's where he has called me to press in and pursue my passion to see the ministry of reconciliation demonstrated in the local church by the gathering of people from diverse backgrounds, cultures, and ethnicities. That this practical, on-the-ground ministry of reconciliation is the natural outworking of our covenantal theological commitment.

It is my joy to be a pastor in the PCA. I might be representative of one percent when it comes to my ethnicity, but by the grace of God, I'm part of the 100 percent of us here in this church called by Jesus Christ to love the Lord our God with everything: heart, soul, mind, and strength. And to love our neighbors as ourselves; called by Jesus to bear witness to the mystery of the Gospel—that he reconciles contraries and brings them together into a mystical union that practically works itself out in their loving, serving, and submitting to one another.

The Apostle Paul made a prayer request for and a charge to the diverse Roman church in Romans 15. He said, "May the God of endurance and encouragement grant you to live in such harmony with one another, in accord with Christ Jesus, that together you may with one voice glorify the God and Father of our Lord Jesus Christ" (15:5–6). Then he charged them with these words, "Therefore, welcome one another as Christ has welcomed you into the glory of God" (15:7). Yes, I may be the first African American moderator of the PCA General Assembly, and it's notable; historic even. But the charge remains the same: "Welcome one *another, the way Christ has welcomed you, into the glory of God."* May this be the tenor of our church.

---

1. Matthew Anderson, *Presbyterianism; Its Relation to the Negro* (Philadelphia: John McGill White & CO, 1897), 22–23.
2. Anderson, *Presbyterianism* , 28.
3. Anderson, *Presbyterianism* , 29.
4. Mission to the World is the mission agency of the PCA. https://pcanet.org

A MEAL TOGETHER

RONNIE GARCÍA

Ronnie Garcia is a graduate of the United States Air Force Academy (BS), the University of Arkansas (MS), Covenant Theological Seminary (MDiv), and is the Senior Pastor of Iglesia La Travesía. He was sent to San Juan, Puerto Rico to plant the first PCA churches on the island. He has begun an internship program aimed at identifying, training, and equipping bilingual Latinos for ordination and other ministry positions in the PCA. Ronnie and his wife, Amanda, have four children.

———

According to the New Testament, what does the Kingdom of God look like? When the kingdom advances and comes upon the people of God, how do we know? What are the signs? What is the shape? Theologians answer this question in a few ways, but I like to think it takes the shape of a table, a round one. It looks like a Jew and a Gentile joyfully sitting around the table, warmly looking into each other's eyes, *enjoying a meal together.*

One of the Bible's primary metaphors for the consummation of God's kingdom is a banquet—or at least its inauguration begins with a meal. God's people are to imagine a table filled with savory foods, choicest wines, and chairs filled with friends from every nation. It is a meal with people enjoying one another. These are former strangers who are reconciled to one another. But perhaps more extraordinary, they even *like* each other.

I love this biblical imagery. It resonates with me. It is easy for me to envision because I have sat around a table with savory food many times in my life. It is part of my Mexican family culture. This is not something we did on special holidays. This was an occurrence every single night.

My father's parents immigrated to the United States from Mexico in the 1940s. He is a Chicano.[1] In 1971, my father married my mother, who at the time was living in her hometown Monterrey, Mexico. Although my mom is an incredibly bright and capable person, she could barely speak English and received formal education only through eighth grade. She preferred to stay home with my brothers and sister while we were young. My father worked—all the time. We did not have a lot of money, so my mom did the same thing she had done since she was nine years old. She cooked meals from scratch. I never tasted store-bought tortillas or salsa until I went off to college.

Our family rarely went to restaurants because it was too expensive, but I didn't notice because the banquet my mother offered at our humble dining table was far better. To my delight, the smells and tastes of those mini-banquets were only possible because of the unique background of my family. My White friends understood this, and they would often invite themselves over for tamales or arroz con pollo.

These were sweet memories uniquely informed by my Mexican-ness. Why do I say Mexican-ness? I am racially Mexican, but my family in Mexico would only see me as a gringo.[2] At the same time, I stood out in my immediate culture. Different color skin. Different family culture. Even a different aroma in my house. I have all the markings of a Mexican, but my Spanish was broken, and honestly, my self-identity was and still is American. I am an American, but there is an undeniable Mexican-ness to who I am. I liked it that way. But that same Mexican-ness became the occasion of painful experiences that sobered me up to a racially charged world.

My Awakening

I grew up in the suburbs of Houston in an area that at the time was predominantly White. I remember one day running an errand with my mom. We were in the car, returning home. I sat in the passenger seat, feeling the heat of the Texas summer and staring out into nothing, not unlike other ordinary fourteen-year-olds.

That moment of tranquility was interrupted as a white truck rear-ended my mother's car. The accident did not appear to be serious, perhaps nothing at all, but it was worth pulling over so both parties could evaluate the damage. My mother looked at me, smiled, and with her thick Mexican accent, she said to me, "Stay in the car, I'll be right back."

I didn't think much of it, because I was enthralled by Selena's hit song, "Como La Flor." That moment was disturbed when I began to hear a masculine voice shouting at my mother in an aggressive tone. My mom is 5' 3." She looked like an ant standing in front of this towering, White man. He yelled at her, "Go back to your country, you stupid spic! You don't belong here!"

Within a second, a deep anger welled up inside of me, and I burst out of the car, "Mom, get in the car, now!" She could see I was serious, particularly because I jumped right into the face of this man. It did not matter that I was 5' 8," 135 pounds soaking wet. I began to threaten this man with every scary thing I could possibly think of: "I will literally rip your eyes out of your head and feed them to you if you so much as say one more thing to my mother!"

He was caught off guard by both the perfect clarity in my English accent, and the clarity of detail in my threat. He could see the crazy in my eyes, and he ran to his truck, burned rubber, and sped away. I returned to the passenger seat, and my mom and I drove home in silence. But as the adrenaline subsided, the emotions came. I cried quietly. The tears kept falling. I couldn't get the lump out of my throat. The beautiful part of my Mexican-ness was also now the occasion of a painful experience. It was disorienting and confusing.

Racism As Protest

What was that man so angry about? Why did my mom not belong? Surely this man would have loved to sit at our table and partake of my mom's banquet, wouldn't he? Honestly, it would not surprise me if this man had a Mexican neighbor whose friendship he enjoyed.

So what is happening?

There are no easy answers. Racism is complex, just like the human heart.

I give thanks for the discussions on racism as evaluated through structural sin. Those conversations have been incredibly helpful. I do not have much to add in that regard.

But I do want to contribute one category of discussion that perhaps is under-appreciated: Racism as protest. That is to say, racism is aroused (and nourished) in a given person when his or her privilege is divorced from the idea that there is one who gives the privilege. When a person sees their privilege as the result of their own work (instead of a gift), they will protest any threat (or perception) of others diminishing that privilege. Could this be a way of understanding experiences against me, or even my own heart?

Many in the media who do not want to use the word "sin" suggest racism (or hate) can be overcome with education. Frankly, education is not the problem. In his book *A Stone of Hope*, Professor David Chappell makes the same point:

The thinkers who were active in the black movement—at least the ones for whom I was able to track down an extensive intellectual record—believed that the natural tendency of this world and of human institutions (including churches) is toward corruption. Like the Hebrew Prophets, these thinkers believed that they could not expect that world and those institutions to improve. Nor could they be passive bystanders. They had to stand apart from society and insult it with skepticism about its pretensions to justice and truth. They had to instigate catastrophic changes in the minds of whoever would listen, and they accepted that only a few outcasts might listen. They had to try to force an unwilling world to abandon sin—in this case, "the sin of segregation." The world to them would never know automatic or natural "progress." It would use *education* [emphasis mine] only to rationalize its iniquity.[3]

Deeper, unseen, sinful motivations in operation at a heart-level are not dethroned by education. Let me explain using the Apostle Paul's discussion in Romans 9–11. This passage of Scripture is particularly helpful because it shows Israel's racism was not simply an intellectual problem. It was their way of protesting God's grace—a threat to what they saw as their self-earned privilege. If true, this framework can be an important contribution for our present discussions on race. It gives us specific language for the dynamics in our racially divided hearts.

Significantly, one of the most hopeless aspects of our national conversation on race is the charge of inevitable racism. This is painful for any one of any color. That is, you are racist no matter what. What if, instead of saying, "no matter what," we label specific patterns for which we can repent? My hope is that if we have a million ways of repenting specifically, then our will to fight racism will not be curbed by unhelpful versions of identity politics, but rather a genuine desire to see God's kingdom come through meaningful, personal repentance. Admittedly, that is a tall order, and these three chapters in Romans are some of the most difficult passages in the New Testament. I will not attempt to explain the details. I simply want to leverage the pastoral concerns that Paul has for Israel to see where there is overlap with our present-day experiences.

Israel was a people of incredible privilege. Notably, it was not the case that they were intrinsically superior to other peoples. Instead, God loved them and showered them with grace (see Deut. 9:4ff). He even brought the world's Savior through them. But through the centuries prior to Christ's arrival, the source of their privilege was confused with performance and, perhaps especially, pedigree. John the Baptist even warned, *"And do not presume to say to yourselves, 'We have Abraham as our father...'"* (Matt. 3:9). This is as if he were exhorting, "Don't you dare play the superior race card!"

Sadly, that is precisely what happened. Israel began to erroneously believe their privilege was the product of their circumcision, or lineage, or other national identity markers. In Romans 9, Paul makes two Old Testament references to illustrate the idea that they are the *"children of the promise"* not the *"children of the flesh"* (Rom. 9:8). Paul illustrates this with two sets of brothers, Isaac and Ishmael and Jacob and Esau. In both cases, privileges are given to the child of the promise, not the child of the flesh. Here, there is no logical, racial, or meritorious connection between the one who is expected to get the privilege and the one who actually receives it. The Jews have nothing to point to inherent in themselves. God's sovereign election is an embodiment of sheer grace. It's not determined by national or racial pedigree.

Broadly speaking, Israel almost completely failed to allow this reality of privilege (by grace) to shape their self-understanding. The consequences were disastrous. The Apostle Paul was stunned. He was speechless and filled with profound grief. He laments, *"I have great sorrow and unceasing anguish in my heart"* (Rom. 9:2).

The promised King of Israel has finally come to his people, and yet they rejected him. Meanwhile the King's table is filling up with Gentiles. Why is this? The easy answer is their lack of faith.

But when we inspect their lack of faith, we find more. The emotional composition of their lack of faith is laced with resentment. The Jews absolutely resented the Gentiles, as if they were saying, "Go back to your unclean countries! Go back to your religion! You don't belong here! You are ruining and defiling everything!"

Can you imagine hearing their protest? On the outside it is a lack of faith, but on the inside it is protest. Can you visualize it? Vertically speaking (to God) the sin is lack of faith, but horizontally (to people) it is racism. The root problem is not Jewish skepticism. The problem is they do not like what is becoming of their religion.[4] In their own minds, they worked hard for their privilege, and the Gentiles are all too conveniently coming in at the eleventh hour [5] and ruining their nostalgic, historic memory with new cultures and practices. For those who perceive themselves as having worked to build their religion and thus their salvation, the concept of grace through faith is massively uncomfortable.

This notion of protest for understanding present day race relations can be highly instructive for interpreting our own hearts. What if one important ingredient of racism is the emotional protest against the changes in the very world we worked so hard to build? Again, race is quite complex, but I suspect that Paul's lament of Israel's skepticism helps us to identify a parallel protest in our own hearts. Racism takes on a specific form of protest that can be identified and repented of. How is this true in twenty-first century American churches?

From Ancient Israel to Modern Houston

American identity is deeply tied to our sense of being self-made. There is an industrious spirit prevalent in the American psyche which leads us (collectively) to believe that we are a product of our own making,[6] a naïve meritocracy of sorts.

However, we are a country of incredible privilege. This privilege, for better or for worse, has produced nostalgia toward our country, our towns, and our neighborhoods. So what happens when this particular vision of America appears to be becoming a distant memory due to cultural shifts? I am suggesting racism is fueled by a silent protest in our hearts.

I grew up in the city of Houston, which presently is wonderfully diverse. It was not as diverse in the late '70s and '80s when I was a kid. As I mentioned earlier, my family lived in a predominantly White area. My parents represent the immigrants who moved north to Texas looking for work.

We, too, were quiet and hard-working, but my family was not particularly welcomed. Why not? We represented change. My mother spoke English with an accent, and it provoked sarcasm and condescension from others. The fancy term for it is "micro-aggression," but we didn't think of it like that. We just wanted to survive. Nevertheless, what we experienced was a residue of racism that permeated every aspect of our lives.

People simply felt uncomfortable with immigrant Mexicans. The general discourse I would hear from the White community is something like this: "This is not the Houston that I grew up with. I feel like I am an outsider in my own home." When the White folks looked around their city, they saw the stores, communities, and schools that they built. In their minds, Houston was a city built by their grandparents and great-grandparents. And now their neighborhoods were being inhabited by foreigners. So Mexicans, like my family, were moving into the cities—cities we did not build—and were benefitting from the culture built by White people. And merely by our presence, the culture was changing. This change provoked resentment. It provoked a type of protest, even if just an emotional one.

What is at the heart of the protest? It was *too easy* to get the privileges of Houston. What does that mean? It means it was *too easy* to benefit from the city of Houston without having built or invested in her. It was *too easy* for Mexicans to enter and become citizens of Houston. We were like Gentiles who were getting all the privileges of being a Jew—through faith alone—without centuries of investment. The eleventh-hour grace was painful, especially, if you saw yourself as somehow deserving (or having worked for) the privileges of Houston. And so the people were filled with resentment and racism, and they began to abandon the city[7] in order to find enclaves where only other White people resided.

Imagine a toddler playing with a toy. A second toddler comes along and wants to play with the toy, too. The first toddler resists sharing until the parent demands that he shares with the second toddler. So, what does the first one do? He abandons the toy and finds something else because he would rather give up the toy than share it with a new kid. It is a form of protest. Moving out of the city, and everything in between, is a form of protest. Racism is a form of protest. It is an expression of resentment. For those who perceive themselves as having worked to build their city (or church) and thus working for their privileges, the idea of gracious integration and accommodation is massively uncomfortable.

It Is More Complex Than That

We would be foolish to limit our analysis of racism to the single filter of protest. It is far more complex than that, and most certainly this does not explain all scenarios. I offer this one framework principally as a complement to other more sophisticated sociological and theological studies.

But there are two principal benefits of this framework. First, as I mentioned earlier, it gives us language for specific introspection. It gives us something concrete to work with. The more we strive to shift the conversation of racism away from the meta-level, the more hope and encouragement we will find fighting against it in our communities, churches, and even our own hearts. Racism is not an ethereal cloud, or an abstract thing. It is actions and sinful attitudes which can be redeemed with repentance and thoughtful community participation. But when racism feels inevitable, people quit trying. I want to give God's people vocabulary for identifying and fighting against racism in their hearts.

The second benefit is that everyone gains from this framework—everyone. My wife, Amanda, is White and grew up in a small town in West Texas. When we lived in Little Rock, Arkansas, she volunteered in a Crisis Pregnancy Center. One day, a sixteen-year-old White girl came to the center. She had been kicked out of her home by her parents because she was pregnant. But there is more to the story—her boyfriend, Brandon, was a young Black kid, and her parents would not accept a bi-racial grandchild. She did not want to abort the child, but her options were limited. This young lady, clearly distressed by her parents' racism, lamented, "I can't believe they won't accept us. Brandon and I truly love each other. Why can't my parents look past the color of his skin? It's not like he's Mexican. Yuck. My boyfriend is not dirty."

Amanda is, of course, married to me, and she sat there speechless. What became evident to her was racism is a human problem. I have been the victim of racial slurs by as many Black people as I have been by White or Asian.

And lamentably, my extended family and I have perpetuated racist attitudes as well. This causes me great grief, but I am not naïve to the reality that racism is uniformly a problem among all human beings. The language of protest, arguably, allows us to more quickly identify it.

Black Christians, Hispanic Christians, and all Christians, can (and should!) read Romans 9–11 and see their own racist sin in the sin personified by God's people. While we read God's Word, God's Word reads us and exposes our sins—even as they are depicted in others. The Bible is given to the whole of God's people, people from every tongue, tribe, people, and nation.

Both the Need and the Hope of Repentance

What does the Kingdom of God look like? It looks like a Jew and Gentile enjoying a banquet together. This is what the Apostle Peter believed too.

Peter, a Jew, boldly proclaimed the Gospel. He passionately followed Christ. And he ate with Gentiles. It was beautiful. The kingdom was advancing.

But then the Jews arrived and "...*he* [Peter] *drew back and separated himself...*" (Gal. 2:12). Paul would not have any of it (Gal. 2:14). The banquet simply could not go on until there was repentance. Repentance was the key.

And why, precisely, is this good news? Because God can do something about it. Racism is not inevitable! We can repent! The call to repentance is not a broken record. It is assuming a posture of hope. We have the dignity of overcoming our structures and making changes. God has given us the gift of repentance. We *can* change. It might be slow, but God will have his way with his church. Every single Christian is invited to be earnestly self-suspicious. We must be committed to truth-telling, not only at the meta-level, but first at the heart level. And to be clear, everyone—every color, every gender—has the opportunity to self-analyze and repent.

What are your fears? What vision of the "good ol' days" are you afraid you have lost because there are new faces of color at the banquet table? Why are you so angry at people different from you? How are you protesting? What are you afraid of losing? "*What do you have that you did not receive?*" (1 Cor. 4:7) Are you harboring resentment toward people of other races and cultures?

Where can you exchange your protest with exclamations like this:

"I'm glad you are here! You belong here! This table is better with you!"

---

1. An American and especially a man or boy of Mexican descent. Merriam-Webster, s.v. "Chicano (n.), https://www.merriam-webster.com/dictionary/Chicano
2. A foreigner in Spain or Latin America especially when of English or American origin; broadly : a non-Hispanic person. Merriam-Webster, s.v. "gringo (n.)," https://www.merriam-webster.com/dictionary/gringo
3. David Chappell, *A Stone of Hope:: Prophetic Religion and the Death of Jim Crow* (Chapel Hill: The University of North Carolina Press, 2004), 3–4.
4. This is a significant claim. This could be further established by a survey of the Gospels and Acts: e.g. Matt. 3:9, John the Baptist's aforementioned comment; Mark 11:17, "*... My house shall be called a house of prayer for all the nations.... But you have made it...*"; in Acts the early Jewish church simply can't get its head around Gentile inclusion, epitomized in Peter's encounter with Cornelius; almost humorously, God has to give him the "Kill and eat" vision *three times*, and Luke recounts the story *twice* for his listeners. The point isn't to humiliate the Jews, but to 1) show how deeply embedded covenantal/ethnic privilege is and, therefore, 2) how compassionate outsiders should be and 3) how sober and self-critical insiders should be. It's almost a shame they have to have a council (Acts 15) to address it.
5. This is a reference to Jesus' parable in Matthew 20:1–16 which, in my estimation, has everything to do with privilege and protest.
6. In 1 Corinthians 4:7, Paul exhorts, "*What do you have that you did not receive?*" Even if we have worked hard, who gives us our health? Who gave us our work ethic? Who gave us a love for work? Who gave us the opportunities, that we might seize them?
7. It is well documented that White flight is the result of race, but multiple other reasons significantly factor in as well. This essay is not intending to be reductionistic, nor discarding the expansive research in that area.

RACIAL RECONCILIATION

WILLIAM EDGAR

William Edgar was raised in France and educated at Harvard and the University of Geneva. He has taught at the Faculté Jean Calvin in Aix-en-Provence, France, and has been Professor of Apologetics at Westminster Seminary in Philadelphia since 1989. Edgar has written extensively on apologetics, music, African American aesthetics, and French Huguenot history. He directs the jazz band Renewal.

———

Although much progress has been made in North America, there is still a long, long way to go. There is no question that racial discrimination is still a shameful reality. Some of it is in surprising places.

A well-documented study on racial discrimination in health care by law professor Barbara A. Noah[1] shows the different ways, some subtle, others not so subtle, wherein people of color, particularly African Americans, are less likely to receive access to medical treatment than White people. PBS (Public Broadcasting Service) recently aired a program on the care of autistic children. It was clear that special needs African Americans receive far less attention than special needs Whites.

Health care is not the only area where discrimination exists. People are surprised when a scandal breaks out as it did at the University of Oklahoma, where it was discovered that student members of the Sigma Alpha Epsilon fraternity were reciting racially-charged chants. What was particularly alarming is we tend to think that education is supposed to diminish racial resentment, and that the millennials are meant to be exceptionally tolerant. As he investigated this and related stories, Sean McElwee found that racism today is not so much in the Bull Connor-type[2] of hatred as it is in the institutional cultures of our different establishments. As he put it, "Modern racism isn't cross-burning (though that still happens). It's the Texas Department of Housing and Community Affairs only approving tax credits for housing in neighborhoods that are majority people of color and denying the credits in neighborhoods that are majority White."[3]

Racism is hardly limited to North America. For years it was assumed that China was free of racial prejudice since it had not colonized other countries based on claims to civilize the less enlightened races. But recently keen observers have identified what might be categorized as "internal colonialism," the uneven effects of development within a nation-state which exploit the minority groups within the society.

Around ninety years ago, Chinese reformer Kang Youwei advocated giving special medals with the imprint *improver of the race* to Asians who married Blacks. He wanted to advance the cause of cultivating more beautiful colors. He was trying to hide the fact of prevalent racism which exists in China, even to this day, against the darker people. In an in-depth study, anthropologist Frank Dikötter found that there has been a longstanding prejudice by the Han people against minorities, who tend to be darker-skinned.[4]

Is Race for Real?

Strictly speaking, race cannot be defined physically. Yes, people's skin colors are different, and certainly there are minor traits belonging to the interaction of certain people groups with their environment. But even modern evolutionists agree that there is no such thing as a pure race, nor does human diversity preclude intermarriage with any other member of the human species.[5] French geneticist Albert Jacquard argues that because of "inter-fecundity" and other commonalities, race classification has become virtually impossible. In fact, he contends that individual diversity is so great, race categories are of little use.[6]

Christians should be glad for these findings, although we already have good enough reason to believe in the unity of the human race: our common paternity in Adam. Evangelical scholar Elizabeth Y. Sung agrees. After a great deal of research into the different disciplines which have explored race, she concluded, "Research within and across these disciplines, especially since the mid-twentieth century, has led to the conclusion in mainstream scholarship that discrete, biologically constituted 'races' do not exist as such."[7] Sung goes on to take issue with a number of exegetes who, in her judgment, use the category of race improperly to make sense of various divisions described in the Scriptures. She argues for using ethnicity, rather than race, to uncover the dynamics of this issue, and as a way forward to eradicate racism.

How is it, then, that we talk of racism and race-based prejudice? Ethnicity does make some sense. It refers to ancestry, culture, language, national origins, and the like. So, for example, we may speak of Jewish ethnicity, even though it is possible to convert into Judaism or out of it. Some ethnic labels are more vague than others. We speak of Asian but that would include Indians, Indonesians, Koreans, Chinese, and many others from that continent. These are people groups that are very different from one another.

When our family lived in France, we were often called Anglo-Saxons, even though as far as I know I carry no blood from the Anglos nor from the Saxons (my family was a mixture of Celtic and French Huguenot).

In her response to Elizabeth Sung, Valerie Landfair asks whether ethnicity serves the purpose of deconstructing race.[8] Since prejudice is expressed against various ethnic minorities, and that is often based on traits such as skin color, countries of origin, language, etc., what functional difference does it make to substitute ethnicity for race?

Landfair then forcefully argues that race is real, but that there are answers for racism. The only real remedy, she argues, is to find our true unity as God's image bearers now renewed by the Holy Spirit. This does not erase identity, but transcends it. Here is how she puts it:

In conclusion, I label myself as an African American woman created in the image of God and joint-heir with Jesus. My roots connect me to Christianity in Africa before the European missionaries and African enslavement, the civil rights movement, the black empowerment movement, the Black Lives Matter movement.

She goes on to say that the only way to eradicate racism is through lived-out Spirit baptism in divine love, based on Scripture.[9]

The Prejudice Is Real

Landfair appears to be right. Racism won't go away just because we are mistaken about it as a category. The fact remains that people are prejudiced. We make adverse judgments about other people, or groups of people, based on assumptions that come from various places.

The Bible is well aware of this unfortunate human trait. At times it simply describes different cases. For example, in recounting the story of the woman at the well, Gospel-writer John almost casually editorializes that the Jews have no dealings with the Samaritans (John 4:9).

There was an ancient and complicated history to this prejudice. Early in the monarchy Samaria and Israel split, and they often disagreed about crucial issues such as worship. Samaritans occasionally intermarried with pagan people such as the Assyrians, for which they were resented. By the time of Jesus, the division had crystallized into a difference over which place, Gerizim or Jerusalem, was the authorized location for true worship. Interestingly, the Lord tells the woman the Jews are right on this issue, though both would need to modify their views in light of the radical fulfillment of the Old Testament in the age of the Spirit (John 4:16–26).

The story of Esther recounts the way in which Haman nurtured an obsessive hatred against Mordecai and the Jews. He lost all taste for the great feast to which he was invited. As the narrative puts it tersely, *"Yet all this is worth nothing to me, so long as I see Mordecai the Jew standing at the king's gate"* (Esth. 5:13).

And need we be reminded that the Jews have been the victims of the most persistent and heinous prejudice throughout history, culminating in the Nazi extermination policies?

The most persistent example of prejudice in the Bible is the division between Jews and Gentiles. We can note the case of Peter who needed special convincing in order to bring the Gospel to the God-fearer Cornelius. His views were challenged by a vision of a dining canopy with formerly unclean foods on it, and the command to eat them (Acts 10:9–16).

It is important to observe that Peter was not wrong in terms of the

Old Testament administration. But the Gospel changed everything, and Peter needed to learn that from now on God was opening up salvation to the Gentiles, without respecting their background. As we know, at one point Peter lost his nerve and drew back from the Gentiles out of pressure from the circumcision party (Gal. 2:11–14).

Can there be ethnic traits? And can they be negative? With great care not to engage in essentialism, that is, tying certain traits to biology or race as such, we may answer in the affirmative. Many are positive or at best harmless. Italians make the best pasta. Or Korean women are strong (perhaps having been the agents of resistance during various occupations has lent this kind of characteristic tenacity to them). Some traits are more negative. The Bible tells us *"all Cretans are liars"* (Titus 1:12). There is obvious poetic hyperbole here, but there are cultures more adept at deception than others.[10] Others are debatable. Irish people have tempers. Jews are good in business. If there is any truth at all to these, we must be sure to identify the origins of such traits with historical circumstances, not race.

Some epithets are clearly harmful, because they are based on genetic fallacy. Asians are good in math and science. Blacks are good athletes or good musicians. Such epithets have led some to fear and others to revere people from these backgrounds. The only reason for the impression that Asians are good in math and science is because of the cultivation of discipline and achievement in those communities, particularly when they have been immigrants.[11]

People can be disciplined for all kinds of reasons. In certain Asian societies there is great significance placed on honor, often rooted in a Confucian social fabric. Losing face or being shamed are greater worries than in certain Western cultures, where guilt and pardon are more the worry.

Blacks often do excel in sports and music, not because they are essentially more qualified, but because circumstances have forced them to look for success in the rare places that have allowed them in.[12] So if there is any truth to these traits it is because of religious, historical, and cultural circumstance, not race.

Now, that does not make the prejudice less real when it highlights these traits. Being aware of the social nature of stereotyped character-istics, rather than believing them to be essential, is a first step toward avoiding prejudice. Awareness identifies caricatures, stereotypes which are more determinist than Christian. Determinism asserts there is no way out since these traits are tied to the biology of the person who doesn't have freedom to change. A Christian view refuses to give in to determinism. It believes God can affect change against all the odds.

Basic Causes

Can we identify some of the basic causes that lead to race prejudice? I believe we can.

There are presenting issues and deeper underlying issues. Here is a partial list.

Xenophobia

The word means "fear of the stranger." Most commonly, xenophobia refuses to let people not originally from a particular group or place belong. The simplest version of this prejudice is nativism. Nativism argues, for example, that particular immigrant groups, say Roman Catholics, or Italians, or Poles, cannot be true Americans because they did not arrive first. The error of this approach is egregious, but it has occurred a great deal in our history.

I remember objections to electing John F. Kennedy president. We were assured he would open the door for the Vatican to control America! The objects were never that, if anything, he was a fairly secular person. The fear of "the other," or xenophobia, is often the irrational source of our prejudice that Americans ought to look a certain way —our way.

The English professor and writer Moustafa Bayoumi[13] shares how people often ask him where he is from. When he answers that he was born in Switzerland, grew up in Canada, and now lives in Brooklyn, he observes their incredulity. Black people have a long history of having to convince blind White folks that they are as American as anyone else. The great jazz composer Duke Ellington often pointed out that America was built by the blood, sweat, and tears of Black people.

There can be historical reasons for xenophobia. I can remember my mother telling me she could never trust a Japanese person. The basis was their treachery in bombing Pearl Harbor in 1941. This was understandable, and yet had no bearing at all on the demeanor of Japanese descents living in the United States. It did not matter that most Japanese Americans had never set foot in Japan. My mother thought they could simply not be trusted, and that indeed they might all be involved with a subversive plot to overthrow the American government. That was a commonly held view in that generation. Indeed, just two months after Pearl Harbor, President Roosevelt issued Executive Order 9066 authorizing the round-up of over 100,000 Japanese Americans to put them in internment camps.

When we were living in southern France, we found a good deal of xenophobia toward the Maghrebin population. There were historical reasons for this, even though it was not justified ethically. The Maghreb, or Greater Maghreb, is an area in Northwest Africa comprising the former French colonies of Tunisia, Morocco, and Algeria. The common language is Arabic, thus many French people simply call them *les arabes*. Throughout the twentieth century, the Maghrebins were often recruited as manual workers in France. The greatest wave immigrated to France in the years after the war, when most of these countries became independent. The French residents in the Maghreb were often expelled, taking nothing with them but the clothes on their backs. And so resentment built up between the French, particularly the *pied noirs*, former colonists in Algeria, and these Maghrebin workers, who were given special advantages for coming to the motherland. Today many North Africans are living in the poorest, most crime-ridden parts of French cities. Even the children born in France are never likely to be considered French. My friend and colleague John Leonard worked for a decade as a pastor in Montpellier, trying to help French people change their attitudes toward the Maghrebins. Even when they had become Christian believers, the prejudice was still there.

Intermarriage

Closely related to xenophobia is the fear of mingling blood. It was not so long ago that mixed marriages were illegal in the United States. One of the most famous cases testing the law is *Loving v. Virginia* (1967). Mildred Jeter of mixed African and Native American descent married Richard Loving, a White man, in Washington, DC. The couple moved to Virginia, where they were arrested and convicted for violating the state's miscegenation law. The judge, Leon M. Bazile, a devout Roman Catholic and deeply imbued with Southern culture, argued that such a marriage was wrong because, as he said in a now infamous statement, "Almighty God created the races…. The fact that he separated the races shows that he did not intend for the races to mix."[14] The case went to the United States Supreme Court, where a unanimous verdict nullified the lower court's verdict, citing a violation of the Fourteenth Amendment and calling marriage one of the "basic civil rights of man."[15]

America was not the only place banning interracial marriage. The Nazi régime forbade both marriage and sexual relations between Aryans and non-Aryans. The notorious Nuremberg Laws of 1935 included such a law "For the Protection of German Blood and German Honor." Violation was called "race-disgrace" and could lead to deportation to a concentration camp.[16] South Africa had similar legislation against interracial marriages, though with less severe consequences.

What was the justification for the fear of mixing the races? In most cases, and clearly for Nazi Germany, it was the belief that being White was superior. In the American South after the Civil War, there were various reasons for laws against intermarriage. One of them was the belief that Whites were superior. For example, in Alabama it is patent that such laws were an attempt to preserve White sovereignty in the face of the emancipation of Black people. Scholar Cheryl Harris has shown that Whites sought many ways to preserve their Whiteness, and for many reasons—economic, psychological, and pragmatic. For example, many argued that it would be harder for racially mixed children to grow up and be educated. Harris found that Whiteness was considered property to be defended.[17]

Christians are not exempt from such views. A number of years ago, I officiated a wedding between a White man and a Chinese woman. The Chinese parents were adamantly opposed to the union. I will never forget one of the arguments I heard. It would be better to marry another Chinese person, even if he were an unbeliever, because we can fix that. I am happy to report that today they have changed, but not without much pain for the young couple.

Meritocracy

Another variant is the notion of perceived injustice. Why should some races be given preferential treatment and not others? Take the example of affirmative action. This policy, known as "positive discrimination" in the United Kingdom, and "employment equity" in Canada, seeks to favor people from disadvantaged groups who have suffered from discrimination, and make the path to education or employment easier for them. While we should not say all opposition to these strategies are racist, it is worth considering how such policies can lead to reverse discrimination: keeping qualified people who have worked hard for their achievements out of the running.

I have spent some time helping with interviews for Harvard University. The administrators told us to look for intellectual capacity. But they also insisted Harvard did not want an entire class of 1600s on the SAT exams, which they could easily find if they wanted to. They were looking for a well-rounded class, which included athletes, musicians, creative writers, scientists, and the like. They want young people whose achievements could be measured by other standards than just test scores.

We were told that after students have arrived, they often change their mind about their majors, some moving out of the sciences and into the humanities, or from large departments into smaller ones. They were looking for character, leadership, the ability to get along with others, and so forth. And they were looking for ethnic diversity. The result is that an otherwise seemingly well-qualified candidate might be denied in order to accept a minority candidate who might not have the high test scores but would contribute to the overall social goals desired by the university.

Affirmative action is a difficult issue. Some of its opponents just think it unfair. Others are not so upset about qualified people not making it, but about the message it sends to the less qualified: you don't have all the skills, but we feel sorry for you because you've been disadvantaged. Westminster Seminary, where I teach, used to have an inner city campus made up mostly of minorities. There were all kinds of tuition breaks and other resources for students who could not afford the high cost of a graduate education. But at one point our administration suggested eliminating some of the tougher require-ments, such as learning Greek and Hebrew. The students were quite incensed, feeling they would be considered less intelligent and less capable of hard work. So the administration quickly abandoned the idea.

Resentment against those who are given special access is under-standable. Why should good scores and hard work be "penalized"? Indeed, some affirmative action can go to absurd lengths. But the argument on the other side is that in order to achieve a healthy soci-ety, there ought to be allowances made for disadvantaged people. The Bible constantly admonishes us to remember the poor, to provide for widows, and to visit the disenfranchised. And it does not encourage us to ask first how this happened, and then discriminate between the deserving poor and the poor who got there by making bad decisions.

Of course at some point that kind of question does need to be asked if we are to help people for the long term. The point is if we resent people who have not achieved as much as we have, without stopping to ask why, we are likely to be prejudiced.

Envy

Underlying all these manifestations, at the deepest level, prejudice, including so-called racism, is caused by covetousness. It did not take long after the fall of our first parents for this sin to devolve into the murderous comportment of Cain against his brother Abel (Gen. 4:1–8). This sort of resentment is close to the surface in every heart. It may be triggered by an incident, a spoken word, or just a circumstance. For Cain it was that the Lord accepted his brother's offering but not his own. He had not "done well" (4:7). He became jealous, and the jealousy festered. He "let the sun go down on his anger" (Eph. 4:26). Uncontrolled resentment is at the root of all prejudice.

James is a biblical author especially sensitive to prejudice. In his letter he particularly addressed class prejudice, but the principles apply to race as well. Contrary to the "pure religion" of compassion (Jas. 1:26–27), the church is often tempted to show favoritism toward the rich (2:1–13). The fundamental problem with doing so is that you have become judges with evil thoughts, forgetting that God is not only impartial but has often chosen the poor as his choice followers (2:4–5). Furthermore, this church seems to have forgotten it is often the rich who oppress and blaspheme (2:6–7).

The most concentrated passage that deals with human conflict is James 4:1–12. The author goes right to the core of the problem. Why do people quarrel? Because they want something and cannot get it. Even when they ask God for it they ask wrongly to spend it on their passions. Such an attitude compromises everything, making unhealthy alliances with the world and claiming to judge God's law rather than submitting to it.

Is it possible that all the vicissitudes of racism boil down to self-serving jealousy? That is the biblical claim. It may have all kinds of complex manifestations. But it all comes down to envy. More than an inconvenient truth, it is the dreadful diagnosis of our human condition. Envy is the sin that crouches at the door (Gen. 4:7). But there it is, in the heart. Jesus' diagnosis is equally severe:

> *What comes out of a person is what defiles him. For from within, out of the heart of man, come evil thoughts, sexual immorality, theft, murder, adultery, coveting, wickedness, deceit, sensuality, envy, slander, pride, foolishness.* (Mark 7:20–22)

While this language may sound individualistic, the problem is also social and systemic. It can and does apply to groups, even to entire countries. And it is an equal opportunity malady. I have heard arguments that say prejudice can be experienced by anyone, but racism only by White people because racism requires institutional power, which minorities do not have.

I question that. While racism indeed implies power, there is much more to power than institutional backing.

As I argued above, I don't find it helpful to deny the reality of racism simply because skin color bias is an illusion. The evil thoughts listed by Jesus all imply some interface with power. They are wrong, but not illusory, since unfortunately their manifestations are all too real.

Basic Cures

To those who only see in the Bible the singling out of a particular people, say the choosing of the Hebrew people in the Old Testament, they will be surprised to discover that the larger message is on human unity. There is to be sure a recognition of diversity within the unity, but the call to unity is one of the strongest themes in Scripture.

One might say unity is the bookends, between Eden and the New Jerusalem. The original creation of mankind after God's own image tells us humanity is basically one. Paul boldly tells the Athenians that God made from one man every nation (*ethnos*) of mankind to live on the face of the earth (Acts 17:26). And the one Gospel, the one body, the one Spirit unites believers in the one hope (Eph. 4:4). To be sure, this Gospel includes every nation and tribe:

> *After this I looked, and behold, a great multitude that no one could number, from every nation, from all tribes and peoples and languages, standing before the throne and before the Lamb, clothed in white robes, with palm branches in their hands....* (Rev. 7:9)

But the final multitude of the redeemed in the new heavens and new earth is profoundly united.

Declaring this does not solve the practical problems for working out this unity and diversity. Paul delivers a good deal of his teaching on the unity of Christ's body through the Holy Spirit, expressed through the variety of gifts of that same Spirit (1 Cor. 12:4–31). Christians can know jealousy and oppression even though they are inhabited by the Holy Spirit. Many of the instructions in the New Testament are about working out ways to love one another. But they also enjoin us to live at peace with outsiders, to love our enemies, to avoid seeking vengeance (Rom. 12:14–21).

Combatting racism is an enormous agenda. There is much homework to do both inside and outside the church. Christians possess a good deal of capital in order to affect reconciliation in the church.

It is important to recognize the reality of the issues. Until we recognize the potential we all have to be prejudiced we cannot properly become agents of change. As one of my colleagues used to put it, each of us needs to sit at the feet of another culture. I have the privilege of working in a multiethnic jazz band, and there is nothing like a few proactive conversations across the race line to stimulate deeper understanding. But recognition is only the first step.

At a conference on race sponsored at Westminster Seminary, there was an unforgettable moment. A Korean speaker apologized for his prejudice against Black people, and poignantly crossed the stage to embrace his African American counterpart, who also stated that his people had not been innocent either. Such encounters are moving, and they help with mutual understanding. But they are only markers along the way.

More long-term work is sorely needed. One outstanding example of a more durable effort is the Voice of Calvary Ministries in Mendenhall and Jackson, Mississippi. The co-founders are John and Vera Mae Perkins who moved to Mississippi as civil rights activists in the 1960s. John Perkins was arrested and badly beaten by police officers. Remarkably, he understood racism to be perpetrated on Whites as well as Blacks. His best-selling book *A Quiet Revolution*[18] outlines the concrete steps needed to effect change. The remedies he and his team practice include Bible studies for youth, low-income housing for single moms, after-school tutoring, and the operation of thrift shops. Today, there is still much work to be done, but there has been remarkable progress and growth.

Other works concentrate on rebuilding local neighborhoods. William "Bill" Strickland has concentrated much of his effort in the Chateau district of Pittsburgh. In 1987 he created the Manchester Craftsmen's Guild, an art, education, and music ministry that helps young people put their talents to work and give them a sense of their worth and dignity as God's image bearers. Strickland recounts his story and prescribes the path for others to follow in *Make the Impossible Possible* .[19] While it may sound like a self-help organization, its Christian base emerges in all its aspects.

There are astonishing examples of reconciliation with justice at the national level. Few of us who are old enough can ever forget the victory over apartheid in South Africa. In 1994 we witnessed the practice of *Ubuntu*, or "humanity toward others," triumph over seemingly intractable racial hatred. The move forward to a post-apartheid world was relatively peaceful thanks to the quiet diplomacy of Christians.

Washington Okumu, ambassador-at-large for the Forum for the Restoration of Democracy in Kenya, a strong Christian, came to help out at the behest of local religious leaders in South Africa. He made a great difference. He was able to persuade sworn enemies Nelson Mandela of the African National Congress (ANC) and Mangosuthu Buthelezi of the Inkatha Freedom Party (IFP) to guarantee each other a place at the table in the new coalition government. The turning point was at the Jesus Peace Rally in the King Park Stadium, when these leaders came together under a common umbrella. The transition was also made possible by the establishment of the Truth and Reconciliation Commission in 1995, headed by Anglican Archbishop Desmond Tutu.[20]

The Christian church is a critical place to effect reconciliation with justice. Some of the issues are not easy. What end-product are we looking for? Should the population of the church reflect the resident demographic, or should efforts be made to seek out minorities from outside the local area? Should music be of one style or a sampling from different styles?

Though such questions require a good deal of reflection, recognizing the challenges of ethnicity and our tendency to be prejudiced is the proper beginning. For example, something is amiss if a church only picks White elders when the local community is racially mixed.

Something is amiss if a church only uses Western classical music when the local community is diverse. My own church has struggled to blend music for the taste of older people with the tastes of younger people. It often feels like sampling to me, rather than a concerted effort to find styles that everyone can embrace. Perhaps newly composed music is a healthy answer, although not every church has the capacity to write new music.

Church unity is difficult but not impossible. I know of one church in Chattanooga, Tennessee, where a relocation confronted people with a choice: whether to stay and struggle with people different from them, or leave. They decided to stay. Now New City Fellowship is a bastion for racial reconciliation. Among their mission statements is the declaration of the application of the Gospel to their present racial and ethnic situation. Among the fourteen principles about the nature of racial reconciliation are:

- It is the assertive correction of circumstances, not simply a desire to get on with things and forget about the past.
- In the life of the local church, it is the active desire to include people through understanding and learning new cultures and enlarging the cultural scope of worship forms as long as they are biblical.
- It is the necessary attitude change that brings people to become like Jesus and take the form of a servant to each other, and to other people groups.[21]

If we are going to see more progress, the most important consideration is to strive for maturity in the power of the Gospel, *until we all attain to the unity of the faith and of the knowledge of the Son of God"* (Eph. 4:13). Striving means hard work. Striving means mutual accommodation. Striving means believing that the Lord will grant us to see progress, because he cares about it far more than we do.

---

1. Barbara A. Noah, "A Prescription for Racial Equality in Medicine," *Connecticut Law Review* 40, (2008): 675. See also her "Racist Health Care?," *Florida Law Review* 48, (1996): 357.
2. Theophilus Eugene "Bull" Connor (July 11, 1897—March 10, 1973) was an American politician who served as Commissioner of Public Safety for the city of Birmingham, Alabama, for more than two decades. He strongly opposed activities of the American Civil Rights Movement in the 1960s. Wikipedia, s.v. "Bull Connor," https://en.wikipedia.org/wiki/Bull_Connor
3. See various reports, including http://www.pbs.org/newshour/updates/americas-racism-problem-far-complicated-think/.
4. Frank Dikötter, *The Discourse of Race in Modern China* (Hong Kong: Hong Kong University Press, 1992).

5. See, for example, "The AAPA Statement on Biological Aspects of Race," *American Journal of Physical Anthropology* 101, (1996): 569–570.

6. Albert Jacquard, *In Praise of Difference: Genetics and Human Affairs* (New York: Columbia University Press, 1984).

7. Elizabeth Y. Sung, "'Racial Realism' in Biblical Interpretation," *Ex Auditu* 31, (2015): 5.

8. Valerie Landfair, "Response to Sung," *Ex Auditu* 31, (2015): 22–26.

9. Landfair, "Response," 26.

10. Titus 1:12 is known as Epimenides' paradox, since this poet was himself Cretan, and thus would logically be included in the company of liars. But the context makes it clear that Paul is simply quoting a local proverb for its rhetorical force, not as sociological data, in order to prepare his young disciple for the difficulties for the elders of managing their unruly flock.

11. African Americans are perceived as less disciplined. If they are, it is because they were brought here against their will and most often were beaten down in order to destroy their will power.

12. The film comedy *White Men Can't Jump* is a tongue-in-cheek response to the caricature that Blacks are better ball-players than Whites.

13. A writer and professor of English at Brooklyn College, City University of New York. Wikipedia, s.v. "Moustafa Bayoumi," https://en.wikipedia.org/wiki/Moustafa_Bayoumi

14. Wikipedia, s.v. "Loving v. Virginia," https://en.wikipedia.org/wiki/Loving_v._Virginia

15. This case is well studied in Fay Botham's *Almighty God Created the Races: Christianity, Interracial Marriage, & American Law* (Chapel Hill: University of North Carolina Press, 2009), 159–178.

16. The Nazis based their race theories on the work of French aristocrat Arthur de Gobineau (1816–1882), who argued in his 1,400 page book, *An Essay on the Inequality of the Human Races* (1848), for the superiority of aristocrats over common folk, owing to their greater Aryan blood, less corrupted by the inferior races from the Alps and the Mediterranean.

17. Cheryl I. Harris, "Whiteness as Property," Harvard Law Review 106, no. 8 (June 1993).

18. John Perkins, A Quiet Revolution (Barrington, IL: Marshalls, 1985).

19. Bill Strickland, Make the Impossible Possible (New York: Broadway Books, 2007).

20. I have written about this settlement in *Does Christianity Really Work?* (Fearn, UK: Christian Focus Publications, 2016), 56–60.

21. See http://www.newcityfellowship.com/racial-reconciliation.

LOOKING JUSTLY
PHOTOGRAPHY, RACE, AND GENDER

ELISSA YUKIKO WEICHBRODT

Elissa Yukiko Weichbrodt is Associate Professor of Art and Art History at Covenant College in Lookout Mountain, Georgia. Her research and teaching explore how visual art and culture can shape and expand our engagement with marginalized identities. Elissa has degrees from Covenant College (BA) and Washington University in St. Louis (MA and PhD). She and her husband, Noel, have two sons, Ezekiel and Miles.

———

[All photographs referenced in this essay can be
easily found with a Google search for keyword or artist.]

———

Bodies press together in a tightly cropped, black-and-white photograph. Two rows of figures stretch across the image's middle ground, striding toward the viewer. In the back row we catch glimpses of two helmeted soldiers and a few men wearing light straw hats. The front row consists entirely of young women with neatly coiffed hair and crisply pressed dresses. But all eyes are trained on the lone figure in the foreground: another young woman in an immaculate, full-skirted shirt dress, clutching a book tightly to her chest with her left arm as she walks alone. Her expression is implacable, and her large sunglasses hide her eyes from us. The clear visual separation from the rest of the figures in the photograph encourages us to recognize her visible difference. Her skin—far darker than anyone else's in the photograph—contrasts strongly with her bright, white dress. Just behind her left shoulder, a White girl squints her eyes and opens her mouth in a snarling, ferocious yell.

Photographs possess an internal, visual logic that creates meaning for viewers. In this image, the Black girl's body is visually separate from and set in contrast against the rows of White bodies behind her. The photograph announces her otherness, her separation from the majority. But while she carries herself with visible dignity, the White girl behind her screeches in unsuppressed rage. The photograph suggests a moral reality that mirrors this visual contrast.

You have seen this image before: the 1957 photograph of Elizabeth Eckford walking toward Little Rock High School while Hazel Bryan screams over her shoulder. It appears in the "Civil Rights" or "Desegregation" section of history textbooks and in television specials on race in America. This is the kind of photograph that we tend to see not as artwork, but as a document, an objective witness to historical events. This image seems to need no interpretation. Its meaning seems evident on the surface. There is no apparent symbolism to decode or expressionist gestures to unravel. We might also be inclined to declare the image an unambiguous success—the photographer captured a raw moment of racial hatred, and responsible viewers respond with appropriate outrage.

And yet historical photographs like this one do not live exclusively in the past. Instead they play an active role today, shaping both our cultural memory and our contemporary attitudes toward others. As Christians, we should be especially aware of how historical photographs impact our ability to *see* and thus *do* justly to our fellow image bearers.

This particular photograph of the desegregation of Little Rock Central High School in Arkansas did have an immediate and powerful cultural impact. A similar image taken by Will Counts was published on the evening of September 4, 1957, in the *Arkansas Democrat*, and one taken by United Press photographer Johnny Jenkins ran the following morning in the *Arkansas Gazette*.[1] Jenkins' image was quickly picked up by the *New York Post*, the *New York Times*, the *Chicago Daily News*, and the *St. Louis Argus*, and it stoked an outcry over the treatment of Eckford and the other eight Black students who were barred from entering Central High School by the National Guard. In 1964, Eckford and some of these other students became the self-congratulatory focus of a short film, *Nine from Little Rock*, commissioned by the United States Information Agency to demonstrate America's racial progress over the last seven years.[2] Within another decade, the still photograph functioned as a kind of shorthand for the ultimately successful battle for school integration.[3] When faced with photographic proof of racism, kind-hearted White viewers—or so the story goes—rallied to support the cause of desegregation.[4]

Although we might possess a much more nuanced understanding of the events leading up to and following the desegregation of schools after *Brown v. Board of Education*,[5] the photograph maintains a particular kind of power. It asserts its objectivity and its truthfulness. Since the invention of glass plate negatives and albumen printing in the mid-nineteenth century, photographic images have been easily and cheaply disseminated. Whereas the singularity and originality of an oil painting or marble sculpture implicitly emphasizes its status as an artistic creation, photography's reproducibility aligns it with machine culture.[6] Relatively few, if any, visible traces of the photographer's hand is evident in the finished print.

In addition, photographs create what cultural critic Pierre Bourdieu describes as the "reality effect."[7] We typically think of photographs as indices. We expect a physical relationship between what is in front of the lens and what ends up on the negative. Visual accuracy further binds the photograph to reality. A photograph of a flower looks like a flower, whereas a painting of a flower—one made by a three-year-old, for example—might not always resemble the thing it purports to represent. The perceived realism of the photograph, its correspondence with our lived experience, gives it the appearance of being natural rather than a social or historical construct.

And yet, photographs also conceal things from viewers. First of all, there is a visual erasure. A photograph as a still image can only represent a split second, a fragment of a much longer series of events. The photograph of Elizabeth Eckford tells us nothing of the decades long struggle of Black parents demanding a better education for their children or the repeated, patient legal challenges leveled by NAACP lawyers against segregated schools.[8] The photograph does not show us that Eckford had been accidentally separated from the other eight Black students of the Little Rock Nine and turned away at the door of the high school by National Guardsmen. It does not show us that Bryan, a fifteen-year-old wanting attention, had wandered to the front lines in search of the spotlight, not out of particular political conviction.[9] It certainly does not show us the relatively rare White families who welcomed the Supreme Court's injunction.[10]

Johnny Jenkins, the photographer, chose to crop his image rather tightly, literally excising any greater sense of context. Another photograph from that day, taken by Will Counts, offers a wider view of the same antagonistic procession. In Counts' image, the crowd feels more diffuse and less threatening. The contrast between Eckford and her White peers is diminished.

But this famous photograph also conceals through its iconicity. We see it simultaneously as a historic document and a transcendent symbol representing something outside of itself. The photograph's ubiquity contributes to its status as an icon. Today it appears in textbooks, museum displays, and the first page of a Google Image search for "school desegregation," always functioning as a symbol of America's supposed moral triumph over Jim Crow and racial inequality. It declares, "This is what we overcame." In actuality, the photograph is not about Elizabeth Eckford as an individual; she is a stand-in for an entire race, social class, historical moment, and set of virtues.[11]

It is this iconicity that can also make this photograph dangerous. As Martin Berger reminds us in his recent book *Freedom Now! Forgotten Photographs of the Civil Rights Struggle*, the photograph of Eckford and Bryan made it "too easy for the millions of White Americans who saw Eckford's image in the newspapers to imagine that race was primarily an interpersonal problem, here, of racist White schoolgirls—and to ignore its rootedness in laws, practices, and institutions that were considerably harder to address."[12] Today the seemingly straightforward nature of the photograph might suggest to us that its work is complete, that the struggle for racial justice, like the specific moment depicted in the image, is a thing of the past.

And yet, this image continues to work. It asserts and naturalizes certain expectations about race, class, and gender, assumptions that guide our engagement with the world today.

Images are neither created nor viewed in a vacuum. They are always referencing other images as a means of accruing, or sometimes undercutting, authority. As viewers, we each carry a mental archive of images. We might not be able to name all the images, and some of them might only exist as half-remembered shadows, but nevertheless we are constantly interpreting and categorizing images in relationship with those things which we have previously seen.[13]

Some artists and viewers are more conscious about this relationship than others, but images do remain in conversation with each other whether or not we acknowledge it. We might liken our archive to a Google Image search in our brains. If we input something as innocuous as "sunset," a host of highly saturated photographs appear, all of them vaguely familiar and all of them reinforcing what a "good" or "photo-worthy" sunset looks like. Indeed, when we see a brilliant, pink and gold sunset in person, we say, "That looks like a photograph."

The Google Image search analogy extends to other examples as well, with perhaps more culturally loaded implications. A search for "wedding," for example, brings up some images of wedding bands and bouquets, but photographs of thin, smiling, young, White, heterosexual couples dominate the results.

Our visual archives are particularly potent when it comes to identifying and policing bodies. In his important 1986 essay, "The Body and the Archive," photographer and theorist Allan Sekula observes that the photographic archive contains traces of the bodies of "heroes, leaders, moral exemplars, celebrities, and those of the poor, the diseased, the insane, the criminal, the nonWhite, the female, and all other embodiments of the unworthy."[14] That is, photographs teach us what heroism, morality, and fame *should* look like, and they do so largely through contrast. *This* is what is respectable; *that* is what is not. Every photograph we see, including the image of Eckford and Bryan, is understood in relationship with the archive of photographs we have already seen.

A significant body of scholarship explores the ways in which photography, since its inception, has been used not only to shape racial bias, but to construct the very notion of race. Artist and theorist Coco Fusco writes, "Rather than recording the existence of race, photography *produced* race as a visualizable fact."[15] Nineteenth-century anthropologists and naturalists created a set of visual tropes that codified racial difference. By emphasizing certain physical characteristics, posing bodies in particular ways, and framing the image with text, photographs offered "proof" of racial difference.[16]

One particularly well-known example is a set of fifteen daguerreotypes commissioned by naturalist Louis Agassiz during his time at Harvard University. Agassiz, along with many other scientists in the mid-nineteenth century, held to the notion of polygenesis: the belief in multiple, separate creations for each race. Hoping to build a photographic archive that demonstrated quantifiable differences between races, Agassiz visited a plantation in South Carolina and selected various slaves to be photographed. Some slaves were photographed standing, fully nude, in frontal, profile, and rear views. Others, still nude, were photographed from the waist up, with front and side views. With their clear lighting, calm faces, blank backgrounds, and direct poses, the images asserted cool, scientific objectivity.

For Agassiz, the photographs allowed for the sustained and detached scrutiny of Black bodies, akin to studying a pinned insect under a microscope in order to detail its particular features. But, crucially, Agassiz was not just looking to catalogue differences. He located those differences within a racialized evolutionary hierarchy, where Blacks occupied a position above an orangutan and below a classical ideal.[17] These photographs thus served as visual proof of Blacks' fundamental inferiority to Whites, a conclusion Agassiz expected to be plainly legible to anyone who looked at the images.

Photography later served as a counterpoint to Agassiz's claims when W. E. B. Du Bois exhibited a series of 363 photographs of affluent, polished young Black men and women as part of the "American Negro" exhibit at the 1900 Paris Exposition. Like Agassiz, Du Bois believed the photograph offered empirical evidence of the economic, social, and even moral conditions of Black subjects in Atlanta. But unlike Agassiz's stripped, flattened bodies, Du Bois' subjects were elegantly dressed and beautifully poised, employing the conventions of middle-class portraiture rather than anthropology. Adopting a three-quarter pose, surrounded by rich drapery, a pedestal with books, or a gilt chair, Du Bois' sitters asserted their status, education, and taste.

These images also make meaning for us through the context of the archive. Even if we have been taught about the moral repugnance of racially based slavery, we struggle to see Agassiz's subjects as individuals rather than types. The visual codes those daguerreotypes utilize are more akin to how we photograph objects for an eBay auction than how we snap a photograph of a friend. Du Bois' images also engender an archival tension. A female sitter's skin tone and hair texture might locate her closer to Agassiz's images of the so-called inferior body, but her clothing and posture insist we categorize her, instead, with images that define noble, upstanding bodies. The disjunction occurs when we realize our archive of such publicly honored figures consists predominantly of White bodies.

Returning to the photograph from Little Rock, we can see how Eckford's attire, posture, and demeanor present a subject much more like those exhibited by Du Bois. Within our visual archive, Eckford corresponds to our notion of what a "deserving" or "respectable" woman looks like. Indeed, in his coverage of that day in 1957, journalist Bob Considine describes her as "aristocratic."[18] Wearing a crisp, neatly ironed dress and pressed hair, Eckford mirrors the poised, fresh-faced models in a Sears catalog, a picture of American wholesomeness.

We must also recognize what categories Eckford resists. She is not the hyper-sexualized, exotic Josephine Baker, dancing in a banana leaf skirt in Paris. Nor is she the desexualized, unattractive Mammy of plantation lore. Side-stepping two stereotypes most often granted Black women, she instead presents herself as non-threatening to White culture's proclivities or social mores.[19] The photograph's more subtle argument constructed through the archive is that Eckford can be assimilated into good White society without much fuss or uncomfortable adjustment on the part of dominant culture.

But Eckford's body also contributes to another archival category of Blackness, that of the noble Black body in pain. The subject has a long history in photography, embodied clearly by a famous 1863 abolitionist *carte de visite* that features the scarred back of freedman Gordon. Here, according to art historian Martin Berger, we see a "Black body damaged by brutal southern Whites, in an effort to galvanize the sentiments of northern liberals."[20] Berger argues that this same visual formula of "inactive Blacks and active Whites," bodies that do not strike back but willingly bear the marks of disgrace and even violence, dominates the most well-known and frequently reproduced images of the Civil Rights movement. It was *this* body that Martin Luther King, Jr. and others in the Southern Christian Leadership Conference would find to be particularly effective in their nonviolent direct actions against segregation. And it was this stoic, seemingly passive body that other activist groups, such as the Student Nonviolent Coordinating Committee and later the Black Panthers, largely rejected in favor of representing self-fashioned agency, much to the discomfort of dominant White culture.[21]

Although Eckford is in the foreground of Jenkins' photograph, it is the screaming girl behind her who is in the sharpest focus. While we may sympathize with Eckford, we prefer, regardless of ethnicity, to disassociate ourselves from the raging Hazel Bryan in the background. The sun illuminates Bryan's face from the side, outlining her ferociously gaping mouth. Her eyes pinch together, and she glares at Eckford's back while striding forward forcefully.

Unlike Eckford, Bryan does not seem to be upholding notions of middle-class respectability. Rather than smiling primly like the Sears catalogue models, Bryan releases a torrent of emotion in a very public space. In doing so, she visually aligns herself with another set of images, photographs commissioned by French neurologist Jean-Martin Charcot in the late nineteenth century. Charcot's photographs of women under his care at the Salpêtrière mental hospital in Paris construct a visual language of insanity manifested through hyper-emotionalism. In one series of images, for example, Charcot documents a *hysterique* patient as she opens her mouth wide in a primal scream. In another series, a woman in a nightgown makes a series of exaggerated, emotional facial expressions. While the images might be humorous in some contexts, Charcot, like Agassiz before him, offered them to the public as scientific documents—visual diagnoses of women deemed unfit to be in society. Certainly, few would look at the Little Rock photograph and attempt to diagnose Bryan with a psychiatric disorder. And yet, our photographic archive categorizes her as "other," someone outside of polite society. Bryan's public expression of rage functionally denies her social class and her gender. She is not acting as a lady ought.

Indeed, she was not acting as a White person ought. White viewers of this photograph in 1957 were quick to disavow Bryan. An article in the *Fresno Bee* described her as having "her mouth open in hate like a dog's" and a letter to the *Milwaukee Journal* called her "a disgrace to the female sex."[22] Even segregationists like John Wells, editor of the pro-segregation newspaper the *Arkansas Recorder*, distanced himself from Bryan, who soon transferred to another high school.[23] Bryan had disregarded the unspoken conventions of middle-class Whiteness, and in doing so she was publicly classified as "White trash," a label that signified not only a low economic status but low *moral* status as well.[24] Journalists covering the story called Bryan, and others agitating against desegregation, "scrawny, rednecked men," "slattern housewives," and "harpies."[25] By 1959, Bryan's reputation was cemented by a *Times Literary Supplement* piece's assertion that the "ugly faces" of "rednecks, crackers, tar-heels, and other poor White trash" would be the ones remembered from Little Rock.[26]

Bryan's image joins an archive of photographs that suggested a moral dimension to the bodies of those considered "White trash." Some of the most powerful images come from a 1937 book, *You Have Seen Their Faces*,[27] written by Erskine Caldwell with photographs by Margaret Bourke-White. The book's text explores and criticizes the devastating effects of the sharecropping system in the South. The Bourke-White photographs, however, carry the book's position and are arguably what made it a bestseller.[28] Each photograph is accompanied by a caption bracketed by quotation marks. Although the captions are written by Erskine, they create the impression that the subjects were speaking directly to the viewer.

Slender, relatively healthy White farmers emerge as the most sympathetic figures in *You Have Seen Their Faces*. Actively working in the fields, or looking heroically up at the sun, they acknowledge their hardship but vow to press on. "We manage to get along," says a woman holding a plow handle and gazing into the distance contemplatively.[29]

Bodies that do not conform to this type, regardless of race, are treated less generously. In one closely cropped image, a White woman with weather-worn skin and dry, cropped hair squints into the harsh sun, grimacing at the viewer. She holds a filthy child who raises a dirty hand to touch his mother's chin. His gesture, in turn, draws attention to her cracked lips and uneven teeth. "Snuff is an almighty help when your teeth ache," the caption reads.[30] Together, the image and caption link the woman's economic poverty, moral turpitude, and her physical deterioration.

Declaring Hazel Bryan and the other White protestors at Little Rock Central High School to be "White trash" allowed the majority of the White American public of the 1950s to remove themselves from any real responsibility in the increasingly violent struggle for Black civil rights. Racism could be explained as a personal problem, perpetuated by morally flawed individuals. The more uncomfortable work of examining the racial biases of social structures could be downplayed or even ignored.

With historical distance, we might now recognize the shortcomings of such an attitude. But Johnny Jenkins' photograph of a noble, stoic Elizabeth Eckford and a screaming, animalistic Hazel Bryan continues to affect us. An apparently simple, documentary photograph can establish certain ideas of race and gender as unequivocal and natural. It teaches us that certain Black bodies deserve our concern, and certain White bodies deserve our derision. And it does so quietly but powerfully. As Christians, called to recognize and dignify God's image in all people, we must work to acknowledge how our own archives may have hampered or distorted our love for our neighbors.

So how might we look more faithfully?

First, we should work to seek out photographs that might disrupt or complicate our understanding of race as a historical construct. For example, in 1956, one year before desegregation in Little Rock, the Black photographer Gordon Parks went to Mobile, Alabama on assignment for *Life* magazine. Once there, he documented the realities of the Jim Crow South through the experience of Mr. and Mrs. Albert Thornton, Sr. and their multi-generational family. But on this assignment Parks used color film, a departure from the cool black-and-white photographs typical of documentary photography.

In one image published in *Life*'s photo essay, "Restraints: Open and Hidden," we face a glass storefront window plastered with advertisements for banana splits, ice cream sandwiches, and butter pecan ice cream.[31] On the left half of the photograph a Black man supports a young girl around the waist as she tiptoes to drink from a water fountain. Three other little girls, similarly dressed in pastel frocks, cluster around, presumably waiting their turn. In the right third of the photograph, two young Black women, wearing matching black sleeveless shirts, full printed skirts, and oversized white pearl earrings stand beside a second water fountain. This second fountain bisects the composition almost perfectly in half, a column of strangely empty negative space. Across the front of the fountain we read in big block letters, "WHITE ONLY."

We might find this image to be unexpectedly poignant and upsetting. Color images like this one create a greater sense of immediacy than the black-and-white images we associate with historically distant documents. This image, like the rest Parks took while on that assignment, focuses on the mundane experiences of the Thornton family in Mobile. They sit on the front porch, go to the theatre, chop wood, and play outside. The boycotts, protests, and brutal acts of retaliation occurring at the same time in Alabama remain unseen. But it is this prosaic moment at the water fountain that speaks powerfully of the constant, insistent ordering of life along racial lines. Parks presents the Thorntons not as victims of White violence but as active agents, choosing how they will negotiate a Jim Crow world.

Parks' images can help us follow Lawrence Levine's injunction in his essay, "The Historian and the Icon." Writing about documentary photography in the 1930s, Levine reminds us that we must not forget that photographic subjects have lives outside of the photographic frame.[32] Their stories exist prior to and after the moment of the photograph. For him, the tensions and ambiguities found in documentary photography prove their "essential soundness as guides for the historian."[33] Acknowledging the complexities and even the contradictions of photographic subjects' lives is a good disciplinary practice for historians, and it should especially serve as a model for those of us who are Christians. Parks' photographs offer what might be new material for our visual archives, and they encourage a more robust imagination of lives lived outside the iconic image.

Second, we should thoughtfully examine how contemporary news photographs, like their predecessors, continue to shape and reshape our expectations of socially appropriate expressions of race and gender. Consider, for example, the range of photographs published by both the mainstream media and social media users following the death and subsequent protests over the shooting of Michael Brown in Ferguson, Missouri. A single photograph of a Black teenager, couched within a much larger archive, could encourage you to view him as perpetrator or victim, as violent thug or earnest young man.[34]

After Brown's death, media outlets initially published a formal photograph of Brown wearing a green and red robe and mortar board for his high school graduation. As unrest grew in Ferguson, however, media organizations and news bloggers increasingly turned to another photograph of Brown, a more casual snapshot of him standing in front of a worn brick façade, wearing baggy bleached jeans and a red Nike muscle tee. His left hand hung by his side, but his right hand was raised in front of his chest, with his thumb and first two fingers extended. Shot from below, Brown seemed to loom over the viewer, staring down with an implacable expression.

This second photograph resonated with a long-established archive of photographs that depict Black men as monstrous. The red sports jersey, oversized pants, and hand gesture located the image alongside stereotypical photographs of gangbangers, and indeed several prominent, conservative bloggers explicitly used the image as proof that Michael Brown was a gang member.[35] The implication, then, was that there could be no real mourning, much less outrage, over Brown's death.

But not all photographs are so easily categorized. Some of the most iconic images to emerge from recent protests over systemic racism are powerful because of the inherent tension between the visual references they make. These tensions should arrest us, disrupting our inclination to see the photographs as simply records or icons.

In a photograph by Robert Cohen, taken on August 13, 2014, in Ferguson, Missouri, we are initially blinded by the white trail of smoke and light that bounces across the middle of the composition. We follow the pulsating glow up to the hand of Edward Crawford, a young man lunging forward, preparing to fling the ball of fire, a canister of tear gas shot by police, out of the composition. He wears a baseball tee printed with the stars and stripes, a quintessential representation of heroic patriotism. And yet, potential dissonance emerges between his attire and his long, swinging dreads, so often mistrusted by the dominant culture that claims the American flag as exclusively their own. He becomes a threat, not only to imagined bystanders but to American values at large. But can we also see how Crawford's torqued body resembles the one carved by Italian Baroque sculptor Gian Lorenzo Bernini? Can he also be a young man preparing to release a rock against a giant?

Or consider the photograph of Iesha Evans taken by Jonathan Bachman on July 9, 2016, in Baton Rouge, Louisiana, during a protest following the fatal police shooting of Alton Sterling. Bachman's view of the protest is eerily empty. Evans stands in profile just to the right of the center of the image, alone in the middle of a road. Her arms are pulled toward her body, and her hands loosely cradle her keys and her phone. She wears a patterned summer dress that flutters around her perfectly still and straight body. Two bulky figures, clad in black armor and wearing black helmets with large, clear visors, rush toward Evans from the left of the composition.

Contrasting with Evans' poise, the police officers are caught mid-movement, scrambling to a halt. Again, the image raises a host of references. One commentator observes that the image reminded him of a scene from Star Wars, a stand-off between a Jedi warrior and faceless Storm Troopers.[36] But Evans is also the stoic, patient body so familiar from Civil Rights photography, the passive figure in need of help. She is in many ways another Elizabeth Eckford, embodying a particular notion of what acceptable femininity and Blackness might look like in opposition to an anonymous and thus easily vilified show of force.

It does not take a vast knowledge of art history and visual culture to begin looking more faithfully. When looking at historical or contemporary news photographs, we should simply but self-consciously ask ourselves, "What is my initial response to the people in the image?" With whom do we choose to align ourselves? Who are we critical of?

Rather than merely accepting those responses as natural, we can question why we might feel this way. Perhaps we can answer that question with a specific history or set of images. Perhaps we cannot. But the act of acknowledging that a single photograph is part of a larger, complex web of meaning can stymie the seductive notion that photographs tell us all we need to know. Bringing others into conversation about such images can help broaden our archives and encourage us to look carefully at images we might be prone to ignoring. Such conversations also offer a more concrete way of tackling issues that can otherwise feel elusive and abstract.

It takes work to excavate these images, to uncover the histories that direct the seemingly natural ways that we categorize the figures within these photographs. And yet, with so much at stake, can we do otherwise? These photographs, and our responses to them, are indelibly shaped by the thousands of other images competing to define not only the past but how we should relate to it. As theorist Coco Fusco observes, "We... create and use photography to see ourselves; by looking at pictures we imagine that we can know who we are and who we were."[37] But it is a great injustice when Elizabeth Eckford's or Hazel Bryan's or Edward Crawford's or Iesha Evans' identities as image bearers of God are subsumed into political iconicity or are used to further uncritical attitudes toward dominant notions of race, gender, and class. If we can acknowledge both the limits and the power of photographs and our relationship to them, we might find that it is our finitude that makes us better able to see and to love our neighbors.

---

1. David Margolick, *Elizabeth and Hazel: Two Women of Little Rock* (New Haven: Yale University Press, 2011), 60.
2. Margolick, *Elizabeth and Hazel*, 147–148.
3. Margolick, *Elizabeth and Hazel*, 71.

4. Martin Berger, *Seeing Through Race: A Reinterpretation of Civil Rights Photography* (Berkeley: University of California Press, 2011), 107.

5. Brown v. US

6. See Walter Benjamin, "The Work of Art in the Age of Mechanical Reproduction," *Art in Modern Culture: An Anthology of Critical Texts*, eds. Francis Frascina and Jonathan Harris (New York: HarperCollins, 1993).

7. See Pierre Bourdieu and John B. Thompson, *Language and Symbolic Power* (Cambridge, Mass.: Harvard University Press, 1991).

8. Martin Berger, *Freedom Now! Forgotten Photographs of the Civil Rights Struggle* (Berkeley: University of California Press, 2014), 21.

9. For more on the story of the women in this photograph, see David Margolick, *Elizabeth and Hazel: Two Women of Little Rock*.

10. Berger, *Freedom Now!*, 21.

11. Robert Hariman and John Lucaites, *No Caption Needed: Iconic Photographs, Public Culture, and Liberal Democracy* (Chicago: University of Chicago Press, 2011), 88.

12. Berger, *Freedom Now!*, 21.

13. For a discussion of intertextuality in text and image see Julia Kristeva, *Desire in Language: A Semiotic Approach to Literature and Art* (New York: Columbia University Press, 1980).

14. Allan Sekula, "The Body and the Archive," *The MIT Press* 39 (1986): 10.

15. Coco Fusco, "Racial Times, Racial Marks, Racial Metaphors," *Only Skin Deep: Changing Visions of the American Self*, eds. Coco Fusco and Brian Wallis (New York: Harry N. Abrams, 2003), 60.

16. See Shawn Smith, *American Archives: Gender, Race, and Class in Visual Culture* (Princeton: Princeton University Press, 1999).

17. Brian Wallis, "Black Bodies, White Science: Louis Agassiz's Slave Daguerreotypes," *Only Skin Deep: Changing Visions of the American Self*, eds. Coco Fusco and Brian Wallis (New York: Harry N. Abrams, 2003), 175.

18. Margolick, *Elizabeth and Hazel*, 72.

19. It's important to note that Eckford's choice of wardrobe was a very purposeful one. Photography was playing an important role in the emerging Civil Rights movement, and confrontations like this one were, at least to some extent, intended to be captured. King, Jr. See Berger, *Seeing Through Race*.

20. Berger, *Seeing Through Race*, 29.

21. Berger, *Seeing Through Race*, 143.

22. Margolick, *Elizabeth and Hazel*, 87.

23. Margolick, *Elizabeth and Hazel*, 87.

24. For more on the history and moral implications of the term "White trash," see Nancy Isenberg, *White Trash: The 400 Year Untold History of Class in America* (New York: Viking, 2016).

25. Isenberg, *White Trash*, 251.

26. Isenberg, *White Trash*, 252.

27. Erskine Caldwell and Margaret Bourke-White, You Have Seen Their Faces (Atlanta: Brown Thrasher Books, 1995 [1937]).

28. Alan Trachtenberg, "Foreword," *You Have Seen Their Faces* (Atlanta: Brown Thrasher Books, 1995), v.

29. Caldwell and Bourke-White, *Faces*, 16.

30. Caldwell and Bourke-White, *Faces*, 49.

31. See Robert Wallace and Gordon Parks, "Restraints: Open and Hidden," *LIFE*, September 24, 1956, 99, https://books.google.com/books?id=70cEAAAAMBAJ.

32. Lawrence Levine, "The Historian and the Icon: Photography and the History of the American People in the 1930s and 1940s," *Documenting America: 1935–1943*, ed. Carl Fleischhauer (Berkeley and Los Angeles: University of California Press, 1988), 20.

33. Fleischhauer, *Documenting America*, 22.

34. For more, see Tanzina Vega, "Shooting Spurs Hashtag Effort on Stereotypes," *New York Times*, August 12, 2014, https://www.nytimes.com/2014/08/13/us/if-they-gunned-me-down-protest-on-twitter.html?_r=0.

35. See, for example, Jim Hoft, "BREAKING: Ferguson's Michael Brown PICTURED Flashing GANG SIGNS," *The Gateway Pundit*, August 14, 2014, http://www.thegatewaypundit.com/2014/08/breaking-michael-brown-was-a-local-gangster-seen-flashing-gang-signs/, and The Conservative Treehouse, "Travon 2.0 Redux – Comparing Mike Brown and Trayvon Martin Similarities...," *The Last Refuge*, August 15, 2014, https://theconservativetreehouse.com/2014/08/15/trayvon-2-0-redux-comparing-mike-brown-and-trayvon-martin-similarities/.

36. Jonathan Jones, "The Baton Rouge Protestor: 'A Botticelli nymph attacked by Star Wars Baddies,'" July 12, 2016, https://www.theguardian.com/artanddesign/2016/jul/12/baton-rouge-protester-botticelli-nymph-attacked-by-star-wars-baddies-iesha-evans.

37. Fusco, "Racial Times, Racial Marks, Racial Metaphors," 13.

DISPELLING THE MODEL MINORITY MYTH
EMBRACING FRIENDSHIP WITH THE AFRICAN AMERICAN COMMUNITY

MOSES Y. LEE

Moses Y. Lee is the pastor of Rosebrook Presbyterian Church in North Bethesda, Maryland. He earned degrees from the University of Maryland (BS) and West-minster Theological Seminary (MDiv, ThM). He writes for The Gospel Coalition *and the* SOLA Network. *He and his wife, Rachel, have the joy of raising their son, a fifth-generation Presbyterian.*

———

[An earlier version of this essay was published as "Asian Americans, MLK, and the Model Minority Myth," in the *The Witness*.]

———

On October 4th, 2016, a baseball fan attacked Baltimore Orioles left fielder, Hyun Soo Kim, during a game by throwing a can full of beer that barely missed his head while shouting racial slurs at him saying, "Go back to your country, Kim!" Immediately, Adam Jones, the Baltimore Orioles center fielder, came to his defense by confronting the racist fan while facing anti-Black racial slurs himself. Jones had confronted racist fans before when someone threw a banana at him in the middle of a game.[1] But the fact that he defended his South Korean teammate at the risk of being attacked with racial slurs himself not only demonstrated tremendous courage, it also represents the way

African American communities have stood up for Asians and Asian Americans throughout our shared history.

A Very Brief History of Asian America

Though Asian immigration to this country can be traced all the way back to 1815, the government tightly controlled the flow of Asian immigration, which eventually resulted in the exclusionary laws of the late-nineteenth and early-twentieth centuries. These laws severely limited the immigration of Asians and other non-White ethnic groups and prohibited Asian immigrants and their American-born descendants from property and business ownership. In 1922, the Supreme Court went further and classified Asians alongside African Americans as people of color, which designated them as victims of segregation. These discriminatory actions reached its pinnacle when President Franklin D. Roosevelt ordered the internment of over 100,000 people of Japanese ancestry throughout the country. The government continued to view Asian immigrants as unfit for US Citizenship until post-WWII.

By the 1960s, countless riots and lynchings all across the country destroyed not only African American lives but the lives of Asian Americans as well. To add insult to injury, a White sociologist named William Petersen conjectured the model minority myth[2] during the civil rights movement to divide and conquer ethnic minorities and perpetuate White supremacy. But change came for Asian Americans practically overnight. In the course of several years, the government abolished immigration quotas and outlawed the segregation of Asian Americans, loosening the grip of systemic racism toward Asian Americans. But this begs the question, who or what can be attributed with the progress Asian Americans enjoy today?

The Primacy of African American Activism

From my experience, Asian Americans know little about Asian American participation in the civil rights movement. Asian American civil rights groups tended to glean from or have many parallels to the Black Power Movement. These groups also held sympathies to various forms of socialism with many prominent Asian American leaders of the movement, even studying under Mao Zedong in China and Kim Il Sung in North Korea.[3] But more importantly, the Asian American community lacked a voice that merged a robust Augustinian anthropology of body *and* soul with nonviolent civil disobedience. Indeed, what Asian Americans were really missing in the 1960s was a distinct Asian American *Christian* voice. For such a model, Asian American believers must look to none other than Martin Luther King, Jr (MLK). Too often though, Asian Americans view MLK as someone who only fought for African American rights and not as someone who is a part of our legacy too.

Asian Americans are greatly indebted to the African American community for leading the way, for the sacrifices they have made, and for the progress they have accomplished for *all* people of color. In other words, the benefits all minorities enjoy today are, by and large, the fruit of African American civil rights activism. They selflessly protested not just for their own rights, but for the rights of people of color all around the world. They protested the killing of innocent Vietnamese civilians during the Vietnam War and led the charge for immigration reform that opened the door for millions of Asians to immigrate to the US. This directly correlates with the exponential growth of Korean Presbyterian immigrants throughout the 1970s and 1980s. In short, Korean Language Presbyteries in the PCA would not exist, nor would most of us even be here to participate in this conversation about racial reconciliation, were it not for the African American community and their contributions to Asian American rights during the civil rights movement.

Even though Asian Americans continue to express little to no gratitude, African Americans continue to stand up for Asians and Asian Americans on issues of whitewashing and cultural appropriation all the while risking persecution from White supremacists and even racist Asians and Asian Americans.

We apologize. You deserve better. We should do better and God has given us that chance in the PCA with Overture 43[4] (repenting of sins of omission regarding racial injustices). So how can Asian American believers begin to rightfully honor the African American community, especially within the PCA? What steps can we take to join them in their continual struggle for justice and equality, not just for African Americans but for all people in the US?

During my teens and even into my college years, I bought into the model minority myth and believed hard work can take you anywhere you want in this country, regardless of your race or ethnicity. I used to believe that others who did not benefit from the system simply lacked the willpower or ambition. I used to believe that President Obama was proof of this.

The model minority myth falsely highlights Asian Americans as an ideal minority, purposely contrasted against African Americans and Latino Americans, in order to suppress potential political activism through stereotyping. But the model minority myth is just that, a myth. When we dig deeper into the origins of the myth narrative, it becomes clear that the model minority myth seeks to tame Asian Americans and put us in our place. It creates an artificial us-vs-them mentality that divides minorities and weakens our unified ability to influence society. It actually reinforces "the bamboo ceiling" that prohibits Asian Americans from becoming central arbiters of power in American society.[5] As reported in the *Pacific Standard*, the model minority myth perpetuates the discriminatory belief that Asian Americans are only useful as long as our influence on the community is minimal, but the moment our achievements set the standard for the majority culture to follow, we are treated with disdain.[6]

This deep-rooted stereotyping and manipulation should upset Asian Americans, but some have found it safer not to speak out or have concerns about being divisive. Still others simply cannot observe this myth playing out in their own lives. Some even go as far as to say we should not be angry for suffering these particular injustices. Surely, the Scriptures have a thing or two to say about the legitimacy of *righteous* indignation.

The truth is, many of us have been cajoled into the illusion that we have joined the majority culture at the adult table when in fact we have merely been appointed the head of the children's table to keep the other minorities in check. We are flaunted as a model minority for other minorities to follow while still being discriminated against when a seat at the adult table becomes available. How will we respond? Will we continue to avoid the same intensity of discrimination African Americans and other minorities face by continuing to play the game? Or will we refuse to play the game and choose the way of the cross and suffer with other minorities until all Americans experience true equality and justice?

Start the Conversation with the Older Generations

It could seem presumptuous to advocate for racial reconciliation while not acknowledging a history of racism between African Americans and Asian Americans. Many Korean Americans can still recall the Los Angeles riots of 1992 and the hardship members of the Korean Southwestern Presbytery endured because of the looting by local African American residents. We acknowledge their tremendous pain and loss and want to honor their resilience. But could it be possible that both parties misdirected their anger and disappointment?

In order to respectfully engage the older generation of Asian Americans, we must first establish a common ground between our two peoples. Along with other minorities, Asian Americans and African Americans belong to a social construct that establishes an uneven playing field for all people of color. And while we share a mutual frustration with the system, we tend to blame the wrong source. Indeed, the fault lies not with African Americans, Asian Americans, or other minorities, but with the majority culture's social construct that pits us against one another. Hence, we all have much to gain if we work together instead of just looking out for ourselves as the model minority myth wants us to.

For members of Korean Language Presbyteries, we have been given an opportunity to start this conversation with the older members of our presbyteries. These efforts can even apply to the older members of our respective congregations. Not only will our engagement alleviate some of the tension between Asian Americans and African Americans, it may even prove to be a time of healing and reinvigorate Asian Americans to get more involved in their communities. But if communicating these ideas can be challenging due to various language and cultural barriers, fortunately, crowdsourcing and social media have provided us with resources for the older generation to understand.[7]

Give Honor to Whom Honor Is Due

The time to recognize sacrifices the African American community has made for Asian Americans is long overdue. Some Asian Americans have tried, but this remains far from our cultural norm. Ironically, many Korean American churches and families still celebrate national holidays from our mother country whose history and language we barely know, and yet we fail to properly honor individuals like MLK whose impact on our lives is much more tangible in our new home country. As we instruct our immigrant congregations how to engage American culture, we must remind them that today's generation of Asian Americans is able to thrive in this country not because of willpower or ambition, but because of the path paved by the blood and tears of African American believers.

Rejoice with Those Who Rejoice, Weep with Those Who Weep

As the African American community leads the charge for equality for all Americans, they unfortunately continue to bear the brunt of the racist attacks in our country. Hence, every step of progress made by African American activists benefits all Americans, while every instance of abuse toward the African American community endangers all Americans. Racism makes no exceptions and neither should our celebration of headway made by others. Therefore, as we disciple the members of our congregations to be more faithful in the workplace and in our communities, we must encourage them to embrace our African American coworkers and neighbors in their pain and celebrate with them in their victories.

---

1. Sarah Harvard, "Baltimore Orioles Adam Jones and Hyun Soo Kim Attacked with Racial Slurs and a Can of Beer," *Mic*, October 05, 2016, https://mic.com/articles/155947/baltimore-orioles-adam-jones-and-hyun-soo-kim-attacked-with-racial-slurs-and-a-can-of-beer#.K79W7R59O.
2. "The term 'model minority' has often been used to refer to a minority group perceived as particularly successful, especially in a manner that contrasts with other minority groups...In particular, the model minority designation is often applied to Asian Americans, who, as a group, are often praised for apparent success across academic, economic, and cultural domains—successes typically offered in contrast to the perceived achievements of other racial groups." See "The Model Minority Myth." *The Practice* 5, no. 1 (2018). https://thepractice.law.harvard.edu/article/the-model-minority-myth/.
3. Erika Lee, *The Making of Asian America: A History* (New York: Simon & Schuster, 2016), 303–04.
4. https://byfaithonline.com/wp-content/uploads/2016/06/Overture-43-clean.pdf
5. Jane Hyun, *Breaking the Bamboo Ceiling: Career Strategies for Asians: The Essential Guide to Getting In, Moving Up, and Reaching the Top* (New York: Collins, 2005).

6. Anjali Enjeti, "Ghosts of White People Past: Witnessing White Flight From an Asian Ethnoburb," *Pacific Standard*, August 25, 2016, https://psmag.com/news/ghosts-of-white-people-past-witnessing-white-flight-from-an-asian-ethnoburb.

7. "Letters for Black Lives," *Letters for Black Lives*, October 3, 2016, http://www.lettersforblacklives.com/.

ECONOMIC RECONCILIATION AND RACIALIZED ECONOMIC DISPARITY

EREKE BRUCE & DANIEL MURPHREE

Ereke Bruce spent seventeen years in the PCA serving as a Ruling Elder, pastoral intern, and a candidate for Gospel ministry in the Northern California Presbytery. He has also served as a campus minister with Campus Crusade for Christ (now Cru) at the University of Hawaii at Manoa. He recently left the PCA in order to attend a multiethnic church due to frustrations and a desire for his children to be affirmed in their God-given ethnic identities.

Daniel Murphree is an Associate Pastor at New City Fellowship, Saint Louis. He and his family serve on the mission field in Southeast Asia. In addition to an MDiv, he has a BA and MA in International Studies in Southeast Asia and has presented papers on Buddhism, Race, and Refugees at the University of British Columbia, Cornell University, and the University of Washington. He is a PhD candidate at the Oxford Center for Mission Studies.

―――――

"I don't understand, Moshé. Why don't they listen to me?"

"What do you mean Daniel? You're White, and they're Black. Of course you're going to have to work for it."

Moshé's response hinted at something I had already expected.

It was both clear and straightforward. I [Daniel] joined the AmeriCorps organization because of their vision for helping an impossible situation of blight and underprivileged African Americans. At the time, I was compelled by a strong sense of White guilt, savior complex, and some nascent forms of economic justice.

While an undergrad, I began the process of "waking up." In one seminar class, I was assigned to work with an African American woman to do a collaborative presentation on a classical, liberal scholar.[1] While preparing for the class, she brought up the subject of prejudice and White privilege. I balked.

I was the son of a career military non-commissioned officer. I had been to daycare with a very mixed group. I was first called a "wigger" in the fourth grade.

Surely, we were beyond racism? Surely, I was not a beneficiary of it.

She began telling me of redlining laws, inheritance laws, effects of the GI bill for people of color, why the non-commissioned branch of the armed forces had a disproportionate number of minorities while the officers remained mostly White.

It was hard to deny.

My undergrad colleague had begun prying my White eyes open to aspects of systemic racism, something I had benefited from. So I did the most radical thing I could think of:[2] I joined the AmeriCorps and lived on-site as a resident guard of the property. The house was built in 1804, during the height of slavery. It was less than two miles from historic trading platforms for Whites (and freedmen) to sell their slaves. Pigeons infested the attic, the plumbing was dismal, and both mice and gunshots kept me up at night. However, these were the exact conditions in which many, if not all, of our students were accustomed to living.

––––––

"Come on, Moshé. You know I hear the same gunshots they do. I've been robbed and broken into. Haven't I earned enough street credit yet?"

"Bro, you're just a tourist. They know you can leave anytime. For us, this is home. There is no out."

––––––

John Perkins' model of Christian community development (CCD) seeks to address the situation that Moshé had put his finger on. Not only are White people disproportionately advantaged compared to African Americans as a result of racism, but they often engage in acts of reconciliation from positions of unexamined privilege. While well-meaning, the vast majority of White Christians who engage in urban ministry and other acts of reconciliation do so with little empathy for the deep-rooted economic conditions that create and perpetuate systemic racialized poverty.[3] Perkins summarizes, "It is clear in Scripture that God works constantly to transform people who then reflect the fruit of the Spirit... But if you don't live in the urban community and allow it to become a part of you, you might see what needs fixing but you won't understand the reasons these problems have developed."[4] Perkins therefore acknowledges that White Christians might have many insights about restoring impoverished communities.

However, Perkins also emphasizes that those who have embraced the dominant culture's narrative of success enter into racialized narratives of "how to become successful." While they have intentions of racial reconciliation, they do so from an observer's standpoint. They're able to engage as little as desired with the perennial ability to escape to the safe confines of their own economically restrictive communities. On the other hand, African Americans who are victims of racialized economic disparity cannot simply "get out," regardless of how hard they work, how intact their families are, or how professionally (a term that often describes having straight hair, fair skin, and other aspects of White culture) they present themselves.

Perkins gives too much credit to dominant culture perspectives. He's too kind. White Christians in the position to offer advice based on their observations, having benefited from racialized economic disparity, have little to no understanding of the African American experience.

In short, the African American experience, just like the White experience, provides the worldview-shaping categories that come to define the Black- or White-normative experience. Such advice ignores the uniqueness of White peoples' access to the very system that produced their economic success. This ultimately makes their advice unhelpful and can undermine reconciliation.[5]

Regardless of these pitfalls, Perkins' model does supply the Christian with the means of pursuing reconciliation: relocation and redistribution. This chapter seeks to introduce these components of reconciliation into the vernacular of Christian racial reconcilers.

What does relocation and redistribution have to do with reconciliation? It situates the American Church in historical context. It actualizes the Gospel through repentance and truth-telling. Specifically, it exposes the accumulation of wealth by White Christians and their churches as a result of racialized historical realities.

This seems hard to hear, and it is. Truth-telling is a critical component of peace (shalom) negotiations between grieved parties and has been used to great effect internationally between conflicting groups.

Though still a work in progress, South Africa's Promotion of National Unity and Reconciliation Act 34 of 1995, is an apt example of how integral truth-telling is to the work of societal reconciliation and national healing. As the shameful blight of apartheid came to an end, the government of South Africa began the difficult work of rebuilding a nation that had been torn to pieces by what many have said was the most precise system of racial segregation and oppression in the modern world. Indispensable to this work was the Truth and Reconciliation Commission, which was chartered to establish "as complete a picture as possible of the causes, nature, and extent of the gross violations which were committed during the period."[6]

This kind of hard, painful truth-telling on a national scale has never been done in the United States or its churches. We've not provided an accurate and complete record of both victims and beneficiaries of the Middle Passage, chattel style enslavement of African Americans, Jim Crow Laws, Housing Discrimination, etc. This leaves the average American, White and Black, ignorant of the oral and written histories that serve to explain our inevitable arrival at the segregated nation and church we are today.

Unless there is integrity in the telling of US histories around racially reinforced economic subjugation and the church's intentional or unintentional profiting from that subjugation, there can never exist honest, shalom-like reconciliation.[7] How is it that a White, Presbyterian Church in America (PCA) in rural Virginia is able to build a brick, modern sanctuary costing several hundred thousand dollars, while the congregation of African Americans who have been worshiping together less than a half-mile away, for a longer period of time, with more congregants, can barely afford their wooden, single-room church?

From whence did that economic disparity come?

For Southern and Northern churches alike, given such a large percentage of White wealth is inherited, what social conditions derived that accumulation of wealth? Moreover, for those engaged in racial reconciliation, how do we justify ongoing lifestyles and salaries to those with whom we wish to be reconciled?[8]

Truth-telling requires us to ask these questions. For White Christians, absent any national or societal effort to tell the truth about the past, redistribution and relocation are the only ways to adequately acknowledge the history of White people's advantage over African Americans and White people's categorical gain at the racialized expense of Blacks.[9] This best reflects the repentance exemplified in Matthew 5:23–24: *"So if you are offering your gift at the altar and there remember that your brother has something against you, leave your gift there before the altar and go. First be reconciled to your brother, and then come and offer your gift."*

Without the acknowledgement of specific sins, verbal repentance around those sins remains steeped in Gnosticism. We might be willing to write blogs, books, or sermons about reconciliation, but without the substantive actions of relocation and redistribution derived from truth-telling, it is little more than lip-service in an effort to alleviate guilt.

Relocation and redistribution require us to do something with our godly sorrow in a way that will cost something for the systemically advantaged (White people) and provide restoration to the systematically disadvantaged (people of color). This reparation is much more consistent with the biblical paradigm of economic provision envisioned for the body of Christ. Without relocation and redistribution, our respective roles in living out a reconciled, repentant faith will continue unexamined: our salaries, excessive; our living standards, indulgent; our membership, elitist; our church and private schools, segregated; and our reconciliation, gnostic.

What we hope to achieve in this short chapter is to set the framework for why redistribution and relocation are vital for understanding our denomination's (or similar denominations') particular idiosyncrasies. We must become aware of ways in which we conform to a racialized cultural narrative, deeply rooted in a cultural elitism that is impossible to achieve without the economic suppression of African Americans.[10]

We then hope to provide modalities of a new ecclesiastical model that seek to address racialized economic disparities and suggest ideas for moving forward. By the end of this chapter, we hope White Christians will begin introducing economic and spatial categories in their conversations on racial reconciliation. For the most part, we assume the reader is already convinced of the biblical mandate to pursue racial reconciliation.

Not Out of the Blue: Economic Justice in Law, Gospel, and Epistle

Perkins bases his call to redistribution and relocation in Scripture, citing both distributive justice laws (see Lev. 25) and prophetic indictments on the wealthy (see Isa. 58) for the method in which they accumulated and maintained their wealth in the Old Testament (OT).[11] Those familiar with the Torah's federal framework might anticipate a potent application: these indictments rang true not just for the individuals who were in the original audience, but also for their posterity and their posterity's participation in that unjust accumulation of wealth. The text then remained codified for future generations as a text read in the synagogue. This suggests that the OT had generational accountability in mind even with regard to specific injustices. This is a critical hermeneutic for conversations about redistribution and relocation.

In the OT, justice (*mishpat, dikiosunē* [LXX]), or the establishment of "right-relationship" is seen in the context of shalom. Perkins summarizes, "Justice is being good stewards of God's earth and resources."[12] OT scholar Christopher Wright also argues that shalom is not the absence of struggle or conflict, but rather the presence of an unfolding, active justice.[13] When poverty exists, especially as a result of racialization, the application of justice requires an active consideration of the ways our pursuit of wealth impacts others. Wright considers economic injustice this way: "Finally, the end product of the economic process is also manipulated unjustly. Claims of ownership are privatized and regarded as absolute, unfettered by any sense of transcendent responsibility for others."[14]

Justice, then, requires us to become aware of the poor, the causes of economic disparity in the body of Christ, and then engage in acts of repentance to remedy ways wealthy Christians have become wealthy by generational and systemic misuse of God's people and resources.[15]

This is not a new reading of the Bible. Economic restoration/redistribution among believers has always accompanied the Gospel message. This theme is prominent in the Gospel of Luke. Luke's recording of the Beatitudes and the Lord's Prayer both show an unambiguous orientation of Jesus' message of redress for the poor, especially those impoverished as a result of institutionalized injustice. Luke 6:20 states plainly, *"Blessed are you who are poor* [hoi ptochoi], *for yours is the kingdom of God."* Luke 11:2–4 records Jesus' prayer succinctly, *"Father, hallowed be your name. Your kingdom come.* [How?] *Give us each day our daily bread, and forgive us our sins* [hamartias], *for we ourselves forgive* [aphiomen] *everyone who is indebted* [opheilonti] *to us. And lead us not into temptation."*[16] Through the use of Greek words which are unambiguously associated with economic conditions, both the Beatitudes and the Lord's Prayer direct the reader toward economies of scale by focusing on a restoration meant to be realized on a communal, church-wide level.

This theme is exemplified on an individual level with Zacchaeus. When presented with the Jesus who emptied himself of all entitlements and glory, he makes his first act of worship an act of reparation. Zacchaeus makes an unqualified redistribution of the economic gains he had achieved. He had the opportunity to claim he was merely doing the commonly ascribed practice at the time. He could have justified his wealth as part of a well-established Roman tax system, or as the fault of the individuals for not taking advantage of the tax code. Yet, when the Lord of the universe breathed life into Zacchaeus' bones, his first act of obedience to the King was to redistribute half of his possessions to the poor and a four-fold payment of reparations. This response does not mention whether Zacchaeus' economic prosperity was justified. Luke had every opportunity to record whether or not Jesus thought this act was extraneous and excessive to Gospel-repentance. He did not.

The reader might even expect Jesus to redirect the conversation to what his response should have been. Something like: "Zacchaeus, what matters is that you have repented in your heart." Jesus did not do that. Instead, Luke shows Jesus' response to Zacchaeus' actions as an immediate response: *"Today salvation has come to this house"* (see Luke 19:1–9).

In the Book of Acts, the motif continues. Luke argues in order to show Theophilus that the body of disciples were obeying the apostles' teaching. He writes, *"all who believed were together and had all things in common. And they were selling their possessions and belongings and distributing the proceeds to all, as any had need"* (Acts 2:44–45).

Acts encourages readers to aspire to the ideal of Christian community. Luke's point is that Jesus' divine reconciliation to humanity always requires racial[17] and economic[18] reconciliation among his people. As Christ's church lived out the themes of Christ's *kenosis*, reconciliation to God required a downward mobility of the wealthy in resources (ethnically or economically privileged) and an upward exaltation of the marginalized (ethnically or economically underprivileged).

The Apostle Paul also assumes this orientation of the Gospel toward the poor. In his admonition to the church at Corinth, he critiques the elitism and economic segregation visible in the sacraments. The Lord's Supper was a celebratory meal where the wealthy brought out of their abundance, and employees were able to sit across from the table from their employers as equals.[19]

If ever there was a church body where it would be permissible for communities to segregate into a homogeneous church growth model, the Corinthian church would have been it. There were sizable groups of wealthy, working-class, Jewish, and Gentile members.

Paul's admonition could have been to gather into similar demographic groups so they could more acutely address the common problems relevant to each group. However, this was not only imprudent, it was anathema to the Gospel.

In one fell swoop, Paul focuses the conversation in 1 Corinthians 12 on the nature of the body of Christ. Shifting the conversation from admonishing the church around the use of gifts, he writes, *"For in one Spirit we were all baptized into one body—Jews or Greeks* [ethnic distinctions], *slaves or free* [economic distinctions]*—and all were made to drink of one Spirit"* (1 Cor. 12:13). To apply Paul's analogy *mutatis mutandis*, a largely White, upper-middle class church (or denomination) is about as healthy a church as a body with a defective, large eye. Similarly, a large African American church lacks the health of a body with a nose, even though the cause for this unhealthiness has more to do with the predominantly White church intentionally excluding African Americans (see 1 Cor. 12:17). This is a theme picked up elsewhere, such as in Paul's discussion of the Lord's Supper (1 Cor. 10–11), the reallocation of resources from Corinth to Jerusalem (2 Cor. 8–9), and rebuking ethnic exclusivity in Antioch (Gal. 2).

How then does redistribution relate to racial reconciliation? The Bible affirms what most people who aren't in the dominant culture have always known: one does not *happen* to be poor in the same way that one does not *happen* to be rich.

Wealth is influenced by the social network one is forced into by birth. Modalities of belonging, borrowing, market access, debt forgiveness, and inheritance, are various means of circumscribing wealth accumulation. The creation of false narratives of meritocracy prevents White Christians from critically examining our own cultures of entitlement.

In the American context, access to the market, home loans, inherited wealth, and credit (among other factors) have historically been made available to White men. They have excluded women and people of color. Luke and Paul would be ashamed. Indeed, our economic, housing, and educational systems are built upon institutionalized, systemic, and historical racial exploitation and exclusion.[20] These historical realities must be dealt with in order to move forward in reconciled relationship.

In light of this biblical theology, if we take Perkins' relocation and redistribution to be intrinsic to reconciliation, the Bible then compels us to examine the following questions: 1) Does racialized economic disparity exist in the body of Christ? 2) Do I or my people perpetuate economic systems that are racially exclusive (intentionally or not); or, how did it get this way? 3) How might I repent in a way that moves toward biblical shalom in various areas of racialized disparity?

Becoming Aware of Racialized Economic Disparity: Racialized Disparity Exists

We must change our narratives. African Americans are poorer than White people. Yet this call to redistribution and relocation is not a racialization of poverty. Such efforts to racialize poverty have already been mobilized by White people to the detriment of African Americans.

One well-known example is the "welfare queen" envisioned as a Black woman by the Reagan administration in the 1980s. This became a repeated media trope. One case of welfare fraud by a woman in Chicago came to be applied to all African American women receiving welfare. This served as the Republican rally cry for welfare reform, propagating a stereotype of the African American women as mostly lazy, while the data revealed (and continues to reveal) a different reality.[21] The welfare trope has continually been exaggerated for African American communities in efforts to racialize poverty.[22]

In contrast to the exaggeration of African American poverty by the media, the disparity in income, opportunity, and living standards between African Americans and White people is real, but it is not due to laziness. A 2016 census report revealed that, while more White people are impoverished in terms of gross income, African Americans are twice as likely to be impoverished than White people.[23] On the aggregate, an African American male typically earns seventy-one cents for every dollar a White male earns.[24] The education gap, that great argument for meritocracy, between African Americans and White people is equally concerning. Of the African Americans who do attend a four-year university, they graduate $7,400 more in debt than their White counterparts.[25]

In 2014, for African Americans with college degrees, the rate of unemployment was 12.4 percent, compared to 5.6 percent for all college graduates between 22 and 27 years of age.[26] In 2016, the unemployment rate for African Americans was 8.9 percent, compared to 4.9 percent for Whites. That's nearly twice as high.[27]

This reveals something about the social networks through which most businesses make their hires. Overall earnings of African Americans in 2016 were much lower than that of White Americans, with median wealth for White Americans at $171,000 compared to a median wealth of $17,600 for African Americans.

Re-read that sentence.

Of inherited wealth, based on a 2015 report by the Federal Reserve, the average White family inherits $236,495 compared to only $82,940 for Black families.[28] Taking assets into account, a Black family's net worth is less than 15 percent of a White family's net worth.[29]

Racialized economic disparity exists.

These societal trends manifest themselves in our local churches, suggesting the American church is a model of cultural norms, not a reformer of them. Our respective churches serve as cross sections of these societal dynamics. For example, the average salary of a pastor in the Presbyterian Church in America (PCA) is roughly $100,000, according to a 2016 voluntary survey by the PCA's Administrative Committee. One pastor in the denomination makes nearly $1,000,000 per year. This means our ministers serving on domestic and foreign fields, on average, earn more than $40,000 more than the median US income and more than $60,000 more than the median African American income.[30]

This data does not even compare the average salary of a missionary serving in their own context. So unless racial reconciliation is limited only to those minorities who are higher up the socio-economic ladder, White Christians will inevitably encounter these social disparities. It is therefore incumbent on the socially advantaged to both acknowledge and address these disparities, birthed from inequality, if they desire reconciliation.

Becoming Aware of Racialized Poverty: Understanding Its Causes and Ways White People Contribute

It has often been said you cannot know where you're going until you know where you've been. This axiom speaks to truth-telling, and it is essential to the work of racial reconciliation. Truth-telling is indispensable when it comes to racialized economic disparities because so much of our history is shrouded in revisionist narratives of the past. A 2016 McGraw-Hill history book, for example, revises the truth and refers to the men and women brought to the US under chattel slavery as immigrants.[31] The faces, families, and stories of this nation's oppression against Black citizens are as little known to and unremembered by most of us as the nearly 4,000 Black Americans who were brutally, inhumanely, and publicly lynched throughout this country[32]

Similarly, historical facts that detail the economic exploitation of African Americans have been revised which contributes to ongoing racialized economic disparity. One of the many fallacies of American exceptionalism is the idea that poor African Americans are poor due to their own laziness or some other factor.

If one rejects the idea of ongoing, systemic racism, laziness is the only explanation for poverty. This is problematic for a number of reasons. Not only is it historically ungrounded, it also refuses to acknowledge the systemic privilege of being born with or assimilating into Whiteness. In an attempt to dispel these myths, what follows is a condensed outline of some key historical facts regarding the African American experience, which have contributed to sustained economic disparity: theft of labor, the exploitation of the fruits of that labor, and the systematic exclusion of African Americans from the means of generating wealth, among others.

We must fully appreciate our shared racial history in the United

States. If we truth-tell about economic reconciliation, then we must talk about how some in this country were able to accumulate the resources needed to acquire and transfer wealth, while others could not. The Church must participate in this conversation because it has been present and participated throughout all the history to which we refer. Christians participated in the market, made investments, bought property, attended universities and seminaries, and inherited wealth within a society and an economy that was arranged to devalue the lives, labor, and worth of African American human beings, while placing premium value and providing benefits to those who could be classified as White. The racialized economic disparities documented here are the direct outcomes of these historic arrangements.

Hence, predominantly White churches and denominations have historically accumulated wealth, resources, status, prestige, and influence in this country, while the majority of Black churches and denominations still have little. This dynamic was and is true for seminaries, colleges, communities, and families. This is our shared history, both within society and within the Church.

Starting with the enslavement of African Americans in the United States, the ability to accumulate wealth was a rigged system exclusively benefiting White, property-holding (slave-holding) men. Enslaved African Americans were tabulated as nothing more than property and used as a population-basis from which slave-holding states could garner more White representation in Congress. Enslaved African Americans received no property, wages, inheritance, or restitution for their labor, while the nation was transformed into an economic powerhouse due to the millions of human beings who had no choice but to work for free. This also fueled growth in the convergence of booming industries on which their labor depended. Cornell University historian Edward Baptist writes:

By 1860, the eight wealthiest states in the United States, ranked by wealth per white person, were South Carolina, Mississippi, Louisiana, Georgia, Connecticut, Alabama, Florida, and Texas—seven states created by cotton's march west and south plus one that, as the most industrialized state in the union, profited disproportionately from the gearing of northern factory equipment to the southwestern whipping-machine.[33]

Baptist's book, *The Half has Never Been Told: Slavery and the Making of American Capitalism*, is an ambitious work of history. It attempts to quantify the sweeping financial benefits Black enslavement provided to the nation and its enabling of American participation in global industrialization. Baptist's work can serve as a useful resource in truth-telling as the Church seeks to understand the costs and benefits of the institution of slavery and how far more hands than just those that held the whips were complicit in maintaining and profiting from the free labor of Black Americans.

Far from the common belief that only southern, slave-holding states benefited from the institution, the economic beneficiaries of free Black labor range far and wide. From universities who held and sold enslaved persons both for labor and for raising capital,[34] to banks and financial institutions who used slaves for loan collateral and the selling of insurance and investments,[35] the American institutions who gained financially from slavery are wide-ranging. Harvard Professor Sven Beckert puts it this way:

Slavery was just as present in the counting houses of Lower Manhattan, the spinning mills of New England, and the workshops of budding manufacturers in the Blackstone Valley in Massachusetts and Rhode Island as on the plantations in the Yazoo-Mississippi Delta. The slave economy of the Southern states had ripple effects throughout the entire economy, not just shaping but dominating it.[36]

Revisionist arguments like "my ancestors were too poor to own slaves" (and many others) can be answered. Even though your ancestors weren't slave owners, or never whipped an African American, or even if they worked toward abolition—if they attended a university, if they were legally employed, if they could purchase a home or land, if they could pass on their property through inheritance, if they financed a home or business through institutions like Chase, AIG, or Bank of America, if they engaged in any of the other unencumbered movements of free men, then they participated in the prosperity and freedoms *only* available to White people and ultimately *denied to*, and *derived at the expense of*, African Americans.

This does not necessarily mean one's ancestors were explicitly racist (though it might). However, it does mean they participated in a society that gave them a pass, while it violently oppressed others. Some were able to live lives freely, whether rich or poor, by their own self-determination, while millions of their fellow citizens did not even have the freedom to choose their own names or keep their own children. It also means the onus is on the beneficiaries of that system to right the wrongs of racialized economic disparity.

Following slavery, African Americans still faced an additional ninety-one years of political, social, and economic injustices (in the North as well as in the South) which further solidified their disenfranchisement and alienation from the normal means by which White individuals and families were able to freely pursue, accumulate, and transfer wealth.[37] Local authorities could legally harass and arrest African Americans for vagrancy if they could not prove they were employed. These policies were widely known as Black Codes. For those unable to prove their source of employment, jail, chain gangs, and hard prison labor often awaited them, simply for not having a job.[38]

This emerging system of laws in the South further prevented Blacks from acquiring wealth while holding them hostage to a racialized economic framework based on sharecropping which all but eliminated the possibility they could own or work their own land, or benefit from their own labor. Those imprisoned could then be exploited, without pay, to farm the land, build roads, or other similar civil projects. Even states who today pride themselves on being progressive (e.g., Oregon) would go on to pass Black Codes, attempting to prevent free African Americans from settling there.[39] These are realities that must be truth-told especially when we hear arguments like, "we don't have any African Americans that live near us."

From the later part of the nineteenth century until the mid-twentieth century, African Americans were denied equal treatment under the criminal justice system, denied equal housing opportunities, denied employment opportunities (except for agricultural labor and domestic work), denied equal educational resources, and in some states, even denied their constitutional right to vote as provided for in the 15th Amendment to the US Constitution.

The oft-heard refrain that Blacks should just "pull themselves up by their bootstraps like everyone else did," falls flat in the face of truth-telling about our history. For example, President Franklin D. Roosevelt's New Deal provided tremendous wealth building opportunities like the reduction of home foreclosures, the creation of affordable mortgages under the new Federal Housing Administration, and sweeping new labor laws to undergird and promote the working and middle class. However, New Deal policies were also riddled with racial exclusions that would provide a massive helping hand to White Americans while nearly shutting out African Americans from the emerging new economic growth.[40] For example, the Federal Housing

Authority's underwriting manual "prohibited lending in neighbor-hoods that were changing in racial or social composition," directly causing the values of homes in Black neighborhoods to plunge and making Black Americans undesirable as potential home buyers. The new suburbs developed policies preventing them from moving there, so as to "promote property value." These are the same suburban communities that are predominately White to this day, both in population and church attendance.[41]

Even African Americans' service in World War II did not change their racial reality once they returned to the United States. Civil rights leader Hosea Williams said, "I had fought in World War II, and I was once captured by the German army, and I want to tell you the Germans never were as inhumane as the state troopers of Alabama."[42]

When these Black servicemen did return they were met by the same rigged systems that were designed to reward and benefit Whites but not them. No lenders would lend to them to purchase outside of the red-lined map areas designed to keep Blacks confined to ghettos where they would have no chance of accessing the wealth building mechanisms that were inherent in the Servicemen's Readjustment Act of 1944.[43] In fact, as the nation funneled new mortgages into the suburbs, further isolating those stuck in inner cities, fewer than one percent of all home loans went to African Americans.

This cursory telling of the truths about our history is far from exhaustive. We do not have enough time to explore all of the more discreet and even lesser-known injustices that remain. Injustices committed to shutting African Americans out of participation in society continue to have a lasting impact on the livelihoods of millions of Black people and communities. Injustices such as the stealing of land legally owned by Black families,[44] the destruction of entire Black towns and communities,[45] mass incarceration and drug laws that disproportionately and unequally punish African Americans, the increasingly segregated public school system that continues to limit Black students' access to quality educational facilities and resources,[46] and many others.

My [Ereke's] own family history includes the account of my maternal ancestors who owned a significant amount of land taken away by local Whites after my family attempted to defend themselves from illegal trespassing. Because they had no legal recourse in the criminal justice system and no physical defense against local mob rule, their land was stolen. The outcome of these racist actions results in a shift in wealth building resources and opportunities, away from African American hands and into the hands of the White people, Christians included. It has shifted educational dollars and resources away from poor communities and into zip codes whose property taxes can afford to develop "good schools," as opposed to urban ones. It allows for White Americans to live far removed from their fellow Black citizens, physically, economically, politically, and socially, all while believing the only thing separating them is differences in culture and a little hard work. Attempts at racial reconciliation will remain impotent and ineffectual without a truth-telling about where we've been and the shared history that has brought us to the fractured state we find ourselves in today.

We who hold dear the covenantal nature of God's dealing with mankind—who can so effortlessly attest to Adam being our head in depravity and to Christ being our head in redemption and reconciliation to God—should also be able to understand how we are all inheritors of actions and events from the past. Occurrences we personally had no participation in, but the results thereof, are attributed to our account, whether for good or for bad. As people born of imputed sin, we believe our inherited state before God must be answered, either with God's just wrath or with atonement by the one who was without sin. We believe atonement was made in the work of our Lord Jesus, who provided justice and reconciliation by satisfying the wrath of the one who was offended by our sin.

We of all people should be able to understand how we are all heirs of legacies passed down from history, some built upon peace and some built upon enmity. Some built upon truth and justice, and others upon built upon lies and repression. We of all people, who believe in the grace of God as the fount of every blessing and that which draws us to his throne, should not be fearful to come near, confess our sins, and seek to be reconciled one to another even as he has reconciled us to the Father. If the cross teaches us anything, it should teach us that reconciliation comes at a cost. It is not an apology, a wink, and a nod. It hurts. There is blood, and there are tears. Because true biblical reconciliation must reach back into the past and account for that which tore us asunder, that which caused the offense. True reconciliation cannot be unclear about the cause of the enmity, so that it can ultimately be clear about the atonement that must be made.

Becoming Aware of Repentance: How Agents of Reconciliation Might Pursue Economic Reconciliation

We must change our narratives. This section will outline concrete examples of how we, as a church moving toward racial reconciliation, might engage in acts of relocation and redistribution. The point here is to provide talking points and ideas. Suggestions here are not definitive. We will provide three categories of ways for Christians to relocate and redistribute. These address the personal and systemic effects of racialized economic disparity. These examples will require White Christians to significantly challenge their modalities of ecclesiology, sense of entitlement, and sense of risk, as it will inevitably cost them something.

Relocate Your Education

As we have done in this chapter, it takes some work to uncover the disparities that exist because of historical racism. These lost narratives must become part of our truth-telling. This not only builds education but also empathy vital for the cultivation of humility and the suppression of defensiveness.

Modify homeschool, seminary, Christian, and at-home education to include the full, gritty story of the US experience. Have your children read *The Slave Narratives* or other works by African Americans? If you take your students to visit Washington DC, make the African American History museum part of the required tour.

Do your seminary graduates understand why men like Martin Luther King, Jr. went to a liberal seminary as a result of conservative, evangelical denominations' commitments to segregation? Do they read his writings?

In your church history exams, require candidates to articulate the history of churches like the African Methodist Episcopal church, or identify historically significant POC (people of color) in the formation of your own denomination.

Can you lessen the importance of a college degree or seminary degree for those already engaged in pastoral ministry? The English bible has roughly 900 translations. Unless the person is working at a seminary in some other relevant field, learning to navigate different English commentaries, translations, and software is enough.

Do you know your local history? Are there POC where you live? Where are they? Why are they not there?

When moving out to the Pacific Northwest, I [Daniel] was surprised to hear church elders claim that racism was not as bad out here because they did not have to go through slavery, reconstruction, or segregation. I spent thirty minutes on a search engine and, sure enough, there were not only Black Codes discouraging African Americans from moving out here, but redlining was actively practiced. Additionally, there was a roundup of Chinese Americans who were marched out of the city.

Know your local history.

Relocate your education about material wealth. Simply because you are materially blessed, is that really because God has blessed you? Or is it the result of something more insidious? Did you inherit land that has been in your family for generations? If so, you likely benefited from being White, and you possibly benefited from the theft of land and labor. Instead, relocate how you perceive wealth and your own family's complicity in a corrupt system. Work toward redistributing that wealth in ways that restore justice (see examples below).

One final example—if you are able to afford private education for your children, consider whether or not the private education you provide reinforces segregated classism. Take personal responsibility in making the same school accessible for several African Americans (not just one, to avoid tokenism). Even if your church is attached to a private school, adopt a local public school and offer tutoring programs and provide funding for teaching materials and electronics.

Ultimately, recognize that POC, by virtue of their experiences, have powerful insights on wealth that White people desperately need. Seek out and submit to minority leadership on issues you might find uncomfortable. If you are not intentionally befriending African Americans and submitting to their needed wisdom, you reinforce a narrative of White sufficiency.

Relocate Your Personhood

This is Perkins' most pressing point because of how it requires the wealthier believer to wrestle deeply with systemic poverty once they move into an economically depressed area. All of a sudden, an established family moving into an impoverished area becomes acutely aware of things like school accreditation, crime rates, job availability, public transit, city and county taxation bases, and other issues that personal wealth might shield one from encountering.

As one relocates, intentionally resist gentrification. As a personal example, one of the authors bought a four-family apartment in which he and his family lived. He was careful to make sure to make capital improvements on the property in ways that did not increase the building's tax-rate. This allows him to offer units to hipsters and the urban poor alike, creating a mixed community of city-dwellers, with more than enough rental income to cover the mortgage. It has contributed to neighborhood stabilization and a rich environment for all.

On a corporate level, this carries implications for where we locate churches, offices, and seminaries. If White people are willing to commute thirty minutes to come to your church, ask why POC who live fifteen minutes away do not come to your church. Befriend and submit to POC leadership in your own denomination. Befriend and submit to POC leadership working with the urban poor. Relocate your church programs to partner with these churches. Do what they ask you to do, not what you want to do. Relocate half of your church's workdays to do work projects they want you to do.

Redistribute Your Finances

This is the most difficult request, especially for pastors, campus ministers, and missionaries in well-to-do denominations. Voluntarily take a more realistic paycheck. Use the "excess" to create more positions of scholarship and pastoral ministry. When we approve salaries using the formulaic "to be free from worldly concerns," we segregate ourselves from the global poor, let alone the poor the next block over. Redistribution and retroactive justice are such established themes in the biblical narrative, that the dissonance created by asking the question "How much is too much?" reveals the profound ways we have assimilated into the narrative of eighteenth century America, largely based on the supremacy of the White property-owning male.

Do not hear what we are not saying. We are not calling all pastors to live in poverty. Quite the contrary. We are calling pastors in well-to-do denominations and churches to take a more commensurate salary and create ministry positions and sponsorships for POC so that *they* do not have to live in poverty. Unless one is living and working in an area with an extremely high cost of living, campus ministers, missionaries, and pastors ought not to make or have to raise in excess of $90,000 per year.

For example, in Saint Louis, Missouri, not only are the majority of White evangelical churches commuter churches (thus negating the argument of how expensive it might be to live where the church is located), but one can live very comfortably on less than $75,000 per year. Yet most of the pastors the author knows makes in excess of $90,000–100,000 per year. This reinforces classism and White sufficiency as these pastors are often given prevalent voices when engaging the urban-core. It is a scandal for urban poor to see these men lead a prayer or sermon in efforts to be reconciled, while never learning the desperation behind "give us this day our daily bread." Meanwhile, African American city pastors are often working separate jobs so that they can pastor on the side. Is it even possible to imagine what a redistribution of our churches' finances would look like in a way that moves reconciliation forward? This is the kind of imagining required if Perkins' model will ever succeed.

Here are a few real-world examples of what this might look like: Cru (formerly, Campus Crusade) asks several of their White missionaries to mobilize their networks to raise an additional amount for their "salary." This amount is then used to offset the amount that qualifying Cru missionaries have to raise in an acknowledgment that they often do not have access to the same networks, generational wealth, or expectations of White communities. Rather than have a missionary couple raise over $100,000 per year, with over $24,000 per year wrapped up in insurance and administrative fees, bureaucratic entities should ambitiously require their administrative staff to become more efficient, while simultaneously giving an equal "administrative" percentage to the salary of a minority working in the same field. Yet this is an imperfect example, as recipients of these "scholarships" have often reported feeling patronized and demeaned.

Business owners can choose to redistribute some of their profits to intentionally hire POC from underserved communities or in neighborhoods where the unemployment rate is substantially higher than in White communities (often the case). If a minority pastor in a city church is able to vouch for a potential employee, work with them.

In St. Louis, in one effort to bring White suburban pastors into relationship with African American urban pastors, the conversation immediately broke down after the African American pastors said to the White pastors, "Many of your people can give our people jobs.

Many of our people want to work but cannot find good jobs because of schooling, minor criminal offenses, and other things. Are you willing to do that?"

Several of the White pastors responded by saying it is not their policy to serve as the go-between with their parishioners and their financial details. The urban pastors left, feeling dejected and frustrated. Meanwhile, thinking it was a positive experience, the suburban pastors regularly requested more meetings and did not understand why the urban pastors did not want to keep meeting.

Institutions have also made progress in repairing their relationships with African Americans by offering free tuition to descendants of slaves and by endowing several professorial chairs to be filled by visiting scholars who are minorities. Every seminarian I (Daniel) know had to compile a FAFSA sheet. Seminaries could adopt a sliding scale tuition rate and/or mobilize scholarships exclusively for minorities.

Additionally, one need not reinforce paternal tendencies by creating a Professor for African American Studies. Instead, create a position that allows the filler of that position to speak authoritatively on myriads of issues, such as a Professor of Systematic Theology. These are a few examples of what redistribution might look like in our communities. Whatever the look of it, redistribution will typically cost something for the White Christian, and rightfully so.

———

Justice is never approximate. It is acute and personal. It is the God of the universe taking on flesh and entering into our brokenness, head first. Jesus, through thirty-three years of being made under the law, imputes the breaches and the cause of those breaches onto himself. The major difference here is God did not cause our brokenness. We did. When we enter into our brokenness, we do not enter as saviors but as the guilty. White Christians today continue to take advantage of pre-existing laws, networks, and societal White normativity to further wealth. Justice requires an unmitigated movement from the victimizer toward the victim, and not by proxy.

Perkins has provided the categories needed to pursue racial reconciliation. However, it is impossible to understand the need for categories like redistribution and relocation without a cursory examination of how the church has come to look the way it looks. A racial reconciliation without substantial consideration of how White normativity and supremacy has created and maintains systemic disparity, especially among those with whom Whites desire to be reconciled, is gnostic and paternalistic in nature. It refuses to deal with the power dynamics created from that disparity. If believers are to pursue reconciliation, they must truth-tell the gritty, personal histories of this country with their ledgers open. The specifics remain to be fleshed out, but surely the same body that loves to debate finer points of theology can introduce tangible ways to bring justice to racialized economic disparity within the body of Christ.

---

1. John Rawls, if memory serves me right.
2. I was not even in relationship with any African Americans, believers or non-believers. In my arrogance, I did not even ask an African American what I should do.
3. For a social science article on how other ethnic minorities have adopted "White" models of economic success with an extensive bibliography, see: Paul Wong, Chienping Faith Lai, Richard Nagasawa, and Tieming Lin, "Asian Americans as a Model Minority: Self-Perceptions and Perceptions by Other Racial Groups," *Sociological Perspectives* 41, no. 1 (1998): 95–118.
4. John Perkins, *Beyond Charity: The Call to Christian Community Development* (Grand Rapids, MI: Baker Books, 1993), 31.
5. In a recent conversation a PCA elder said the reason there were not many poor people in their church was because most of their congregation is married and has completed high school. When asked to elaborate he simply restated, "The two largest contributors of poverty in the US are fatherlessness and the lack of education." Not only is this correlative data, but it neglects historical causes of economic disparity in the first place.
6. Promotion of National Unity and Reconciliation Act 34 of 1995 (1995), 3–10, http://www.justice.gov.za/legislation/acts/1995-034.pdf.
7. Examples of this are the hagiographies written about our national leaders, with whom we do not even share membership in the Gospel. Instead, our joint membership with people like Thomas Jefferson or George Washington is governed by owning property, being White, and being American. Truth-telling requires us to be honest about their exploits. We might idolize Jefferson's ambition, but ignore the fact it required slavery to accomplish it. This exposes our own pragmatism and White-washed histories in ways that lessens the innocence of things like the American Dream. This truth-telling can only benefit our Christianity, since nationalism often obfuscates Gospel truth. Jeff Corntassel and Chaw-win-is and T'lakwadzi, "Indigenous Storytelling, Truth-telling, and Community Approaches to Reconciliation," *ESC: English Studies in Canada* 35, no. 1 (2009): 137–59.
8. We have rarely been to a gathering of PCA pastors (where the authors are ordained) where several single-malt scotches and cigars were not available. This is just a minor, trivial example of lifestyle disparity. Another example might include how a critical examination of our view of the stay-at-home mom as a paradigm of the ideal Christian household is rooted in White, middle-class lifestyle expectations. African Americans and other minorities rarely had the luxury of a stay-at-home mother-figure, and if they did, it was often because those figures were taking side jobs in the service industry (of White people).

9. Everything mentioned here can, and should, be applied to the American Indian as well. The authors have little experience with reconciliation in that context, so we will focus comments on the context of African Americans as a category of the racialized poor.

10. Both historical and contemporary. Examined below.

11. Justice in the Old Testament was always retroactive and accompanied by economic redistribution. The year of Jubilee in Leviticus 25 offers the most distinct call for a generational redistribution of the land to return it to the original owners every fifty years.

12. Perkins, *Beyond Charity*, 127.

13. Christopher Wright, *Old Testament Ethics and the People of God* (Downers Grove, IL: IVP Academic, 2011).

14. Wright, *Old Testament Ethics*, 152.

15. Perkins, *Beyond Charity*, 129–131.

16. *"Opheilonti,"* a participle, is elsewhere unassociated with *hamartia* and *afikomen*. It is a word used for situations designating indebtedness and economic boundedness to another. Temptation, then, is understood as both economic (that which brings *opheionta*) and spiritual temptation (that which brings *hamartia*). Such a reading exposes how we have trained ourselves to read these passages allegorically, rather than as they plainly are: Gospel renderings with immediate economic consequences.

17. The Jerusalem conferences recorded in Acts 13 and 15; much more explicit in Paul, see 2 Corinthians 5:21–25.

18. See also 1 John 3:17.

19. When I initially ask churches about their health in living out economic reconciliation, generally as a litmus test, I will ask who is on the session: employers, employees, or both? Are janitors and businessmen welcome on the session as equals? This will often portend the difficulty (or receptivity) in having a conversation about racial/ethnic reconciliation.

20. See Thomas Piketty and Arthur Goldhammer, *Capital in the Twenty-first Century* (Cambridge, MA: Belknap Press of Harvard University Press, 2014). Many of our alma maters were built by slaves or funds derived from the slave trade including, but not limited to, Harvard, Princeton, Columbia, Brown, Vanderbilt, William and Mary, and the University of Virginia.

21. More men were on welfare at the time. Today, government assistance is not usually thought of as things like farming subsidies, tax breaks, FHA housing loans, and the like. White people benefit from these programs disproportionately. Even with poverty alleviation programs such as SNAP or TANF, more than twice as many Whites (6.2 million) as African Americans (2.8 million) were lifted above the poverty line by those programs. See Isaac Shapiro, Danilo Trisi, Raheem Chaudhry, "Poverty Reduction Programs Help Adults Lacking College Degrees the Most," *Center on Budget and Policy Priorities*, February 16, 2017, https://www.cbpp.org/research/poverty-and-inequality/poverty-reduction-programs-help-adults-lacking-college-degrees-the.; Franklin D. Gilliam, Jr., "The 'Welfare Queen' Experiment: How Viewers React to Images of African American Mothers on Welfare," *The Nieman Foundation for Journalism at Harvard University* 53, no. 2 (Summer 1999), http://escholarship.org/uc/item/17m7r1rq.

22. Martin Gilens, *Why Americans Hate Welfare: Race, Media, and the Politics of Antipoverty Policy*, Studies in Communication, Media, and Public Opinion (Chicago: University of Chicago Press, 1999).

23. Jessica L. Semega, Kayla R. Fontenot, and Melissa A. Kollar, "Income and Poverty in the United States: 2016," September 2017, U.S. Department of Commerce: Census Bureau, https://www.census.gov/library/publications/2017/demo/p60-259.html.

24. Valarie Wilson, "New census data show strong 2016 earnings growth across-the-board, with black and Hispanic workers seeing the fastest growth for second consec-

utive year," *Economic Policy Institute*, September 12, 2017, http://www.epi.org/blog/new-census-data-show-strong-2016-earnings-growth-across-the-board-with-black-and-hispanic-workers-seeing-the-fastest-growth-for-second-consecutive-year/.

25. Judith Scott-Clayton and Jing Li, "Black-white Disparity in Student Loan Debt More than Triples after Graduation," *Brookings Institution Reports*, October 2016, https://www.brookings.edu/research/black-white-disparity-in-student-loan-debt-more-than-triples-after-graduation/.

26. Janelle Jones and John Schmitt, "A College Degree is No Guarantee," *Center for Economic and Policy Research*, May 2014, http://cepr.net/documents/black-coll-grads-2014-05.pdf.

27. Bureau of Labor Statistics, "Unemployment rate and employment-population ratio vary by race and ethnicity," *The Economics Daily*, U.S. Department of Labor, January 13, 2017, https://www.bls.gov/opub/ted/2017/unemployment-rate-and-employment-population-ratio-vary-by-race-and-ethnicity.htm.

28. Bureau of Labor Statistics, "Unemployment rate," January 13, 2017, https://www.bls.gov/opub/ted/2017/unemployment-rate-and-employment-population-ratio-vary-by-race-and-ethnicity.htm.

29. Lisa J. Dettling, Joanne W. Hsu, Lindsey Jacobs, Kevin B. Moore, and Jeffery P. Thompson, "Recent Trends in Wealth Holding by Race and Ethnicity: Evidence from the Survey of Consumer Finance," Board of Governors of the Federal Reserve System, September 2017, https://www.federalreserve.gov/econres/notes/feds-notes/recent-trends-in-wealth-holding-by-race-and-ethnicity-evidence-from-the-survey-of-consumer-finances-20170927.htm.

30. Semega, "Income and Poverty," Figure 1. Data compared with the 2016 PCA's Administrative Committee's report on the average, nationwide, income distribution for 2016. $101,337 for a full-time Senior Pastor, $92,850 for a full-time Associate Pastor, and $75,788 for a full-time Assistant Pastor. Data was voluntarily and confidentially compiled, meaning that the median incomes for these positions only comprise those who submitted their information for 2016.

31. Manny Fernandez and Christine Hauser, "Texas Mother Teaches Textbook Company a Lesson on Accuracy," *The New York Times*, October 5, 2015, https://www.nytimes.com/2015/10/06/us/publisher-promises-revisions-after-textbook-refers-to-african-slaves-as-workers.html.

32. For further study on the history of lynching in the US, see Equal Justice Initiative, "Lynching In America: Confronting the Legacy of Racial Terror," Equal Justice Initiative, 3rd ed., 2015, https://lynchinginamerica.eji.org/report/.

33. Edward E. Baptist, *The Half Has Never Been Told: Slavery and the making of American Capitalism* (New York: Basic Books, 2014), 350.

34. For more study on American universities that benefited economically from slavery see, Craig Steven Wilder, *Ebony and Ivy: Race, Slavery, and the Troubled History of America's Universities* (New York: Bloomberg Press, 2013). For more information on Harvard University and slavery, visit: www.harvard.edu/slavery. In 2016, Georgetown University was one of the first of the Ivy Leagues to acknowledge that it raised capital in 1838 to pay off debts by selling 272 black enslaved human beings. The Jesuit University has since taken grand steps to reconcile and recompense for its past by naming buildings after some of the 272, erecting monuments, and offering special admissions considerations for descendants. For more information visit www.slaveryarchive.georgetown.edu.

35. For a more complete discussion of this topic and a bibliography related to the global financial impacts of slavery and its contributions to nineteenth-century industrialization see Sven Beckert, "Slavery and Capitalism," *The Chronicle Review*, December 2012, http://chronicle.com/article/SlaveryCapitalism/150787/.

36. Sven Beckert, "Slavery and Capitalism," *The Chronicle of Higher Education*, December 12, 2014, https://www.chronicle.com/article/SlaveryCapitalism/150787. For a full

treatise on the subject, see Sven Beckert, *Empire of Cotton: A Global History* (New York: Vintage, 2015).

37. African Americans faced institutionalized racism without Federal intervention between 1877 and 1965. In 1877, President Rutherford B. Hayes withdrew federal troops from the South, which removed the protections necessary to ensure that the progress made during Reconstruction, including a more equitable share of representation of African Americans throughout all levels of government, would continue. With those federal protections removed, the southern states were allowed to implement policies that would continue to place African Americans in subjugated positions. This period of time came to be known as Jim Crow. It was not effectively challenged and eliminated until passage of the Civil Rights Act of 1964 and the Voting Rights Act of 1965, both Federal interventions.

38. Douglass A. Blackmon, *Slavery by Another Name: The Re-Enslavement of Black Americans from the Civil War to World War II* (New York: Anchor, 2008).

39. Some Oregon laws designed to keep African Americans from settling there were so inhumane that they only lasted a few months, such as the law passed in 1844 requiring that "blacks in Oregon—be they free or slave—be whipped twice a year 'until he or she shall quit the territory,'" The whippings were soon replaced with hard labor. "Oregon Racial Laws and Events, 1844–1959," Oregon Department of Education, 2017, http://www.ode.state.or.us/opportunities/grants/saelp/orraciallaws.pdf.

40. Ira Katznelson, *When Affirmative Action Was White: An Untold History of Racial Inequality in America* (New York: Norton, 2005).

41. Dalton Conley, *Being Black, Living in the Red: Race, Wealth, and Social Policy in America*, 2nd ed. (Oakland: University of California Press, 2009), 37. For more study, see Nancy Denton and Douglas Massey, *American Apartheid: Segregation and the Making of the Underclass*, (Cambridge: Harvard Press, 1998).

42. For more on race and New Deal politics see: Katznelson, *When Affirmative Action Was White:*

43. Conley, *Being Black, Living in the Red*, 37.

44. Andrew W. Kahrl, *The Land Was Ours: How Black Beaches Became White Wealth in the Coastal South* (Chapel Hill: The University of North Carolina Press, 2016); Todd Lewan and Dolores Barclay, "AP Documents Land Taken from Blacks Through Trickery, Violence, and Murder," *Associated Press*, 2001, http://nuweb9.neu.edu/civilrights/wp-content/uploads/AP-Investigation-Article.pdf.

45. Tim Madigan, *The Burning: Massacre, Destruction, and the Tulsa Race Riot of 1921* (New York: St. Martin's Griffin, 2003).

46. Government Accountability Office Report 16–345, "Better Use of Information Could Help Agencies Identify Disparities and Address Racial Discrimination," United States Government Accountability Office, 2016, http://www.gao.gov/assets/680/676745.pdf.

CONFESSION AND RECONCILIATION ARE NECESSARY FOR OBEDIENCE

YES, WE LIVE HERE

RAISING CROSS-CULTURAL KIDS

MARIA GARRIOTT

Maria Garriott and her husband, Craig, began Faith Christian Fellowship in 1981. It is a multiethnic, socio-economically diverse church. They served there for thirty-eight years. In 2019, they founded Baltimore Antioch Leadership Movement (BALM), a regional ministry to multiply cross-cultural disciples. Maria also works for Parakaleo, a ministry to church planting spouses. Maria has an MS in Professional Writing and is the author of A Thousand Resurrections. *Maria and Craig have five adult children and seven grandchildren.*

––––––

When we committed to urban multiethnic ministry in 1981, we just wanted to follow Jesus. I didn't foresee the joy and sorrow, the sweet and bitter, or the delight and despair. Relocating meant raising our children in a multiethnic church in a low-income, Black community. By God's grace, it challenged and changed us all.

I recently asked our five adult children (four daughters and one son) to share their perspectives about this life we lived. I was relieved they didn't say we'd ruined them for life! They didn't say we were irresponsible parents. They didn't regret living in a community where their Whiteness stood out.

They are thankful—with some caveats.

Even with imperfect parents, my children see more gains than losses, and they can articulate their perspectives. Their daily, cross-cultural relationships with friends and neighbors in the Christian community and the community-at-large have been life-shaping in positive ways. They've had the privilege of knowing people from many races and backgrounds who live out their faith daily while pursuing justice and mercy. They've seen people transformed—but not crushed—by suffering. They've gained cross-cultural competence and a greater sensitivity to the poor, and this has impacted some of their career choices. They've learned about poverty and privilege, two issues that still plague America. They've experienced the richness of a church where people from all races, ethnicities, and backgrounds cherish each other and work together. They've seen a biblical ideal brought to life—imperfectly, messily, but at times, gloriously.

We had many reasons not to move into a struggling Baltimore neighborhood in 1981 to start a multiethnic church. Presbytery leaders had asked my husband, Craig, a twenty-six-year-old intern pastor, to lead an urban church startup that was little more than a handful of people, several of whom struggled with significant mental illness. We'd been married a little over a year. Craig hadn't finished seminary yet. Our firstborn, Rebecca, was an infant. We had no urban or multiethnic experience.

Many churches, including several in our denomination, had followed their people to the suburbs, unable or unwilling to embrace changing demographics. What was facilitating this flight of middle-class Whites and Blacks? The post-1960s urban woes: a loss of manu-facturing jobs, an accompanying increase in crime and, not coinciden-tally, the dramatic decline in the quality of a public school education.

We also arrived in time for the sordid introduction of crack cocaine. Baltimore, a largely Black/White city at the time, was histori-cally hyper-segregated. People joked that a racially diverse neighbor-hood was one "where African Americans have moved in, and the last White person hasn't yet moved out." In church-growth circles, the homogeneous-unit principle held sway: "Birds of a feather flock together! White people attract White people. Let the Blacks reach the Blacks. Multiethnic churches don't grow. In fact, they will split along racial lines. And don't worry about reaching low-income people. The Pentecostals do a better job of reaching them."

We heard it all.

So why pursue an idealistic dream of starting a multiethnic church in hyper-segregated Baltimore? Don't mono-ethnic churches also evangelize and disciple people? Hasn't the American Black Church played a vital role historically? Yes and yes. But God's concern for all peoples and nations—and especially the marginalized, the poor, and the vulnerable—is clear throughout Scripture. We can't dismiss this as just another option.

In reconciling people to God, Christ also reconciles diverse people to one another. In the early church, the apostles didn't segregate into ethnic congregations. Instead, beginning with the Jerusalem church, they appointed qualified leaders from the minority community (Acts 6). We don't have to wait until heaven to experience the united worship of all nations, tribes, and tongues (Rev. 7). A multiethnic church displays the unity of Christ's body, his multiethnic bride, and it points to Christ in a fractured, divisive world. If a local community is multiethnic, its local churches should reflect a cross-section of the community. It's possible through the cross of Jesus Christ.

Compelled by the Scriptures and influenced by John Perkins' philosophy of Christian community development and racial reconciliation, we prayed, bought a dilapidated house, and moved in. We believe Jesus promises to work through his servant ambassadors—flawed, naïve, and inexperienced as we were—so that their ministry of presence testifies to his power. Fellow Christians variously thought we were impractical, heroic, misguided, or irresponsible.

God in his providence placed our church, Faith Christian Fellowship, at a crossroads of socio-economic class and culture. He provided a building in Pen Lucy, a low-income, working-class Black community hit hard by drugs, job loss, gangs, and government neglect. It sat one block west of Guilford, one of the wealthiest enclaves in Baltimore, which was then almost exclusively White. Johns Hopkins University, Loyola University, and Morgan State University are one mile southwest, northwest, and east, respectively. It was an ideal setting for a multiethnic church, and an intense setting for an inexperienced, young, White pastoral family.

Our children grew up seeing believers pursue justice and mercy, not necessarily the American Dream (Mic. 6:8). At our church, the economically disadvantaged are not statistics but names and faces, and care for the poor is not an optional add-on. The church is called to welcome the stranger, the immigrant, the orphan, and the widow with both the blessings and costs attendant to this. Church members gathered food and household goods for families displaced by fires. College students and other adults coached our after-school sports leagues to provide healthy activities for neighborhood kids. When birth parents were consumed with addictions, grandparents or aunts and uncles raised grandchildren, nieces, and nephews. Professional men and women cut back their work-hours to free up time to come alongside neighborhood kids. Bible study members pooled their resources to buy a fellow attendee a used car so he could get to both his jobs.

As a pastor's kids, our children had a front-row seat to congregational backstories of transformed lives. Every Sunday, they worshipped with heroes of the faith. The beloved deacon and usher who greets you every Sunday? He's a former drug addict who almost died from a shotgun blast at close range whose life was dramatically transformed by Christ. He took in a neglected teenage girl and is now an adoptive grandfather to her baby.

The woman weeping and calling out "Thank you, Jesus!" during Christmas Eve service? She's a former prostitute and drug addict sheltered by several church members during her recovery.

That quiet man from Sri Lanka? He's a PhD, entrepreneur, and seminary student who chairs our missions committee and makes sure we keep the needs of the "two-thirds world" before us.

That scholarly, middle-aged couple working at Johns Hopkins? They took in an elderly, handicapped man whose home lacked heat and was robbed three times by an intruder eager to take advantage of easy prey.

That young married couple? They are now raising a young teenage boy they met through the church's tutoring program.

Because our children grew up with people who experienced suffering, whether from economic hardship, racial injustice, or other effects of living in a fallen world, they are not blindsided by hardship. Suffering is not considered aberrant or the result of weak faith or an inability to believe in your best life now. Jesus promised abundant life, but he also promised trials, tribulation, and persecution.

Baltimoreans joke about our "city tax," the price you pay for living here: receiving an annual jury duty summons; being mugged on your way home from work; paying $300 after your car was towed because you forgot to move it before rush hour; having a drunk sideswipe your vehicle in the wee hours of the morning; returning home from church to find your front door smashed in. The "city tax" is higher in poor neighborhoods: more stray bullets, more break-ins, more stuff disappearing from your porch.

As our children became adults, they paid their own "city tax." One daughter was robbed, another assaulted and mugged while pregnant, and a third daughter had her car set on fire. These were painful episodes, but they weathered them well.

Urban multiethnic ministry helped equip our children to live in a nation where Whites will no longer be in the majority. Historically, Whites have been oblivious to their status as the dominant culture, while minorities were daily reminded of their subdominant status. (Why was the Crayola "flesh" a pinkish color? Why were all Disney princesses—at least the early ones—White? Why was White culture considered "normal" but Black culture "exotic"?) Minorities have needed cross-cultural competence to survive, yet cross-cultural challenges were optional for Whites.

Because our children had the rare experience—for Whites—of living as minorities, they gained cross-cultural competency. Sitting down for dinner with people from Pen Lucy, Chad, Nigeria, Bangladesh, or Peru was unremarkable for them. Our most outgoing daughter, Melissa, was adept at code switching, customizing dialect to fit various racial or class settings and norms. She flowed easily between her different worlds of school, neighborhood, and church. She worked her way through graduate school waitressing at a high-end restaurant. She moved seamlessly between executives, pro football players, and the low-wage kitchen crew. Our kids didn't have to leave the country to experience other cultures. Neither should yours.

Growing up amidst a multiethnic church in a low-income neighborhood influenced some of our children's career choices, and prepared them to work with diverse peoples in an urban setting. Rebecca, our oldest, works as an emergency room nurse in a hospital near our home. No matter who walks in—the unemployed addict, the yuppie, the tradesperson, the college student, or the immigrant struggling to learn English—she feels she can interact with them honestly without pre-existing notions that entirely block an honest conversation.

Volunteering at church summer camps in the neighborhood gave Melissa a passion for teaching within at-risk communities. She became a special education teacher in a low-income, racially diverse school. It's where a kindergartener tried to sell his peers marijuana for ice cream money; where mommy might have the "dope fiend lean" (a sleepy stagger from her latest heroin hit); where daddy has a rap sheet rather than a resume; where a little boy hates the police because "they took away my daddy." It's a heartbreaking, complicated world.

My daughter knows she can't fix it, but she throws herself into it. Every. Single. Day.

Caroline credits growing up in an urban neighborhood and being raised in a multiethnic church as the two greatest shapers of her life —both personally and professionally. Caroline's interest in race and class led her to pursue a graduate degree focusing on religious and racial identities and hierarchies. She has lived abroad in several countries and married a Spaniard who now calls the US home.

While I grew up oblivious to my privileges of race and class, my children understand this concept. Raised in a White suburb outside Washington, DC, I had only a very vague sense of the privileges I inherited because of race and relative affluence. At my public high school, if you got busted for a little pot, or were pulled over for drunk driving, your parents bailed you out. If you had learning disabilities, parents paid for educational testing, tutoring, or prescriptions. If you suffered emotional trauma, they could rush you to counseling.

But the poor have little access to these interventions and fewer resources to cope with dysfunction or escape the consequences of youthful foolishness. Public defenders don't have time for your case. Schools can't handle the high percentage of special-needs kids, and children act out because their traumas aren't treated.

Living in a Black neighborhood and attending a multiethnic church helped my children understand White privilege. They knew that, unlike their friend Chaz, they probably would not be roughed up by a cop for "loitering" at a bus stop on the way to work. They knew they were less likely to be targeted or profiled because of their skin color, shuttled into special education classes, absorbed into the criminal justice system, or turned down for jobs. When one of our daughters confessed she'd attended a high school party with underage drinking and the police had arrived, my lecture included, "What would have happened if you had been a Black male?" "I know, I know," she sobbed. She knows the juvenile jail system is clogged with Black males arrested for similar minor offenses.

My children realize "rich" is a relative term, and there's a difference between being broke and poor. We were sometimes broke, but we never were poor. Even when we lacked financial capital, we had social capital—a network of supportive, stable relationships, parents or siblings who could lend us money. Many of our Pen Lucy neighbors lacked such social capital.

Caroline says, "I knew I was lucky to have a dad who was actively involved in my life—coming to sports games, eating dinner, building backyard jungle-gyms. Most of the neighborhood kids lived with their moms or grandmothers."

We also had work options. Craig could leave ministry and work in architectural engineering, and I could volunteer less and get a full-time job. We had life skills. We knew how to budget, plan, study, and navigate bureaucracy. Craig can fix cars, plumbing, and houses. I can cook nutritious, cheap food, drive, advocate for my children, and speak English.

Because of their relationships in the neighborhood, my children learned about poverty and privilege. Unwilling to send our children to failing neighborhood schools, we homeschooled or sent the children to various private or parochial schools. Their friends from the neighborhood public school weren't so lucky. They told stories of no textbooks, school fires, and overwhelmed teachers, including one who duct-taped a student to his seat to keep him still.

Our son Calvin says, "Because of my upbringing at Faith and my education at Covenant College, I have a much more holistic perspective on poverty and the complexity of poverty. With that comes a certain level of graciousness [toward the poor]."

Living on an urban pastor's salary in a low-income neighborhood taught my children how to live frugally. As an undergraduate, Caroline worked fifteen–twenty hours per week: nanny, restaurant hostess, or work-study student. The day after graduation, Caroline and her best friend Yejin, a naturalized Korean American, decided to dumpster-dive outside the dorms, knowing their well-heeled peers threw away usable loot on move-out day. As they gleefully retrieved new clothes with tags still on them, a university dean and two parents strolled by. The dean recognized them. "There's something you don't see every day," the dean said dryly. "Two of our recent graduates." Yejin, who would go on to earn a law degree, was unfazed. "Well, Dean Smith, those tuition bills are pretty steep."

My kids remember Faith Christian Fellowship as a racial safe-zone. The church is home to many biracial people and interracial couples who say that at other churches they've often felt they didn't fit in. "I occasionally had people say racist things to me in the neighborhood, but not in the church," our daughter Melissa recalls. Caroline, our third-born, says adults from the church helped ease her internal struggles with being White in a Black neighborhood.

Like most mothers, I desperately wanted to protect my children from the "real world." When I birthed my youngest after nearly twenty years of urban ministry, I wept to think of raising her in this broken world. Untouched by evil, Juliana had not yet tasted pain or betrayal or sickness or violence. She knew only my womb, my arms, my breast, my soft voice and her father's deeper one. Try as I might—and I would try—I would not be able to protect her. I'd again have to trust that God is both sovereign and good.

My family's cross-cultural immersion had a down side. There are thorns in my garden. The racial and socio-economic chasm that Rebecca and Caroline navigated daily to attend a private middle and high school on scholarship was, in retrospect, too wide. Our children felt consumed with the identity of the larger population in Pen Lucy. Rebecca recalls, "It was always hard to be a minority. It often didn't allow me space to fully explore my individual identity."

Caroline says, "Grappling with my Whiteness was painful because I was shy and did not want to stand out from the rest of the neighborhood kids, but also because I didn't know how to identify with what it meant culturally." She immersed herself in books rather than playing outside in the neighborhood, and felt this hindered her from developing social confidence. She told me, "I wasn't taught enough how to protect my own needs and nurture myself in the midst of so many pressing demands. I hated that my dad worked late hours at the church and worried that he might get shot by a stray bullet walking home in the dark."

Rebecca felt the world's ills: "It's not necessarily a bad thing, but a hard thing.… That often felt like a very personal burden." Yet this awareness was also good, Rebecca says. "As I grew older I became more balanced and can appreciate the upper and lower echelons of society. I'm grateful for that."

Minorities are often seen as outsiders, not belonging, or the "exotic other." My children got a taste of this. One parent at the private school where Caroline was a scholarship student gasped when I told her where we lived. "Pen Lucy?! My *maid* lives in Pen Lucy!"

Police stopped Melissa on her way to church: "Are you lost? Where are you going?" She was "walking while White." Conversely, while riding bikes in a nearby wealthy, White enclave, our preteen son Calvin and his Black friend were interrogated by the neighborhood security guard. "We're just checking IDs," the rent-a-cop said. Really? Of ten-year-olds? My daughters were the "exotic other" to little girls in the neighborhood, who loved playing beauty parlor with their long, straight, blonde hair. Most African American women have had similar "exotic other" experiences, as evidenced by one book title: *You Can't Touch My Hair (and Other Things I Still Have to Explain).*[1]

After almost twenty-three years in Pen Lucy, we felt God calling us to move out of the neighborhood to a diverse area a few miles away with a better public high school. When we told our daughters, who were sixteen, seventeen, and nineteen, they objected. They felt their baby sister Juliana, who was four at the time, needed to be raised in Pen Lucy. So Juliana experienced a far less cross-culturally intense upbringing. Although she grew up surrounded by diversity both in the school and neighborhood, she rarely experienced being the only one of her race in the room. For her, wearing the pastor's kid label felt heavier than race or class.

A Complicated Faith

My children have had complicated faith journeys... which is I suppose appropriate because there's nothing simple about following Jesus. Several struggled to find diverse evangelical congregations or church homes when living away. One has decided she is not a Christian. What my children do with the faith is up to them. Though I begged God for this role, I can't be the Holy Spirit in their hearts. But they can't flippantly say the church doesn't care about the poor, or the immigrant, or the marginalized. They can't say Christianity is a crutch to make life easier. They've seen not Marx's "opiate of the masses" but a congregation where many live sacrificially, give generously, and serve joyfully.

While they express appreciation and respect for what we did, our children don't feel called to a similar ministry. Melissa says, "What you were trying to do was very challenging, on the front lines of bridging races. It is very complex and complicated. It's not something a lot of churches want to do. The biggest challenge was raising your family in it. I couldn't do it." Although Calvin doesn't feel called to live in the inner city again, he values his upbringing in a multiethnic church. He says, "The worst thing you can do for yourself is be in an environment where everyone is just like you and you become numb and blind to the world."

The need for multiethnic churches is even more pressing now than it was in 1981. If a community is multiethnic, its churches should reflect this. My children's generation—Millennials and GenXers—wonder why churches don't reflect the same diversity they've experienced in school, the workplace, their neighborhoods, and other settings. Many are eager to put their faith into action and address racism and other societal ills.

The urban multiethnic church isn't easy or convenient. Raising five children in this setting taught me Jesus is drawn to our weakness. That smoldering wick he doesn't snuff out. That bruised reed he doesn't break. He does his best work with the smallest, the youngest, the most inexperienced, and the most timid. He wins battles with slingshots and stones. He incarnates in a stable not a palace, and his ancestors include a prostitute (Rahab), a child conceived in incest (Perez), and a woman from a despised ethnic group (Ruth). He didn't abandon us or our children.

Like every parent, I have a litany of regrets: I wish we'd _____ (fill in the blank). Taken more vacations. Had more family devotions. Picked a different school for that child. Protected family boundaries more.

But I haven't wished we'd never moved into Pen Lucy. Living in the community was a daily leap of faith, a freefall where we'd jumped out of an airplane holding hands, praying Jesus would save us. It forced me to trust that he loved our children even more than Craig and I did. It forced me to depend on God and his Word in ways I never would have done otherwise.

Sometimes I'm tired, and I want easy. I want my desires, my comfort, and my safety to be front and center. I can complain.

Or I can remember:

We cannot protect ourselves.

We cannot comfort ourselves.

We cannot save ourselves.

And that's the point. I keep running smack into this.

Because we have a Mighty God, a Wonderful Counselor, a Savior.

I've bet my family on him.

---

1. Phoebe Robinson, *You Can't Touch My Hair (and Other Things I Still Have to Explain)* (New York: Plume, 2016.

A BURDEN REMOVED

A BIBLICAL PATH FOR REMOVING THE BURDEN
OF THE RACISM SINS OF OUR FOREFATHERS

REED DEPACE

Reed DePace has served as pastor of The Church at Chantilly, Historic First Presbyterian of Montgomery, Alabama, since 2008. He holds degrees from Westminster Theology Seminary in Philadelphia (MAR) and from Ligonier Academy of Biblical and Theological Studies.(DMin).

———

But if they confess their iniquity and the iniquity of their fathers in their treachery that they committed against me, and also in walking contrary to me, so that I walked contrary to them... then I will remember my covenant.
Lev. 26:40–42

Should a congregation repent of the sins of their forefathers?

This was a particularly relevant question for us. First Presbyterian Church (PCA) of Montgomery, Alabama was the first church formally established in Montgomery (1824, we beat our Baptist brothers and sisters by six months; whew!). We've seen lots of blessings from God over our history. In the late 1800s we were key supporters of the Presbyterian missionaries God worked through to bring about the 1907 Pyongyang Revival and the Christianization of Korea. In the 1920s we were a "mega-church" before there were such things, with a membership over 2,000. Even in 1961, our membership was still at a respectable 1,100.

Before I was called to be the pastor of First Church (our nickname) in 2008, the church had moved from its downtown location to a suburban one in hopes that folks more like the existing congregation would join. Yet that hadn't really happened. Official membership was around 100. But the reality was that we had about fifty active members, and many of them were from the Silent Generation, well into their 70s and 80s. The common renewal plan followed by many downtown churches (move to the suburbs) wasn't working for us.

Yet, as often happens with a new pastor, we saw an increase in our ministry over the next few years. By 2011, membership rose to just over 100. It looked like there was a rebirth of new life, that God was going to bless us with more years of ministry. Yet over the next few years, the previous slide toward dissolution continued. By 2015, membership was down in the 70s, with active membership back in the 50s.

The elders at the time agreed that we needed to spend some time investigating why God seemed to be "walking contrary" to us (Lev. 26:41), why he seemed to be cursing rather than blessing our ministry efforts. I conducted a thorough search of our church records (something southern Presbyterians are very good at keeping) back to the very founding of the church (church plant 1821, organized 1824). We had a number of key markers in our history, some interesting, some not so good. In 1857, a grand-uncle of Winston Churchill, Rev. George H. W. Petrie, became the pastor of First Church. In the congregation at the time was the man history records as being significantly responsible for inflaming secessionist fervor among the southern States, William Lowdnes Yancey.

Yet, regarding our current circumstances, it was the records from the Civil Rights era forward that seemed most relevant. Starting in the 1950s our church, both the congregation and leadership, engaged in actions and decisions that are most simply described as racism, a refusal to love our Black neighbors as ourselves. In short, we found a historical connection that suggested why we seemed unwilling to reach the people around. It seemed to begin with our unwillingness in the Civil Rights era to reach Black people in our community.

Oh, First Church wasn't all racist all the time. Some members sought to obey Christ and love our Black, and fellow Montgomerians. For example, Rosa Parks' White attorney was a deacon in our church, and his wife was one of Mrs. Parks' best friends. In the 1960s, even though he suffered for it, one of our ministers accepted the call to be the pastor of a small struggling Black congregation (planted out of our church in the 1880s). Other notable examples were seen throughout the 1950s and '60s.

Yet far more often in this era, our church chose to partake in racial sins. In 1956, about a decade before most other White Churches in Montgomery took this action, our leadership chose to formally block Blacks from membership and service attendance. In 1961, our church failed to offer sanctuary to the Freedom Riders who were attacked at the Greyhound Bus Station. Our building was located half a block away from the station's front door. Rather than taking a reasonable, biblical action, we ignored what was happening. As late as 1974, our elders and deacons continued to affirm their intention to not allow Blacks to join or attend services. Numerous other racist attitudes and decisions littered First Church's history through the Civil Rights era. In fact, these attitudes and actions only began to disappear from our records in the late 1970s.

Yet these sins would occasionally make themselves known after this. An outreach proposal to open up a daycare was actively hindered for the whole of the 1980s, in part, because it would require letting Black children participate in the day care. The dominant debate among the elders in the 1980s and '90s concerned whether or not to reach the surrounding community with the Gospel, a community that was no longer White. While not overt in every discussion, the underlying opposition to including Blacks in outreach meant that almost no witnessing ministries were present. Then in 1999 the decision was made to move to a suburban community where the demographics of the surrounding community matched those of the congregation.

Back to 2015. Despite a number of attempts, witnessing efforts at First Church were met with very little response from the congregation. Comparing this to the research gleaned from our history, we discovered a startling similarity. In the Civil Rights era, First Church refused to reach out to people unlike them: Blacks. By 2015, when most members had never been a part of the downtown church, we had become a congregation that was all but unwilling to reach out to anyone. All might be welcome, but we weren't putting any effort into taking the Gospel to them, White, Black, or the proverbial purple with pink polka dots.

This was the context in which we considered the contentious practice of repenting of the sins of our forefathers. It certainly looked like God was "walking contrary" to us; we were experiencing the fruits of past sins, even though we were no longer racist. Was repenting for those past sins, sins that no one in the existing congregation participated in, God's path to restoring the ministry of the Gospel among us?

The answer to this question is not immediately obvious in the Scriptures. There seems to be a contradiction at play in this question. As many others have noted in recent years, the Bible is expressly clear that God does not impute the culpability of the forefathers' sin on their descendants.

> The soul who sins shall die. The son shall not suffer for the iniquity of the father, nor the father suffer for the iniquity of the son. The righteousness of the righteous shall be upon himself, and the wickedness of the wicked shall be upon himself. (Ezek. 18:20)

On the other hand, there are numerous warnings that God "visits the iniquities" of forefathers on their descendants (Exod. 20:5; 24:7; Num. 14:18; Deut. 5:9; Lev. 26:39–41; Isa. 14:21; Isa. 65:6–7; Jer. 14:20; 32:8, etc.). The notable examples of Daniel (Dan. 9:8, ff.), Ezra (Ezra 9:6–7, ff.), and Nehemiah (Neh. 9:16, ff.), each confessing their forefathers' iniquities, give strong evidence that God both fulfills the warnings and the promises attached to "visiting the iniquities."

The way out of the apparent contradiction here is found in the details associated with the words *iniquity* and *visit*. While more could be said, let me summarize. Being one of three words used for sin in the OT, the Hebrew word translated *iniquity* is used to express sin *with its results*. We are most familiar with the result of culpability: sin makes us guilty before God, accountable to him for our rebellion against his law.

Yet sin has another result, one that is as common as culpability, but not often focused on. In addition to culpability, sin also results in *corruption*. This is the spiritual pollution, the contamination factor attached to sin. Sin spiritually infects others. A significant part of the Mosaic ceremonial law pictures the corruption result of sin:

> And Aaron shall lay both his hands on the head of the live goat, and confess over it all the iniquities of the people of Israel, and all their transgressions, all their sins. And he shall put them on the head of the goat and send it away into the wilderness by the hand of a man who is in readiness. The goat shall bear all their

iniquities on itself to a remote area, and he shall let the goat go free in the wilderness. (Lev. 16:21–22)

Placing his hand on the scapegoat's head was a picture of Aaron transferring the sin of the people onto the sacrificial animal. It was the corruption component that was symbolically transferred, not the guilt of that sin. Another goat sacrificed at the same time (Lev. 16:15–20) carried the guilt-burden of the people's sin. The scapegoat, driven out into the wilderness, was symbolically removing the corruption of those sins, "losing" it in a place where it would never burden the people again.

This notion of the corruption of sin is also relevant in church discipline. One of the purposes of church discipline is to protect the other members of a congregation from the corruption of the offending member's sin. Like yeast in dough, sin has the potential to spiritually infect the other members, encouraging and enabling their own sin:

Your boasting is not good. Do you not know that a little leaven leavens the whole lump? Cleanse out the old leaven that you may be a new lump, as you really are unleavened. For Christ, our Passover lamb, has been sacrificed. (1 Cor. 5:6–7)

The corruption result of sin is so pervasive that there is nothing we can do to avoid it:

We have all become like one who is unclean, and all our righteous deeds are like a polluted garment. We all fade like a leaf, and our iniquities, like the wind, take us away. (Isa. 64:6)

The Hebrew word *visiting* explains how the sins of forefathers corrupt their descendants. The visiting in view is not some sort of social call, as if God were promising to drop in for milk and brownies. Instead, the word refers to a *covenantal visiting*: God visits on people the experience of the blessings or curses of his covenants to those in covenant with him, and their descendants. The Fourth Commandment (Exod. 20:5–6) illustrates the pattern of covenantal visiting succinctly:

You shall not bow down to them or serve [other gods], for I the LORD your God am a jealous God: [covenant curse] *visiting the iniquity of the fathers on the children to the third and the fourth generation of those who hate me,* [covenant blessing] *but* showing steadfast love *to thousands of those who love me and keep my commandments.*

It is quite simple: God gives to the descendants of those in covenant with him the corruption results of their forefathers' sins. If the culpability result of sin is personal (it only attaches to the sinning individual), then the corruption result of sin is *corporate* (it also attaches to those in covenant relationship with the sinning individual).

There are many more biblical details that show this corruption result is basic to the nature of sin. Further, this is nothing more than the historic understanding of the church: God curses the descendants to follow in the sinful footsteps of their forefathers, with the result that they sin in related ways.

This explains why Daniel, Ezra, and Nehemiah were resolute in confessing their forefathers' sins. Reading Ezekiel, they understood that they weren't culpable for those. Instead, understanding the sin's corruption factor, they knew that God's promise of forgiveness was attached to the corruption of those sins. So they confessed, and led their congregations to confess with them. Likewise, in the letters to the Seven Churches of Revelation, Jesus advises certain congregations to corporately repent of sins committed only by some of their members (e.g., Pergamum, Rev. 2:13–17; Thyatira, Rev. 2:18–29; Sardis, Rev. 3:1–6). While not personally culpable for the sins of the few, all the members of these congregations were corrupted by these sins. Corporate repentance, confessing the sins of others to whom they were covenantally related, was Jesus' Gospel-rooted solution.

In 2016, as we explored these things, our leaders were aware of some of the controversies around repenting for sins of forefathers. But as various social justice motivations played no part in our considerations, it was quite straight forward for us. We understood we could not repent *for* sins we did not commit. But could we repent *of* sins, sins committed by those covenantally related to us?

We were shepherding a congregation that seemed to be experiencing problems related to sins of forefathers. For us then, it was purely a matter of Gospel-practice. Did our forefathers commit atrocious racial sins? Yes. Was God visiting the corruption of these sins on subsequent generations, including the congregation under our care? Yes.

Was repenting of these sins—

- acknowledging the wickedness of those sins,
- acknowledging God's righteousness in visiting the corruption of those sins on us,
- trusting that in Jesus there is cleansing from the corruption of these, and
- so confessing the sins of our forefathers,

—the Gospel-rooted resolution before us?

We understand that this *corporate* usage of repentance is outside the common personal usage. We respect that others may come to differing conclusions. That's OK. We didn't apply this principle to make a statement, to persuade others to do likewise. Our sole purpose was to seek God to remove the burden of our forefathers' sins, and thereby bring glory to his holy name.

In the summer of 2016, following the tradition of our Presbyterian forefathers, the elders and I signed a solemn declaration of all these things, particularly identifying our forefathers' sins and our repentance of them. At the beginning of 2017, we entered into a formal period of renewal. We added to our historic name a second name that identifies us with our community: located on the grounds of a historic slave plantation, the name "The Church at Chantilly" declares that this church has been freed from the curse of sin, including all forms of racism. The congregation asked to follow their elders' lead and signed their names to the declaration of repentance. That document now hangs in the entry hallway of our church, right next to a picture of our former downtown buildings for all visitors to see.

In God's providence and through no intention of ours, the story of our repentance was publicized both locally and nationally. This long after the Civil Rights era, and after many other churches took a similar action decades ago, we were not concerned with publicizing our actions. Yet, God honored our efforts in restorative ways. Over the last few years, we have been contacted by numerous former members of our church, and even some of the descendants of former members, all of whom had taken a stand against historic First Church's racism and had been driven out of the congregation for doing so. The experience of asking them to forgive the sins of our forefathers has brought healing and, in some cases, a credible Gospel witness from a church that was previously nothing more to them than a source of hypocrisy.

While our current congregation is small, we are for the first time in over half a century (possibly longer) seeing new conversion growth. In the last year and a half we have seen a good half dozen millennials make a profession of faith and actively participate in the ministries of the church. Sustained weekly witnessing activities have been going on for over a year now. Two-thirds of the congregation have participated in evangelism training, now offered twice a year.

In 2016, we were blessed to partner with Korean brothers and sisters in Orlando, Florida, to plant Montgomery Open Kingdom (Korean, PCA) church. In the fall of 2018, we were blessed to begin hosting a Spanish-speaking (Baptist) congregation, Light to the Nations, reaching Spanish speakers in Montgomery hailing from numerous Central and South American countries. Today all three congregations share Historic First Church's facilities, with multiple worship services, joint children's Sunday School, and numerous joint activities throughout the year.

You might notice that I didn't mention anything about outreach to the Black community in Montgomery. While we maintain strong relationships with sister Black congregations in our area, this is a blessing God has not yet seen fit to grace us with. We prayerfully continue to reach out to the Black community around us, praying for God to raise up a family or two from which he would grace us with more elders and deacons.

Truth be told, we're small enough now (about 40 active, 50 + including shut-ins) that statistically speaking, there is every possibility that Historic First Presbyterian Church of Montgomery might close before she reaches her 200th anniversary. We're ok with that. Repenting of the sins of our forefathers was not some pragmatic church renewal step. It was simply the right thing to do. The corruption of sin is real. In a community filled with so many churches, and the next generation all but abandoning them, turning to God and pleading for his forgiveness from all sins (including those of the past) is nothing more than what Gospel-believing people ought to do. Because in God's providence, some who had lost hope, who had been helped by our forefathers' sins to disbelieve in Jesus Christ, have found a new hope in him through our repentance.

Let me end with one of the most interesting and unexpected examples of this. Vivian is an older Baby Boomer raised in Montgomery, with some background in the hippie movement. She was won to Christ and then spent some time as one of the early English language teacher missionaries in China. In 2016, sensing she only had a few more years in Montgomery before she would need to move to be near family members as health needs increased, she joined our church because she wanted to focus on reaching Millennials.

Like many church members raised in Montgomery, Vivian was a tad suspicious when her pastor and elders first began discussing repenting of the sins of our forefathers. "Social justice" concerns, etc., raised questions about the what and why. Yet as the biblical basis for the action was explained, Vivian began to see that repenting of the forefathers' sins was a godly action completely consistent with living by the faith taught through the Gospel's ministry. She willingly joined her fellow members in signing her name to the declaration of repentance.

At the beginning of the following year, Vivian got an odd query from her brother (living in a western state): did she know about any first cousins still living in Montgomery? The answer was no; Vivian was the only one left from her family in this area, all others having moved away years ago. When she asked why, her brother told her that a DNA test he had completed sent back results telling him that he had a first cousin, one he didn't know anything about, living in Montgomery. He gave Vivian the contact information and left it up to her to do the sleuthing.

Vivian contacted the first cousin, Mattie, and arranged to meet her. I was blessed to briefly meet Vivian's new-found family at one of those first meetings. Gathering at a hospital for a doctor's appointment one of them had, Vivian (White) sat with her new-found cousin Mattie (Black).

The story that unfolded was in one sense rather common here in the deep south. Yet because it was personal for Vivian and Mattie, their meeting was momentous for both of them. Mattie was the daughter of Lily (half-Black/White). Lily's father was Ray, Vivian's (White) grandfather (Poppee). An archetypal story, Lily's mother, Mattie the first, had been the maid in Ray's household. In case you haven't put things together yet, I'll put it in blunt terms: Vivian's White grandfather had raped her cousin's Black grandmother.

As a little girl Vivian remembered her Poppee taking long walks on Sunday afternoons, ostensibly to smoke down at the park, and not coming home till well after dark. Vivian now heard the real story. Her grandfather would walk two blocks down from his house, where his daughter by rape, Lily, would pick him up. He would then spend the afternoon with his Black family. They all resented him; yet, consistent with the times, he was their patriarch, and they had to show him some respect.

You can just imagine Vivian's shock as she learned this family history she had never heard before. She knew that her Poppee, like many southern White men from the first half of the twentieth century, showed common racist behaviors (e.g., Jim Crow era cultural attitudes and acts). But he had raped a Black woman, and had a whole other, Black, family?!

As you might surmise, I was fascinated by the new family history Vivian had to share. But then she revealed a fact that caused me to join her in being shocked to my core. While her Poppee was raping his Black maid, while he was keeping a second family with their daughter, Vivian's grandfather was a respected elder of, yep, First Presbyterian Church of Montgomery!

When we took the action of repenting of the sins of our forefathers, we did not envision the opportunity to express repentance to some of the families that had been hurt by those sins. Imagine our delight when Vivian's family's circumstances surfaced. Here a terrible wickedness, one attached to the name of Christ, perpetrated by a man who had been a shepherd in our church, had come to the fore only after we had taken the action of repenting of our forefathers' sins.

Imagine our delight later that year when Vivian's new-found Black family attended worship with us in the very congregation where their White rapist grandfather was formerly an elder. Imagine their joy as the pastor of that church asked that family to forgive the sins of their forefathers, particularly the rape of their matriarch. Imagine this Black family in Montgomery, Alabama, home of some of the best and worst from the Civil Rights era, receiving the amen-ing applause of the White congregation affirming their pastor's repentance of their forefathers' sins!

We don't expect this isolated act, which will most likely be lost in the shuffle of forgotten history in no more than a decade or two, will have any significant church-wide or cultural-wide impact. Again, our motivation is not pragmatic (for us or others), but declarative, for God's glory, alone. What he may or may not do with our repentance is solely up to him, and that makes our joy all the more complete. Call our actions macaroni art on God's refrigerator. We know he is pleased with our expression of love, and that is enough.

Yet if God does choose to use our repentance to bless our brothers and sisters, maybe what we've learned and experienced may offer an alternative to the unsatisfying paths before us in issues of racial reconciliation. The world demands of us a course to reconciliation that in the end is by man, for man, to man. It will not lead to the only reconciliation that matters, that which is rooted in God's reconciling us to himself through Jesus. Some among us fear this response is a "path to capitulation." Seeing no other alternative, their reaction is to erect a NO to worldly reconciliation so big (wide, high, and deep) that there is no room to take even a first sacrificial step toward biblical reconciliation. What we've learned has blessed us to recognize how the world's either/or paths have been broken in the broken body of our Savior on that cross.

Some discussion and investigation about this doctrine of repenting of the forefathers' sins is well and good. The congregation at the Church at Chantilly, Historic First Presbyterian Church of Montgomery, Alabama, is sufficiently satisfied that God has given this principle in his word to bless his people, that their repentance might show forth his glory, glory that removes the stain of the worst sins, and restores the Gospel's hope in Jesus Christ. In Jesus, the worst of burdens can be removed, including our forefathers' racism. With that, we're grateful to submit to his will and repent. He has removed the burden of our forefathers' sins, and his Gospel is going forth from us!

YOU GOTTA GO TO A CHURCH OR A LIBRARY!

GEOFF HENDERSON

Geoff Henderson serves as pastor of Harbor Community Church in Bradenton, Florida. He has been ordained in the Presbyterian Church in America since 2006, having served as an assistant pastor in Bradenton and Hurricane, West Virginia. He is a graduate of Furman University and has a Masters of Divinity from Reformed Theological Seminary.

———

Some people come to fairly obvious conclusions later in life. I consider myself among such folks. Several friends of mine, leaders at Harbor Community Church, have finally, but fortunately, come to an obvious but regrettable conclusion: we don't have any/many friends of color.

Now this doesn't mean we lack contacts or people with whom we talk at sporting events and fundraisers, or with whom we serve on nonprofit boards. I mean *real* friends we invite into our homes, or meet over coffee or beer with, spend time listening to, and enthusiastically ask questions of.

Friends. Actual friends.

In the movie *Coming to America*, Eddie Murphy's royal character receives a friendly rebuke regarding his pursuit of a queen, "You can't go to a bar to find a good girl. You gotta go to a church or a library."

Perhaps that is wise counsel today for someone in search of a spouse, but does such advice pertain to folks like me who desire diverse friendships? I can't speak as much for libraries. But as a pastor, I think I can speak for churches.

Sunday mornings often represent the most segregated time of the week. And I wish that were simply a media bias, or fake news, or even a coincidence. But after just a little digging, I've discovered this is a sad, intentional fact.

However, I've recently noticed a holy discontent among many pastor friends in the majority culture who honestly feel we've missed out. We've missed out on gifts. We've missed out on hearing new perspectives regarding politics, neighborhoods, and parenting. We've not heard enough disheartening experiences of prejudice, such as a local dentist deviously deciding my friend's tooth removal didn't warrant novocaine. We've also missed out on redemptive stories of forgiveness, hope, and peace.

While late to the party as usual, I can now honestly speak for many of us: "We want in." We don't want to miss out.

As I preached through the book of Acts in hopes of motivating our new church to live on mission, we began to notice a resistance to diversity. Even during the perceived golden age of the early church, God's people appear quite reluctant to appreciate his divine design for a diverse people.

While the Holy Spirit came at Pentecost with quite the tangible display of power, we tend to think he fast-tracked all areas of sanctification. They did become much bolder in their faith. Men who wimped out just chapters before demonstrated Tom Petty-esque "stand me up at the gates of Hell, and I won't back down"[1] courage. But for many other areas, we see much slower growth.

For instance, in regards to missionary work, you know that whole *"go therefore and make disciples"* (Matt. 28:19) stuff? Well, no one leaves Jerusalem until Acts chapter eight. In regards to racial reconciliation, it takes almost twice that many chapters for the Jewish Christians to finally recognize Jesus as the ultimate wrecking ball who destroyed *"the dividing wall of hostility,"* making one new entity out of the two (Eph. 2:14–15).

Fifteen chapters seems a bit long for God's new Spirit-filled people to catch on, doesn't it? Then again, doesn't this hesitation sound at least a little familiar when we look at certain periods in our Presbyterian history? Let's never overestimate our Spirit-quenching ability in any arena, and in any era.

Still, when I see this reluctance in Acts, I actually feel quite hopeful. The Holy Spirit has been there, changed that, and he can turn this ship around. Of course, the ship's turn has to begin with those leading.

During the Q-and-A time of our first informational church plant meeting someone hopefully posited, "Are we going to be a multiracial church?" I scoffed silently, but retorted honestly, "Well, look at us. Do you see racial diversity?"

Four years into this thing called a local church, and now armed with a rejuvenated desire for racial diversity, my new response resembles something like this: "Do you have non-White friends? Let's start there."

You see, I came to the sad realization that one of our two Black church attenders was my only *real* Black friend. Another leader came to the same conclusion entirely on his own. We didn't want it to stay this way.

Dissatisfied with our lack, I reconnected with a Black pastor friend named James with whom I hadn't talked since I first left our area seven years prior. More than a few chapters had passed since we had spoken, but due to a shared love of Jesus and his Church, we met at a local pizza place, and we immediately began to dream about how our churches might more fully display Christ's dazzling beauty.

But like big ships, churches turn slowly. Whether mature hundred-year-old African American churches, or smaller, "toddler" church plants like Harbor, this dream will require gumption and forbearance. And I had no guarantee we wouldn't face the same fate as the bigger ships like the Lusitania or the Titanic: torpedoed by labels of "liberal" from "conservatives" holding onto a truncated Gospel, or sunk by naïvely navigating the icebergs that lay ahead.

Yet God speaks loudly and clearly in his Word, so I needed to get out of the way. I knew I had to trust him to do his work. I didn't have to force a diversity narrative onto the message of redemption in Acts. It is already there. That's what we kept learning as we worked through the book of Acts in our Harbor church.

We witnessed evidence of racism in the unfair treatment of Greek widows in Acts 6. We laughed at how it took a bizarre vision for Peter to realize what Jesus had repeated over and over already:

And he said to them, "You yourselves know how unlawful it is for a Jew to
associate with or to visit anyone of another nation, but God has shown me that I

should not call any person common or unclean." (Acts 10:28)

So I simply watched God reveal his design and convict us in our resistance. The inertia, laziness, and apathy we tend to have in settling for mono-cultural churches exposed our failure "to claim the victory Jesus won," as U2's Bono reminds us in his spiritually rebellious anthem "Sunday, Bloody Sunday."

I preached the text to our congregation and the community, and I followed our denomination's example in repentance. I also confessed that our conservative forefathers kept Martin Luther King, Jr. from their seminaries. They steered him in a theologically liberal direction. One of our Black members shared that Sunday's confession on twitter and immediately heard back: "That's a church I'd like to check out."

To take a positive step forward, I committed to intentionally seek out and share with the congregation more Gospel-centered minority voices. We now use several articles from African Americans in our Elder and Deacon training. That's a small but simple step we needed to take.

Because we already had a fairly successful quarterly discussion with Harbor men and our friends at a local brewery, we used this venue to narrow our topical discussions around race and the Gospel. Eventually, one leader built up enough courage to lead a discussion on the subject of privilege. It went quite well when we framed it in terms of discerning how to love our neighbors.

Then as more and more folks caught the vision, we turned our annual men's retreat into a unified focus on diversity. I asked fellow PCA Black church planter Mike Aitcheson, who has a multiracial, multi-economic (frankly multi-everything) church, to hit us hard with specific barriers we might unwittingly hold up. We soon learned how much Sunday morning segregation had very little to do with geography and more to do with an intentional racially exclusive design. He even shared some blatantly racist skeletons in our closet. Almost immediately, in a way reminiscent of Peter's preaching in Acts, men cut to the heart raised their hands to ask, "What can we do? What can we change?" (see Acts 2:14–41).

The ship was turning.

In the end, we really didn't create any new programs. We worked within the already existing church structure and rhythm. With the momentum from our time at the pub and retreat, as well as with the excitement from within Pastor James' own congregation at St. Paul's

Missionary Baptist Church, we agreed it was time for "my people" to talk with "his people." This would only work if laity took ownership.

At the same pizza place where Pastor James and I rekindled our friendship, seven pastors, staff, and volunteers came together to dream how we might fellowship, serve, and worship together. We all agreed on the need for practical venues to give our people chances to develop long-lasting cross-racial friendships.

I asked several from St Paul's, "Do you have any good relationships with White folks like me?" They laughed, all admitting they had no choice, for even their children had married White folks like me!

This only reaffirmed what I had begun to learn. We in the majority White culture can often spend our entire lives without diverse friendships, while those in the minority have no choice. For the former, such intentional church partnerships might present one of the very few places we have to develop diverse friendships in suburbia.

By the end of our "business" lunch, our dreams had begun taking shape. Pastor James said to me, "Geoff, this is beautiful. Just look at everyone talking." One woman, an expert in her field, listened to one of our member's struggles, and she shared sensitive and helpful counsel.

Everyone was really *listening*. Our table had transformed into a tangible demonstration of God's grace that day. At the pizza place.

We left with an invitation to join St. Paul's annual fellowship picnic. What a great step forward in celebrating the unity we have in Christ! It could give both congregations a taste of what we miss on Sunday mornings. We'll move slowly, but we have considered pulpit swaps and sharing music teams.

Restless to see this partnership blossom, members have regularly requested these very events sooner rather than later. Without a doubt, this Spirit-wrought heavenly impatience from our members reminds me once again of Jesus' promise to pilot the ship.

Why share this story? Two reasons.

First, we can all become relationally "Seinfeldian" at times. We easily limit ourselves to three friends who look, act, and think like us.

We need more and different friends. That day over pizza I noticed something I wished I'd noticed a long time ago: I simply can't afford to only have friends who look like me. It hamstrings me as a pastor, a father, a husband, and a neighbor. And yes, as a friend. Our churches will only grow in diversity as our friendships grow in diversity.

I'm late to the party, but so glad I was invited!

Second, I'm a firm believer in telling stories because stories give us a picture of what could be. We are not too far into Harbor's journey, and I do not know how all our dreams will unfold. Will such efforts and others (learning new music styles, future staffing, etc.) lead to the diversity we desire? How much disappointment will we experience along the way?

We don't know. But because the Gospel frees us to fail, we can take the beautiful risk of dreaming without fearing the outcomes.

Due to the growing number in our circles who have taken this call seriously, I have many mentors and examples of how to navigate these waters. But my hope does not depend upon how well we do this, or in how well others model it for us. The Jerusalem Council in Acts 15 eventually came to the right conclusion. Multicultural ministry and churches flourished.

As loopy as God's people often seem, he doesn't give up on them. The Spirit ends up winning the battles with stuck-in-their-ways sinners. As a result, our hope is in the one who has written the story from Genesis to Revelation. It is a story which begins with one couple, but it ends in one incredibly diverse people.

For churches like ours which lack the depth of desired (though we see small gains) diversity, perhaps partnerships like these will one day serve as a catalyst for diverse growth within? Who knows? One day, maybe for my kids, or maybe for my grandkids, Eddie Murphy's counsel "You gotta go to a church" will be spot on in regard to developing cross-cultural relationships.

I have never felt so high, so encouraged, so hopeful by any church endeavor as I have that day of our pizza lunch. I wrote about in my normally scheduled piece for the Bradenton Herald. I honestly felt what Paul describes in Philippians 2: the encouragement, comfort, fellowship in Spirit. Check, check, check. But soon our schedules filled up, and James didn't return my calls as promptly as before.

I honestly wondered if we needed to find a new church with whom we could partner. But James eventually bridged the absence gap with an apologetic desire to move forward with our plan. Only this time, in the words of Bill Murray in *What About Bob*, we would take "baby steps."

James and I continued to meet, fellowship, and dream together once a month over lunch and always talked concretely about the next step. He and his assistant minister took that first step toward us by representing St Paul's at Harbor's organization service one Sunday evening at the YMCA. And they stayed long afterward for our celebration dinner. In January he came to preach for us the Sunday after MLK Day weekend. Our congregation loved it. Despite a few slight theological and style differences, James has continually reassured both congregations that we both essentially believe the same thing. I found out he preaches expositional sermons and always points everyone to Jesus in the end. Our slight differences only made us sense the unity we have in Christ that much more.

We had hoped to get our entire two churches together for a fellowship time in the Spring but had little time to accomplish anything before the Summer. Not only that, but my family director and I double-booked events on the same day. Knowing the numbers wouldn't quite end up what I had hoped, I simply aimed for getting Harbors leadership (elders/deacons and wives) and music team to fellowship with them one Sunday after their service. St Paul's would provide the food, and we just needed to show up. Even though they had a multi-congregation choir concert at 3 pm, James assured me food would bring enough folks in to make this worth our while. And they didn't disappoint!

As God's providence would have it, we appropriately gathered together with St Paul's immediately after celebrating Pentecost Sunday at Harbor. We had begun to take part of the same story we had read about in Acts. The giving of the Spirit empowered cross-cultural fellowship as it had so many years ago.

Our Harbor family arrived just in time to see one man dancing—as my curious nine-year-old had expected—and hear the preacher point us to Jesus. The fellowship time couldn't have gone any smoother, once some of the St. Paul's Missionary Baptist members told our introverts, "Ya'll gonna have to spread out!" It was beautiful. It reminded me of the day at the pizza place, only on a much larger scale. James invited me up and shared with his people our common beliefs, vision, and the plans for us to get together again. Next time we would have our full congregations. You could even hear an "amen" from the White folks. Not bad, even if ten–eleven months behind schedule.

---

1. https://www.youtube.com/watch?v=xzGNLCJ4_P0

DEAR LORD, PLEASE OPEN MY EYES TO SEE, MY HEART TO CARE, AND MY LIFE TO SERVE!

MARK L. DALBEY

Mark Dalbey has served at Covenant Seminary since 1999 and as president since 2012. He was ordained in the PCA in 1978 as chaplain and Bible instructor at Geneva College in Pennsylvania. He served PCA pastorates in Cincinnati, Ohio and Richmond, Indiana between 1984 and 1999. He holds a BA in philosophy and religion from Tarkio College, an MDiv from Pittsburgh Theological Seminary, and a DMin from Covenant Seminary. He and his wife, Beth, have been married since 1975 and have three grown, married children and eleven grandchildren.

––––––

When I was a child growing up in church, our congregation often sang the prayer hymn "Open My Eyes that I May See," by Clara H. Scott. The refrain includes the phrase, "Open my eyes, illumine me, Spirit divine!" More recently, Michael W. Smith wrote a prayer chorus called, "Open the Eyes of my Heart, Lord."

Both of these songs reflect Paul's prayer for the church (Eph. 1:18): for the eyes of our hearts to be enlightened. Like Paul in Damascus (Acts 9:18), I need the scales of my eyes removed because they keep me from seeing all God wants me to see. Like the blind man Jesus healed who initially could only see people as trees walking (Mark 8:24–25), I need a deeper healing to see people as image bearers of God.

209

The Lord has been showing me more of what it means to love God and love my neighbor. He has done this through his Word, his people, a fuller understanding of American history in general, and the history of the Church in particular.

My wife, Beth, and I are both the products of Presbyterian pastors' homes. My father was a Presbyterian pastor, and Beth's father, grandfather, uncle, two brothers, two cousins, husband, and father-in-law served or serve as Presbyterian pastors. You might say that pastoring Presbyterian churches is the family business. Overall, this has been a great blessing in our lives. Yet, when you add in the fact that these pastoral ministries have taken place in predominantly rural and suburban contexts, our perspective and experience has been somewhat limited by being mostly middle-class, well-educated, and White.

In 2016 Beth and I took the entire month of July off. This was the first time in over forty years of marriage we had taken that amount of consecutive time for vacation. The first half of the time we traveled to the Pacific Northwest, where I was born. The second half of the time we traveled to the Northeast, where Beth was born. During these trips, God opened our eyes to see things we had not seen previously or, if we had, it was only vaguely and in a dim light.

The Pacific Northwest portion of our trip began shortly after the 44th PCA General Assembly in Mobile, Alabama. That assembly adopted an overture on racial reconciliation that confessed our denominational sins of commission and omission related to the Civil Rights Movement of the 1960s. The assembly also formed a study committee to examine the roles of women in the life of the PCA. We left and drove west.

Our arrival in Portland, Oregon, included a stop at a famous donut shop that now sits in the midst of the city's homeless, LGBT, and drug populations. This was followed by conversations over three days with a pastor who had been a high school history teacher and an FBI agent prior to entering vocational ministry. I gained a new awareness of the 110,000 Japanese Americans placed in internment camps during World War II, as well as significant mistreatment of Chinese people connected to the Chinese Exclusion Act (1882–1943). This act imposed almost total restrictions on Chinese immigration and naturalization and denied Chinese Americans basic freedoms because of their ethnicity.

During this part of the trip, I was reading the book *The Boys in the Boat* by Daniel James Brown,[1] which is about the 1936 Munich

Olympics gold medal eight-man rowing team from the University of Washington. We stopped to visit the shell house and the café/museum honoring these men. These depression-era sons of loggers, shipyard workers, and farmers overcame prejudice from elite, privileged rowers in the US, and then they shocked Hitler and the Nazis in a manner akin to African American track and field star Jesse Owens, who won four gold medals at the same Olympics.

God was opening our eyes to see and value people made in his image, people who were often off our radar.

We drove east.

The Northeast portion of our trip started in western Pennsylvania. We visited Fresh Air Camp, where Beth worked one summer when she was in high school. It was a program that brought inner-city children to a camp in the open countryside. It reminded us of issues of privilege and poverty that remain significant to the present day.

We then stayed at a hotel across from the Warren State Hospital. In 1947 the hospital housed more than 2500 patients with mental disabilities. The institution is located near a state park where our families had gone camping over several decades. The only references we remembered hearing about that place were derogatory, comments that made fun of the types of people who lived there. I was struck with guilt, and I repented as I jogged through the beautiful grounds and prayed for the hospital residents and their families.

On our drive to the New York Finger Lakes, we passed through a Seneca Indian reservation and visited a museum there. Two elementary-age Seneca girls joined us, and gave us an impromptu tour. We stayed four nights at a bed and breakfast in Seneca Falls, New York, and took day trips from there. Seneca Falls was the birthplace of the women's suffrage movement at a convention held there in 1848. Seventy-two years later, women were finally allowed to vote in national elections. I was struck with what a difference it would have made in our history if the church had valued the voice and vote of women in a way that impacted our nation from its beginning.

In Rhode Island, we went on the Vanderbilt Cliff Walk and looked through the window of extreme wealth and privilege. This contrasted with the other experiences we'd had on our trip. Driving back to Pennsylvania, there was an accident on the George Washington Bridge in New York City, and we traveled one mile in three hours. As we waited, Beth read aloud three chapters of *Bury My Heart at Wounded Knee* by Dee Brown.[2] I wept as I listened to the repeated accounts of the injustice of broken treaties, forced relocation, and mass killings. When we arrived at the Pittsburgh airport to fly home, we saw an area honoring the Tuskegee Airman. We realized we had come full circle from the General Assembly overture to a reminder of how recent and current racial prejudice and separation have impacted our lives, our nation, and our church.

Reflecting on our journey, we began to name other groups of people who are on the edges of society and often not welcomed into our lives and ministries. These include unwanted, unborn children; born but mistreated children; people with physical handicaps; single people; elderly people; autistic people; divorced people; couples without children; lower-income people; immigrants and refugees; people trapped in human and sex trafficking; next-generation millennials; lay people without seminary training; and many others. The Lord was working in us to make us aware of people made in his image whom we often don't see or, if we do, we underestimate their dignity and value. We began to pray:

Dear Lord, please open my eyes to see, my heart to care, and my life to serve!

How do we make sense of marginalized and mistreated people in our lives, our churches, our nation, and our world? Psalm 146 is a passage of Scripture that has had a significant impact on my understanding of these things. Psalm 146 is one of the best expressions of the compassion and justice of God. It is found in the middle of a hallelujah song that celebrates God's power and eternal reign.

Psalm 146 is the first of five hallelujah songs that close out the psalter, the hymnbook of Israel. The context for these songs is the gathering together of God's people to worship and sing corporately. This psalm is meant to shape and form God's people toward a continual praise and an increasing embodiment of God's character and mission in our lives.

Verses three and four admonish us to, *"Put not your trust in princes, in a son of man, in whom there is no salvation. When his breath departs, he returns to the earth; on that very day his plans perish."* We are to put our trust in God and not in human rulers or governmental leaders. Every four years during our US presidential elections, Christians seem to disregard this admonition. We get caught up in the utopian campaign promises that will supposedly bring heaven to earth if a particular candidate is elected. Government is established as a servant of God for the common good (Rom. 13:4), but "princes die" (or are voted out) and God does not.

By contrast, verses five and six exhort us to lift our eyes much higher, to the only one in whom we can have confidence and complete trust to fully reconcile and restore all things one day (Ps. 146:5–6; Col. 1:20), even as we co-labor with him now in the first fruits of that certain promise. God as creator has power to rule and reign and accomplish his purposes. The one who determined the number of stars and names them also heals the brokenhearted and binds up their wounds (Ps. 147:3–4). Our covenant God keeps faith forever. He has both the power and the desire to execute justice and show compassion.

Psalm 146:7–9 describes what the Lord does. The string of phases is an amazing description of God's active hand on behalf of the displaced, needy, neglected, unwelcome, and often mistreated people. The Lord *"executes justice* for the oppressed," *"gives food* to the hungry," *"sets free* the prisoners," *"opens the eyes* of the blind," *"lifts up* those who are bowed down," *"loves* the righteous," *"watches over* the sojourner," and *"upholds* the widow and fatherless."

This is justice with provision. These verses are reflected in other portions of God's word that underscore his comprehensive gospel of grace and truth that are expressed in justice and mercy for hurting people (e.g., Isa. 61:1–2, Matt. 25:31–46, Luke 4:18–19). Our sovereign king is full of mercy and compassion toward marginalized people. As we sing these words we are to own this same heart for all kinds of people around us. We are called to live in a way that derives and draws from God this source of justice and compassion and expresses his heart, concern, and healing presence in the name of Jesus.

Dear Lord, Please Open My Eyes to See, My Heart to Care, and My Life to Serve!

In a presentation to the Gospel Coalition, Pastor Mika Edmondson pointed out that in its exposition of the Ten Commandments in question 135, the Westminster Larger Catechism lists positive requirements of the sixth commandment.[3] These relate to understanding, caring for, and preserving human life while resisting the unjust taking of the lives of others:

The duties required in the sixth commandment are all careful studies, and lawful endeavors, to preserve the life of ourselves and others by resisting all thoughts and purposes, subduing all passions, and avoiding all occasions, temptations, and practices, which tend to the unjust taking away of the life of any. [4]

I am especially impacted by the phrases "to preserve the life of ourselves *and others*" and "the unjust taking away of the life *of any*." The second great commandment Jesus gave is *"to love your neighbor as yourself"* (Mark 12:28–31), and leading into the parable of the Good Samaritan is the question, *"And who is my neighbor?"* (Luke 10:29).

While I conceptually understand the parable, I am convicted that my definition of neighbor is: mostly people like myself. My experience of life is one of a well-educated, middle-class, sixty-eight-year-old White, Anglo-Saxon, Protestant male raised in a Presbyterian pastor's home. Life in the United States for me has been full of blessing and privilege. This has not been true in US history for Native Americans, African Americans, Asian Americans, Eastern and Southern European Americans, Irish Americans, Jewish Americans, Catholic Americans, female Americans, and impoverished Americans. While there have been many wonderful improvements for many of those just named, the emotional scars and continuing mistreatment are significant. And they are my neighbors!

My narrow definition of neighbor has sadly been reinforced by a less than biblically comprehensive theological perspective. The Fundamentalist-Modernist controversy[5] of the early twentieth century combined a philosophy of escapist separation from this world with a deep suspicion of involvement in social justice issues that was seen as being aligned with liberal theology and a social gospel without Christ. Remnants of this outlook continue today in some expressions of the doctrine of the "spirituality of the church."[6]

The social gospel is indeed a false gospel, but the one true Gospel of Jesus Christ has significant and necessary social implications here and now deeply rooted in loving God and loving neighbor. The core of the true Gospel is indeed individuals who are saved by grace alone through faith alone in Christ alone. But that is not the full extent of what the Bible has to say about the Gospel of the kingdom. Jesus inaugurates that kingdom by proclaiming the prophetic words of Isaiah 61 have been fulfilled in himself, and they include *"...good news to the poor... liberty to the captives... sight to the blind... and set at liberty those who are oppressed"* (Luke 4:18–19).

Dear Lord, Please Open My Eyes to See, My Heart to Care, and My Life to Serve!

As we live and walk in newness of life as an expression of our union with Christ and the indwelling of the Holy Spirit, God will show us our blind spots when it comes to race, gender, nationality, educational level, class, etc. He will do this as an outworking of his pledge to conform us to the likeness of Christ. He will answer the prayer Jesus taught us to pray for God's kingdom to come and his will to be done on earth as it is in heaven. The ascended, reigning, and coming back King Jesus does this now in and through his people as the comprehensive Gospel of the Kingdom goes to the nations, the generations, and into all of life.

Loving God means loving all our neighbors. It means speaking for those who cannot speak for themselves. It means giving a cup of cold water to thirsty people in the name of Jesus. It means telling the good news that salvation, forgiveness, healing, and newness of life are found in Christ. It means showing genuine hospitality and tangible love to fellow members of the human race made in God's image. As we increasingly conform to Christ-likeness, this will happen more and more in all who truly belong to Christ. He does this work in connection with and as an outworking of our faith and trust and union with him.

In the summer of 1972, I had the privilege of being on a summer-long Christian Leadership Study Tour that went around the world meeting missionaries and Christian leaders in more than twenty nations. Before we left for the trip, one of the books we were required to read was *Let My Heart Be Broken*. The recurring phrase in the book was, "Let my heart be broken with the things that break the heart of God."[7]

As I discuss issues of racial reconciliation and compassion and justice for displaced, marginalized, and deeply wounded people, I find myself weeping as I speak. I used to apologize for my tears, but now I don't. God has been showing me more and more what these tears mean. They are tears of sadness and repentance for the fact that things are not the way they should be, including in the church, and how I have been part of a church that has contributed to things not being the way they should be. Yet these tears of sadness and repentance are combined with tears of joy and delight in what God is doing to make things increasingly the way they should be, and for the privilege of participating in that healing and restorative work with him. God has been increasingly breaking my heart as an expression of his heart.

Dear Lord, please open my eyes to see, my heart to care, and my life to serve!

---

1. Daniel James Brown, The Boys in the Boat (New York: Penguin Books, 2013).
2. Dee Brown, Bury My Heart at Wounded Knee (New York: Henry Holt and Company, 1970).
3. Mika Edmondson, "Is Black Lives Matter the New Civil Rights Movement?" The Gospel Coalition, June 24, 2016, https://www.thegospelcoalition.org/article/is-black-lives-matter-the-new-civil-rights-movement
4. Westminster Larger Catechism, Question 135.
5. The Fundamentalist–Modernist controversy is a major schism that originated in the 1920s and '30s within the Presbyterian Church in the United States of America. Wikipedia, s.v. "Fundamentalist–Modernist controversy," https://en.wikipedia.org/wiki/Fundamentalist–Modernist_controversy
6. "The doctrine has to do with the question of the province of the church and the nature and limits of its power, specifically, the contention that, since the church is a spiritual institution, a kingdom "not of this world," its concern and focus should be spiritual and not civil or political." Alan. D. Strange, "The Doctrine of the Spirituality of the Church in the Theology of Charles Hodge," Mid-America Journal of Theology 25 (2014): 101.
7. Richard Gehman, Let My Heart Be Broken (New York: McGraw-Hill, 1960).

THE HURT LOCKER
DEFUSING THE WHITE PRIVILEGE MINEFIELD

LINDSAY BROOKS

Lindsay Brooks has been an elder at Soaring Oaks Presbyterian Church (PCA) in Elk Grove, California, a multicultural congregation. He is a staff apologist and former radio co-host for Apologetics.com, an Evangelical educational organization that seeks to challenge believers to think and thinkers to believe. He is founder and co-host of That Political Theology Show, *an apologetics and public theology video series. He is co-author of the book* Think and Live *and has published articles in the* Journal for Trinitarian Studies *and Apologetics. He is married to Jamiella and has four children.*

———

[This essay is adapted from a chapter in a forthcoming book co-authored with Jamiella N. Brooks.]

———

The 2008 film *The Hurt Locker* follows the heroic acts of an Army bomb squad during the Iraq War. I was struck with the inventiveness of the bombers in rigging and concealing the explosive devices and with the heroism and recklessness of the characters. It occurred to me that we need all that heroism and far less recklessness.[1]

I thought about this when I ran across a video of a protester hurling the phrase "White privilege" around like an accusation.

Famous conservative commentators and churchmen took the protest event to be a real representation of the term. People who talk about White privilege from an anti-racist perspective, and those within the church who talk about it from a racial reconciliation standpoint, were all painted with the same brush, even though none of us define White privilege in that way.

An example of the response offered from within the Church is a document signed by churchmen and academics entitled "Critical Theory and the Unity of the Church." I know and respect some of these people who say, in part:

The notion of "White privilege" is artificial in that many non-Caucasians are similarly "advantaged," while poor Whites often experience problems and disadvantages similar to those experienced by impoverished people of color. While such thinking provides incentives for political activism and a "stick to beat people with," it does little to further careful analysis, productive theological reflection, and mutual understanding.[2]

This petition concerns what it styles as uncritical borrowing on the part of some in the conservative Reformed community of "categories drawn from the 'critical theory' of secular academia."[3]Multiple examples show the great need for skilled communication about the terms surrounding the sociology of racism, like the over-reliance on critiques by Ben Shapiro, Jordan Peterson, or others. But perhaps one more might help. It comes from Anglican churchman Sam Murrell:

> In contemporary parlance, the word "privilege" is employed by the offended group as a weapon against the other. Once someone is labeled as "privileged," he is supposed to realize his rightful place in the "race" conversation is as the silent observer whose liberty to speak has been revoked. The accused and the accuser are no longer equals.[4]

These responses represent the concerns of many of our brothers and sisters. I frame these concerns by calling them landmines, not to malign those who have them, but rather to heighten the care of our approach, and to help us understand that there is work to be done.

Like the soldiers in *The Hurt Locker*, we need to disarm those mines and bring all things under Christ. With such a task, we cannot risk a maverick's mentality. Only a steady hand and great care will protect those who could be harmed by the explosiveness of the matter.

I will begin by clarifying the term itself. I will work with some common objections, and then I'll give an analogy of what I believe to be a biblical approach to White privilege. In the end, I will apply that understanding to certain select objections of special significance.

What Is This Thing That Triggers Such Anxiety?

Privilege

White privilege is, as the name implies, privilege attached to "Whiteness." The privilege side of the term is fairly well understood by most of us. Dictionary.com gives a good definition: "A right, immunity, or benefit enjoyed only by a person beyond the advantages of most: the privileges of the very rich."[5]

Note that privilege can attach to any number of things, and there are several ways to talk about it. I might be privileged in my education, in my ability to speak, or in my Christianity within the social network of Christians. Others might be privileged economically. Privilege is part of life, and it can occur naturally.

Privilege can also occur deliberately and on both micro- and macro-scales. On the micro-side of the scale, a club membership is an artificial structure that is specifically exclusive. It is wholly about privilege. As the old credit card advertisement says, "Membership has its privileges."

On the macro-side, citizenship is a structure formed by people, one that accrues benefits to citizens and denies them to non-citizens. Some of those benefits are obvious: things like voting or running for office. Other more subtle aspects of privilege might include certain psychological conditions, not worrying about belonging to a community, not being concerned about being rounded up by ICE (Immigration and Customs Enforcement) agents, or not thinking getting sick might result in deportation if you go to a hospital.

A person's privilege is a complex mix of natural and artificial, micro and macro, obvious and subtle. This complexity should not preclude us from talking about what privilege might attach to separately, as well as in their situated complexity. The citizenship fears of a well-to-do, English-speaking, educated person might be different from those of a poor, non-English speaking person with a sixth-grade education. We could talk about the various components and factors of these privileges.

To understand how privilege attaches to Whiteness, we should have a grasp of what Whiteness is, how it came about, and what it means today.

In August 2017, I conducted an informal survey of my Facebook friends who are of European descent. I asked:

- When did you start thinking of yourself as White instead of your national heritage?
- Is it important to be proud of Whiteness or do you still celebrate your national heritage instead?
- How often are you aware of being White and not your specific nationality?
- Did your great-grandparents think of themselves as White?

After surveying for three days, seventy people responded, and what they said was helpful in grasping what "White" means to everyday people. I'm also considering how historians and sociologists view the term.

The vast majority of respondents didn't think of themselves as White, and they don't usually unless they are filling out a government form. It comes up if race is brought up in the news. A corresponding majority also understood White to refer primarily to the color of their skin, which is reductively a necessary but not sufficient condition for Whiteness. No one thought Whiteness was something to be proud about. No matter how mixed in the American experiment, this was true even in those cases where Irish heritage or other European heritage was a matter of pride and identity.

Very few of my respondents understood Whiteness as any sort of concept that was constructed in history or having the features of a social imaginary,[6] the contours defined by laws in the service of specific interests at the time of its ascension to prominence in American thinking.

It might initially be useful to approach thinking about what it means to be White apophatically—to start with what it is not. White is not a nationality. No one is born White. White is not a race. It's not even a skin color. No one is from Whitopia. There is no language of Whitish. And no people are organically tied together by a so-called "White culture." Certainly skin tone has something to do with it, but it is a necessary-but-not-sufficient quality. James Baldwin said it well: "No one was white before he/she came to America. It took generations, and a vast amount of coercion, before this became a white country."[7]

David Roediger's book *Working Toward Whiteness* tracks the assimilation process for those European immigrants who came to the US in the early twentieth century. He quotes Henry James, author of The American Scene: "The Italians, who, over the whole land, strike us, I am afraid, as, after the Negro and the Chinaman, the human value most easily produced."[8] Yet since that 1907 work the great grandchildren of Italian immigrants have been fully accepted in the established flow of Whiteness. They were allowed to fully participate in America and its project to increase wealth and prosperity (The New Deal, GI Bill, and the FHA), but Roediger points out that the effort was great and the cost was high.

Historically then, Whiteness has been a moving target. Some people didn't initially get full access to what America had to offer, but they were able to make it work. Italians, Jews, Slavs, and Poles all had to assimilate to claim the full promise of our fair country. Whiteness, seen in this way, is not completely separable from the privilege it represents.

But because White as a racial construct is not rooted in biology, place, language, or culture, anyone can participate in it to some degree. A Black man is able to garner advantage if he talks and dresses a certain way which is often attached to Whiteness. And while his phenotypic expression doesn't get him all the way to White status, he can perpetuate Whiteness with his politics, and choices. Whiteness is in part a scheme of and reward system for homogeneity.

Our understanding of White then is that it is a social construct brought about in order to further specific interests, encouraged by law, supported by propaganda, and hardened into custom. It is not natural, and it cannot be reduced to characteristics transmitted genetically.

Even though the history of Whiteness is enlightening, space prohibits going into the details of the cases of John Punch, Elizabeth Key, Bacon's Rebellion, runaway slave laws, formation of the slave patrol, the shift to maternal parentage for Negroes, and the entire complex of the creation of the social imaginary of White identity— most pertinent to us, the role of the church and Christians in it. I will simply refer the interested reader to the books by Joel McDurmon, Nell Irvin Painter, Ibram Kendi, Anthony Parent, and Sean Lucas.[9]

Being a Beneficiary of Privilege Isn't a Moral Evil

Before moving to how Christians might think of the moral demands of the Bible's prescriptions for us connected with White privilege, it is important to defuse an important mine. Because of the type of presentation that can happen in the context of chanting protestors or twitter wars, our brothers and sisters have learned to associate White privilege with a personal moral rebuke. "Check your privilege," is a commonly misunderstood tactic in dialog. It's often used to end a conversation rather than begin it. As a consequence, many with whom we might engage on the topic have become allergic to the term.

I don't think I can state it any more clearly than this quote from the *Huffington Post*. It has the virtue of being stated by an author from the political left and in a left-leaning publication, so it accounts for the conservative concerns of Evans, the signatories of his petition, "Critical Theory and the Unity of the Church" and Murrell's article:

> Some people take white privilege as a moral accusation against them personally. The existence of white privilege doesn't make any one of us a bad person. No single one of us invented it and we were all born into a world in which it already existed. In a way, it even co-opts us whites. The existence of white privilege does not reflect on the morality of any one of us. Our individual responses to white privilege, however, do.[10]

Especially in the Church, we should avoid taking umbrage when the topic of White privilege arises, which it will since it is sewn into the fabric of our nation.

Murrell's article, quoted above, offers a prescription: "The Church of Jesus Christ should stop attempting to address the mythical issue of so-called 'race.'"[11] Setting aside the strange idea that the peace and unity of the Church somehow depends on not addressing the spiritual needs of the world we are to transform with Law and Gospel or of the body of Christ in its situated-ness, Murrell seems to believe that because race is a social construct, it isn't real.

For a compelling example of the reality of social constructs, think of the social imaginary of what it means to be American. It's real, it has a body of documents and laws, and it consists of systems, which are little more than ideas we simply agree on. It's constructed. It was invented by the same modernist thinkers like Gouverneur Morris who penned the words "We the People," an idea that wasn't shared by all of the "We," then or now. That concept had never been seen before in the history of the world.

As a second example, think of the value of our currency. It is worth what we collectively think it's worth. It may not be backed by gold held at Fort Knox anymore but by a construct called a "government-sponsored security." It still spends just fine.

So it is with race in general, especially of Whiteness. It doesn't depend upon anything concrete like heritage but was formed specifically against other constructs. It has the value everyone thinks it does; it is part of our government, media, history, and custom. Failing to talk about it surrenders the field to the evil one. We cannot let our allergy to the term because of its abuse turn us from dealing with the thing the term signifies: the edification of the saints and the instruction of the nations.

Part of the remedy must be in the definition of terms so we might communicate with one another, which is the focus of this chapter. But also, we need a view of what we are supposed to do here and now with the reality of the thing called White privilege.

As a segue, and to show how this question has been answered in recent years, I offer the conclusion to an article by Jarvis J. Williams, from 2014:

> An appropriate gospel-centered response to the category of white privilege from those who are privileged is neither to deny the existence of white privilege nor to feel guilty because of privilege. Instead, privileged Christians (regardless of their race) should praise God for their privilege, and think prayerfully and carefully about how they can use their privilege in a God-honoring, Christ-exalting, and Spirit-filled way to advance God's kingdom on earth and to make those less privileged happy in Jesus since Jesus used his divine and spiritual privilege to help those who were spiritually disadvantaged. (2 Cor. 8:9) [12]

There is a risk in the forthcoming analogy because another landmine we must defuse is the reduction of White privilege to economic privilege. While economic privilege is certainly an ingredient in the stew, it is not the whole story. It may even be absent from a lot of the discussion of privilege. Nonetheless there is something to be learned about how to apply a Christian view of privilege to Whiteness because we already know how to apply it to economic privilege.

In his first State of the Union address, President Donald J. Trump said, "There has never been a better time to start living the American Dream."[13] That might have sounded strange to young people in places like Eastern Kentucky (with a 25.4 percent poverty rate) or Los Angeles (where nearly four out of ten people live at or near the poverty line). It requires optimism to think if you participate in our nation's structures according to the values inculcated in you (intelligence, hard work, grit, honesty, invention, community mindedness, etc.), you will succeed, be better off than your parents, and leave a running start for your children.

For many however, the optimism was ready and available. The Dow went from just over 20,000 in January 2017 to 24,000 by the end of November of that same year. People with vision and means were setting Bitcoin ablaze with gains of over 1,700 percent. Apple stock was over $900 billion. Housing values were up nationwide about 6.5 percent.

Why were some positioned to take advantage of these market facts and others were left with their nose pressed against the glass, watching the good times roll from outside of the party? It's complex. It involves things like education, intergenerational planning, secure housing, children, etc. It's not just one thing; it's a lot of things.

But Christians understand that when God grants economic privilege to some, there is a corresponding duty. Put briefly, and without a deep *tota scriptura* exegesis: *"Everyone to whom much was given, of him much will be required, and from him to whom they entrusted much, they will demand the more"* (Luke 12:48b).

This passage speaks of a servant's duties while awaiting the return of the master. The picture of the disciple's life is not for his or her self, but as one who is set over the possessions of another (Luke 12:42). It is the guiding principle for the way a Christian looks at all he or she has received from God's benevolence. And what does the master expect? Being a faithful and wise manager of what you are given charge over. This is a moral demand that is contrasted with the abuse of other servants and the use of resources for one's own indulgence. So we see a picture of a manager using the household resources for the good of the household and the other servants. It is not self-indulgence. This stewardship hopes for the pleasure of the master and the possibility of a charge over much more.

In context this is an explanation of a Christian attitude toward material possessions. This comes after Jesus instructs us to be anxious for nothing. He teaches that we should learn from the birds of the air and the lilies of the field that our Father provides our needs. Then he says:

> Fear not, little flock, for it is your Father's good pleasure to give you the kingdom. Sell your possessions, and give to the needy. Provide yourselves with moneybags that do not grow old, with a treasure in the heavens that does not fail, where no thief approaches and no moth destroys. (Luke 12:32–33)

We are left with no doubt regarding the weight of this instruction. It is a duty for us, a command, and not just something that might be nice if we're so inclined. Jesus tells us that the consequences are terrible for not putting his servant's needs ahead of our own use of the resources he provided: *"The master of that servant will come on a day when he does not expect him and at an hour he does not know, and will cut him in pieces and put him with the unfaithful"* (Luke 12:46). Lest we read that and skip over it to the lesser punishments, Jesus next proclaims on those servants who collude with the manager. The NET (New English Translation) Bible note on this explains:

> The verb διχοτομέω (dichotomeō) means to cut an object into two parts. This is an extremely severe punishment compared to the other two later punishments. To translate it simply as 'punish' is too mild. If taken literally this servant is dismembered, although it is possible to view the stated punishment as hyperbole.[14]

In the eyes of the world, Christians are weird. We understand mercy as a duty, and we understand love as a command. We do love and mercy even in the absence of feeling like it because we understand that the Holy Spirit is transforming us and our feelings in the process of sanctification. We do love and mercy because we know what Jesus demands of us, and we want to be like him. Our duty with regard to our wealth and possessions is to show ourselves wise managers. That is analogous to all the ways we are advantaged over others in the household of Christ. How the world might be expected to behave outside the Church is a different question. But here in the Lord's house, what advantage is given to us is given, not for us, but for the good of the household.

Common Objections

There are several mines in this field, including the adoption of bad usage of the term White privilege as definitive, the reduction of White to skin color, the denial of the reality of socially constructed things, and the reduction of White privilege to economic privilege. Now I would like to point out a few more mines that come from real interactions and from the media. It is my hope that I might help think of ways we could respond in our own personal exchanges. With skill and care we might mend the rip in the fabric of the Church caused by the diabolical invention of race, especially Whiteness.

Majority Privilege

Canadian psychologist Jordan Peterson has a presentation against White privilege, a concept he numbers among things he claims as Frankfurt School neo-Marxist infiltrations into the popular imagination. He says White privilege is just "majority privilege."[15]

There certainly is such a thing as majority privilege. The question is whether that privilege is the product of justice, or injustice.

When Frederick Douglass was born, he was a slave. When his owner Edward Lloyd was born, he was a free man. That was definitely "majority privilege." But there's more to it than merely the condition that accompanies population disparity. The whole structure of society and law that supported the difference in the condition of the two men became racialized in the early 1600s. Something called "White" set itself against Mr. Douglass in a way that Lloyd's Englishness did not —nor did Mr. Lloyd's membership in the majority demographic. Since the difference in the two men was racialized, all the laws that supported it and the social structures of custom that reinforced it, weren't about English and African anymore. They were about Whiteness.

However, even if one holds the opinion that majority privilege and White privilege are reducible to one another, it in no way addresses the justice question. For a present day example to counter the reduction to majority privilege, we wouldn't simply say the Yazidi suffering at the hands of Saddam Hussein, and later ISIL in Iraq, is not racialized privilege on the part of Arabs but merely majority privilege. The minority that made up 650,000 of Iraq's 37 million people were systematically massacred, enslaved, and forced into exile.

I understand this example is hyperbolic and crosses the line from mere privilege to out-and-out persecution. It is intended to help us ask how privilege attaches to majority status that doesn't amount to sin. Can we simply police a population more heavily? Can we impose harsher punishments at law? Can we enforce the *de jure* condition under which wealth building is diminished? Are we allowed to reject job applicants based on the name on the resume?

It is difficult to see how the mere fact of being in the population majority is the only reason to create the disparities in privilege we are trying to account for.

It's All a Commie Plot?

In a blog article on the victimization narrative, Joel McDurmon, author of *The Problem of Slavery in Christian America*, quipped:

> I have been confronted multiple times now with the narrative that liberals only use the race issue to gain leverage over Christian America —a watered-down version of the old hard-racist complaint. All of Christian civilization is apparently a victim of George Soros, the Frankfurt School, and "Cultural Marxism."[16]

We see this concern in the "Critical Theory and the Unity of the Church" document ("notions of 'White privilege,' 'White guilt,' 'intersectionality,' and more broadly the power-analysis tradition that stems from Marx, Foucault, and others"), in Murrell's "Why I No Longer Participate in Racial Reconciliation Services" ("The Church cannot continue to trail along behind the world attempting to sprinkle 'holy water' on the latest iteration of Marxism and call it 'social justice.'"), in Jordan Peterson's speeches ("There's an infinite number of dimensions along which people vary, and so then the post-modern question is why would you privilege some of those dimensions over the other, and I would say, well, it sustains your bloody Marxist interpretation, that's why."), and in Ben Shapiro's take on history ("The Frankfurt School decided to change the culture... instead of using class which is difficult... what they would use as a proxy is racial groups, they would use racial groups to tear down the United States...").[17]

This preoccupation with Marxism as a live threat to the Church and to the United States is not new. It has a rather storied past. From the accusations of Martin Luther KingJr., a communist to the hidden reason why political correctness is destroying our freedoms, Cultural Marxism is there behind the scenes. But the term "Cultural Marxism" is a slur against a group of people who were thought to be lapsed Marxists, that is, thinkers who no longer hold to the ideals of Marxism and are Marxist in culture only. It was used this way of the Frankfurt School. We use the term "cultural Christianity" in a parallel way; it's not real committed belief in the Gospel, it's only cultural.

But what about this Frankfurt School? What is its part in the idea of White privilege? Surely the idea of privilege comes from within Critical Theory, which is a Frankfurt School construction, and they were Marxists, right? Well, sort of. The critique of the Frankfurt School as being merely cultural Marxism stems from its critique of Marxist theory as incomplete. So Marx's ideas of historicism, materialism, and class struggle are viewed as wrong.

None of that makes the Frankfurt School the friend of Christianity, but it does give us reason to question why the specter of Marx is summoned to frighten us away from thinking about how we got where we are. Indeed, it seems the Frankfurt School has not had the kind of impact that would suggest it is an engine for shaping culture. Gary North writes about its lack of power to affect culture this way:

> My argument is this: what went on in a handful of Protestant theological seminaries north of the Mason-Dixon line, beginning in 1875, had more to do with the counterculture than either the Model T or the Frankfurt school. This pushes the issue of culture back to where it belongs, namely, theology, which is why I began this discussion with the issue of theology. What people believe about the doctrine of hell has more to do with their behavior than what they believe about the relationship between the mode of production and proletarian revolution.[18]

While the dialectical method of Critical Theory is rooted in Hegel and Freud as a corrective to the flaws in Marx, we are not obliged, therefore, to commit the genetic fallacy that anything that occurs to thinkers in that lineage is therefore bent on the destruction of the Church. But here's the concern stated by Evans: "[The] unity of the Church must not be subverted by dubious and irremediably divisive secular theories."[19]

Evans believes the Church, against which the gates of hell will not prevail, can be subverted. But not by any direct attempt to divide. By an alleged importation of Marxist ideas via "uncritical borrowing" of the term "White privilege," so laden with hidden Marxism that "are powerful centrifugal forces that have the potential to tear not only society but also the church apart." That's how powerful the fear of the Frankfurt School is in the imaginations of our brothers.

But Christians working in this field are perfectly able to do history from within a Christian worldview. We are able to read philosophy and tell the difference between what accords with biblical ethics, and what doesn't. Moreover, the ghost of Marxism seems to disappear whenever the lights are turned on. It's not the destitute Marxism or the impotent Frankfurt School philosophy that divides the Church now or ever has. It's the White supremacy that churchmen knowingly colluded with, and its abiding effects. White supremacy didn't simply disappear in 1964 when Black folk finally became full citizens, or in 1968 when the alleged communist rabble-rouser Martin Luther KingJr., finally silenced forever from his race-baiting ways, or when the Fair Housing Act of that same year finally started the process of undoing segregation and its devastating impact.

We didn't wake up in the '70s and '80s to desegregated churches, neighborhoods, and changed hearts. Why not? Because issues that had previously been bolstered by the law had congealed into ghettos and suburbs. The wealth grown by socialist programs were on one side of the fence, while the other side of the fence stayed where it was —in neighborhoods, in schools, and in businesses.

It is churchmen, the erstwhile partners of White supremacy, who will be best equipped to face these very real matters of privilege in our household. So we can't afford to be frightened out of wisdom in our condition by the specter of failed ideologies.

Some Final Thoughts Regarding My Own Theological Commitments

I am a full believer in the doctrine of total depravity. Every part of the human person is disordered to some degree. Not every evil is as bad as it can be in every person, but there is no part of the human person free of corruption. Those of us in Christ mortify sin daily.

But what does that mean in a racialized world? Everyone is corrupted by racist ideas, and the smartest of us have invented the cleverest, most diabolical ways to serve self-interest.

People always get nervous when I say that, but let's make an analogy to disordered sexuality. In a hyper-sexualized society where the strong prevailing wind is toward the constant objectification of the human person, who is free of its influence? Not everyone is a serial rapist, some of us just dabble in porn, or don't mind watching women raped and prostituted on subscription TV. Many of us engaged in premarital sex. Many women have had abortions. Many people mutilate their bodies to sterilize themselves. Disease is rampant, even the killing kind. And the man who brought the phrase "Just grab 'em by the..." into the national lexicon now presides over us. It's everywhere.

So why is everyone surprised that the besetting sin of our entire American institution, the one that resulted in our bloodiest war, the one that Martin Luther KingJr., killed for, the sin that started the Drug War, and I could go on and on—only this sin is nearly eradicated in our America?

I said that Christians mortify sin daily, and the Bible gives us the impression that it is an ongoing process that requires perseverance and repentance after failure to stand and try again. I encourage us all with the closing of Paul's letter to the Galatians. After exhorting us, among other things, to *"Bear one another's burdens, and so fulfill the law of Christ,"* (Gal. 6:2) we are given encouragement in the long road to come. If the healing of racial strife is of the nature I've portrayed here in this chapter, then we need this message now, as much as any generation has needed it:

> *Let us not grow weary of doing good, for in due season we will reap, if we do not give up. So then, as we have opportunity, let us do good to everyone, and especially to those who are of the household of faith.* (Gal. 6:9–10)

1. Notably, the real bomb squad guys took offense at the representation of their mission and temperament in that movie. There was even a lawsuit, where a soldier who was part of the embedded research for the movie thought, in part, that he was misrepresented and maligned by being portrayed as a maverick.

2. William B. Evans, "Critical Theory and the Unity of the Church," https://theecclesialcalvinist.wordpress.com/2017/08/31/critical-theory-and-the-unity-of-the-church/.

3. William B. Evans, "Critical Theory and the Unity of the Church," https://theecclesialcalvinist.wordpress.com/2017/08/31/critical-theory-and-the-unity-of-the-church/

4. Sam Murrell, "Why I No Longer Participate in Racial Reconciliation Services," Kuyperian Commentary, Jan. 2018, http://kuyperian.com/no-longer-participate-racial-reconciliation-services/.

5. "privilege," *Random House Unabridged Dictionary*, Random House, 2018. *Dictionary.com*, http://www.dictionary.com/browse/privilege

6. I'm using the term here in a way similar to Charles Taylor's adaptation of Anderson's *Imagined Communities*. Taylor uses the example of "We, The People" in the Constitution of the USA: "The United States is a case in point. The reigning notions of legitimacy in Britain and America, the ones which fired the English Civil War, for instance, as well as the beginnings of the Colonies' rebellion, were basically backward-looking. They turned around the idea of an "ancient constitution," an order based on law holding "since time out of mind," in which Parliament had its rightful place beside the King. This was typical of one of the most widespread pre-modern understandings of order, which referred back to a "time of origins" (Eliade's phrase), which was not in ordinary time. "This older idea emerges from the American Revolution transformed into a full-fledged foundation in popular sovereignty, whereby the US constitution is put in the mouth of 'We, the people.' This was preceded by an appeal to the idealized order of Natural Law, in the invocation of 'truths held self-evident' in the Declaration of Independence. The transition was easier, because what was understood as the traditional law gave an important place to elected assemblies and their consent to taxation. All that was needed was to shift the balance in these so as to make elections the only source of legitimate power." Charles Taylor, "On Social Imaginary," Contemporary Sociological Theory (2001), 1–63, http://blog.lib.umn.edu/swiss/archive/Taylor.pdf. My own understanding of how Whiteness takes on the character of a social imaginary follows similar lines, where vague traditional ideas become clear in the enactment of law.

7. James Baldwin, "On Being White... and Other Lies," Essence, 1–3.

8. David Roediger, *Working Toward Whiteness* (New York: Basic Books, 2005).

9. Joel McDurmon, *The Problem of Slavery in Christian America: An Ethical-Judicial History of American Slavery and Racism* (Braselton, GA:: Devoted Books, 2017); Nell Irvin Painter, *The History of White People* (New York: W. W. Norton & Company, 2010); Ibram Kendi, *Stamped from the Beginning: The Definitive History of Racist Ideas in America* (New York: Nation Books, 2016); Anthony Parent, *Foul Means: The Formation of a Slave Society in Virginia, 1660-1740* (Chapel Hill: University of North Carolina Press, 2003); and Sean Lucas, *For a Continuing Church: The Roots of the Presbyterian Church in America* (Philipsburg, NJ: P&R Publishing, 2015).

10. Peter DiCaprio, "Why Some White People Don't See White Privilege," 2017, https://www.huffingtonpost.com/entry/white-prevalence-why-we-whites-dont-see-white-privilege_us_5970cb92e4b04dcf308d2aa1.

11. Sam Murrell, "Why I No Longer Participate in Racial Reconciliation Services," *Kuyperian Commentary*, Jan. 2018, http://kuyperian.com/no-longer-participate-racial-reconciliation-services/.

12. Jarvis J. Williams, "No Title," The Witness: A Black Christian Collective, 2014, https://thewitnessbcc.com/blind-white-privilege-blinded-white-privilege-response-bill-oreilly/.

13. "Trump's State of the Union: 'Never been a better time to start living the American Dream,'" January 30, 2018, www.NBCnews.com,

14. LLC Greek-English Lexicon of the New Testament Based on Semantic Domains. New York, NY: United Bible Societies.

15. Jordan Peterson, "Identity Politics and the Marxist Lie of White Privilege," University of British Columbia Free Speech Club, 2017, https://youtu.be/PfH8IG7Awk0. Dr. Peterson's presentation on White privilege begins at about 1:45:00.

16. Joel McDurmon, "Shelby Steele: Turning Black Victimization White," The American Vision, 2018, https://americanvision.org/15515/shelby-steele-turning-black-victimization-head/.

17. Ben Shapiro, "'Politics on the American Campus' - Ben Shapiro," Hillsdale College, 2016, https://youtu.be/WxKwmy5AGKI. Begins at 34:36.

18. Gary North, "Cultural Marxism Is an Oxymoron," 2014, https://www.garynorth.com/public/12623.cfm.

19. William B. Evans, "Critical Theory and the Unity of the Church," https://theecclesialcalvinist.wordpress.com/2017/08/31/critical-theory-and-the-unity-of-the-church/.

A WAY FORWARD

A HOSPITALITY OF WORDS

SHERRENE DELONG

Sherrene DeLong (MATS, Westminster Seminary California) is working on a PhD in higher education at Azusa Pacific University. She is a contributor to All Are Welcome: Toward a Multi-Everything Church. *She lives in Virginia with her husband and son, and they attend Christ Church PCA in Arlington.*

―――――

Have you ever had someone make an incorrect assumption about you?

Maybe someone guessed you were younger than you really are, or maybe someone assumed you've seen that super popular movie when you actually haven't. Or perhaps you've experienced the more frustrating kind of assumptions, like when you're forty-five years old and get offered the senior citizen discount.

Other assumptions can be downright hurtful. There is a reason why it is culturally unacceptable in the United States to ever ask a woman if she is pregnant. I am still shocked at how often that actually happens.

Take a moment to think about the last time a hurtful assumption was made about you. How frustrated were you? How often did you think about it after it happened?

Depending on the severity of the assumption, you may have been able to let it go. But what happens when that assumption is made about you repeatedly over time? The woman who is asked if she is pregnant more than once or twice is likely to experience a great deal of shame, anger, and hurt. She is likely to be very self-conscious about her choice of clothes (she may never wear those outfits again), the places she frequents (she may avoid places where comments have happened before), and her body itself (she may go on a shame-fueled rampage to lose any semblance of a baby bump).

It's amazing what a few inappropriate words can stir up in the heart of the hearer. Sticks and stones may break our bones, but words can be just as powerful and debilitating.

Now take a moment to think about the person who made the assumption about you. Was the person trying to attack you? Was she intentionally rude and hurtful? The man offering the senior citizen discount genuinely wants to be of service to the guest to help him save money. The person asking about the woman's due date may be genuinely happy for the "expecting" mother and want to share in her joy. Nine times out of ten, the people who make assumptions about us don't mean to be hurtful.

But that doesn't really make us feel less hurt, does it? The not-pregnant lady will be plagued by those well-meaning comments for a long time.

No matter who you are, you've more than likely experienced the hurt that comes from incorrect assumptions from well-meaning people. Unfortunately, if you're anything like me, you may also be one of those who has unintentionally made incorrect assumptions about others. We may not have asked a woman about her due date (I hope not!), but we have unwittingly made other assumptions and hurt those around us, and we probably didn't even know it.

Unfortunately, too many hurtful assumptions about individuals are made unintentionally by God's people against God's people every day. For people of color like myself, the repeated assumptions laced in everyday conversations can be staggering. Though unintentional and well-meaning, the frequent expression of assumptions based on skin color or ethnicity drive a wedge between God's people and hinder the brotherly love we are called to have toward one another in Christ (Rom. 12:10; 1 Thess. 4:9; Heb. 13:1; 1 Pet. 1:22, 3:8; 2 Pet. 1:7).

Do you mind if we pause for a moment? As you think about your own personal experiences with hurtful assumptions, and even start to wonder about ways you may have unintentionally hurt others, would you pray that God would grow empathy in your heart for the people of color around you who experience hurtful assumptions from well-meaning people nearly every single day?

My Story

Like many other people of color, my story is chock full of inaccurate assumptions based on my skin color and ethnicity.

Here's what you need to know about me: I am American. I was born and raised in southern California, and I have never lived anywhere other than the United States. I am also a child of immigrants. Both of my parents were born and raised in India. They were married in India and immigrated to the States in the early '80s, and they are now citizens of the United States.

My husband is American too, but we don't look alike at all. He has blonde hair, blue eyes, and a reddish beard. I have black hair, dark brown eyes, and olive skin. We're both American, but we have very different backgrounds.

My husband and I met in seminary in California. Before attending seminary, my husband was working in Alabama. He had committed to return to his job in Alabama at the completion of his studies, which he did. After I finished my degree a year later, we got married, and I moved from my southern California home to Alabama, where he continued to work.

Let me tell you—culture shock is no joke. I went from heavily populated city life to more rural and small-town country life. I went from seeing Starbucks on every corner to seeing churches on every corner. I also went from a beautifully diverse area with people from all over the world and a variety of languages spoken, to a homogenous area of people whose families have lived there for generations.

I arrived in Alabama devastated by leaving my sprawling Indian family and amazing church family in southern California, but eager to meet people, make friends, and start a new life with my husband. I didn't really know anyone other than my husband, and I looked to church to fill the gap and be my new family.

I'm an extrovert (ENFJ!), so I'm fairly comfortable meeting new people and initiating conversations. It came as a surprise, then, that after my best efforts, I was not making connections and building relationships as quickly as I thought I would.

Seven months later, I found myself at a women's retreat, parched by loneliness and hoping the event would give me a good opportunity to connect with the women who had been surrounding me for most of a year. It was in this context I finally learned one of the major factors contributing to my situation. I shared with two women about my struggle to connect, and they apologetically told me, "We thought you were a mail-order bride! We didn't know you spoke English!"

Initially, I didn't know what to make of these words.

Well, I'm not, so, that means we can be friends, right?

I really believed that once people at church knew the truth, then they wouldn't shy away from me anymore. In a warped way, I received those words with hope for change, and I was desperate for people to give me a chance. Yet as the words of the women sunk in, I slowly realized their assumptions about me were based on my skin color, and behind their unintentional assumptions was a serious questioning of my identity.

Someone who looks like you and is married to a White man must have been ordered via catalog. Someone with your skin color should not speak English. You are not one of us. There is a language barrier between us, so we cannot connect with you. You can be around us, but you are not part of our community. You are too different for us to be friends.

Like the assumptions hidden in asking a woman about her due date because of her size or clothing, the assumptions based on the color of my skin cut me deeply. While the women did not intend to hurt me by their assumptions, the impact of their words became very real to me.

Over time, more and more assumption-filled comments based on my ethnicity would make their way to my ears.

"I'm glad they hired someone… [long pause]… *impure!*"

The woman speaking said this to me to affirm me and to commend the school for branching out in diversity. The underlying assumptions, however, hinted that the previously all-White staff was pure in its homogeneity, a person of color like me is polluted in some way, and adding me to the staff is an adulteration of the natural, clean, and ordinary.

You are contaminated. You are not normal. You are not one of us. They hired you because of your skin color, not because of your education or skills. They took you in so you can be their token person of color to improve their statistics.

I am sure she did not intend to express any of those underlying assumptions. Her choice of words, however, were extremely poor. They hurt. I'm not impure.

On a different occasion, I was sharing with an elder that my parents are from India. As he heard me talking, a puzzled look came on his face. He exclaimed, "Wow! If I talked to you on the phone, I would have never known you were Indian!" He said this to compliment my English skills and neutral accent. Unfortunately, his statement revealed his expectations.

You look like a foreigner who should not speak English. All Indian people have accents. Who you are does not make sense. You are an anomaly.

He did not intend to be hurtful, but the assumptions in his comment impacted me greatly, especially because comments about my English have come from many others before him and many others after.

Even more frequent than the questions about my English is the question, "Where are you from?" When "southern California" is not a sufficient answer, I know the person is not asking about my hometown, but about my skin color. I don't mind people knowing that my parents are from India and why I look the way I do, but when conversation ends there, it is evident the person was not trying to get to know me, but she was just curious about my pigmentation. Once she knows the answers, I have served her purpose, and she moves on.

Sometimes it feels like I am an exotic animal at the zoo. A few people make assumptions and guess what's inside. Others ask or look for the info placard. Even more just stare. In the end, they all end up walking away. This has been my experience being a minority in a dominant culture.

The repeated effect of all these comments and assumptions is wearying. It feels like who I am, the person God has made me, with my particular shade of skin, with my unique family and culture, is beyond true acceptance in the church's covenant community. Even though I am American, my skin color makes me a perpetual outsider, too different to be truly received and respected. Even though I am a Christian, my skin color has become a hang up in the development of meaningful relationships with my brothers and sisters in Christ.

Again, no one stated their assumptions directly to me. No one had to. That is how assumptions work. By definition, an assumption is "a fact or statement taken for granted."[1] These "facts," taken as truth regardless of reality, dictate how a person interacts with someone. When we operate on faulty assumptions, we can hurt one another even when we don't mean to do so. I wholeheartedly believe that none of the individuals who have made assumptions about me intended to be malicious. They did not mean to question my identity or make assumptions based on race. While I'm grateful for the lack of ill-intent, I am weary of how these assumptions erode relationships between the people of God.

When we believe something is true about another person and it is actually false, we sabotage our own ability to love that person well. We interact with that person with a level of pride in our own knowledge, however faulty, and fail to take a posture of humility to care for a person through listening and learning. If a husband gives his wife a circular saw when she is not interested in woodworking, he has neglected to learn about his wife and care for her appropriately. In the same way, when we make assumptions about people because of their skin color or ethnicity, we neglect to love them well and our imposition can cause great hurt, frustration, and angst, especially when multiplied by the number of times it is done by others in the person's life.

While there's no quick and easy solution to this problem, I would like to offer a working theory about how to resist making unintentional assumptions about people of other ethnicities so that the body of Christ can flourish together. We can start by recovering biblical assumptions.

Biblical Assumptions

While false assumptions can hurt, true assumptions can help. The only absolutely true assumptions we should seek to hold about one another, especially about those in the family of God, are found in Scripture.

- Assume the person is made in the image of God and has inherent dignity, value, and honor as a human being (Gen. 1:27–28).
- Assume you are called to love that person with brotherly affection and go above and beyond to show him or her honor (Rom. 12:10).
- Assume you are called to unity with that person as one body (John 17:20–21).
- Assume the person is more significant than yourself (Phil. 2:3).
- Assume you need to be compassionate, kind, and patient (Col. 3:12).

If you look closely, many times, the faulty assumptions made based on skin color or ethnicity actually violate these true, biblical assumptions we are called to hold as the people of God. Assuming someone does not speak English may inadvertently cause you to avoid him, hindering the unity we are called to as one body.

One Sunday morning, a Korean man walked into our church before the service and sat alone in the pew. I overheard a woman saying, "Wow, he's early!" intimating that the only reason he would be present is for the Korean congregation that met later in the afternoon. She didn't realize he was actually our guest from California, my husband's previous pastor, who was there to preach at his ordination service later that evening. Her assumption about who he was stopped her from introducing herself and welcoming him as an honored guest in our community.

Verbal expressions founded upon incorrect assumptions reveal the posture of a person's heart toward his or her neighbor (See Luke 6:43–45). They say, "I am going to interact with this person based on something that I believe I know," (pride) instead of, "I don't know the details about this person but would like to learn from this person directly" (humility). They say, "I am going to make a judgment about this person's identity because of his or her ethnicity" (affirming the value I assign) instead of, "I am going to learn more about this person because he or she is made in God's image" (affirming the value God assigns).

Again, these faulty assumptions are deceptively benign and unintentional, but tremendously powerful when repeated over time. This is the reality of many people of color. Our identities are subtly prodded and probed from countless unknowing people day by day, leaving us bruised and weary. A friend described it as, "death by a thousand paper cuts." Imagine what it would be like for biblical assumptions to be affirmed day in and day out instead! What healing would come from being respected and heard instead of judged and dismissed! The people of God need to pursue such unity and strive to love our neighbors, even in everyday conversations.

Micro-Hospitality

One way to think about avoiding faulty assumptions in conversations is through the lens of hospitality. I know when you hear the word "hospitality," your heart may swell with pride, especially if you're

Southern. You might be known for your hospitality. You may be able to put on a dinner party like no one's business. You may have an elegant home with family heirlooms and custom paintings of your children. You might pull out all the stops for a guest who comes to your home: the silver goblets, the fine china, the perfectly prepared extravagant meal served on your best platters on a themed table-scape that rivals those in Southern Living magazine. Your home is usually pristine, your family is flawless (or at least appears so), and you put your best forward as your guest enters your home. Hospitality? The South has it covered. Or does it?

My husband preached a sermon on hospitality to a church we'd never been to, and I will never forget what a church member said to him afterward: "I love it when I hear sermons on things we're good at. It makes me feel so good." The ironic thing was my husband was preaching on welcoming the foreigner among us, while precious few actually said hello and introduced themselves to me, the "foreigner" with darker skin in the pew. This man's version of hospitality was limited to opening up one's home. While this is an important aspect of hospitality, there is much more to the concept we as a church need to consider.

Scripture challenges our surface level hospitality throughout its pages. Just as Jesus explained that hatred in one's heart is tantamount to murder and lusting after another in one's heart is tantamount to adultery, he also explained that hospitality is more than what is superficially seen. The Greek word for hospitality (*philoxenia*) literally means "love for strangers." Note it is not defined by "entertainment of guests," "kindness toward those in your circles," or "one-time pleasantries exchanged for the sake of politeness." Instead, the focus is on showing love for those we do not know.

This is the opposite of what we are naturally inclined toward, isn't it? We gravitate toward those who are like us and toward those who are familiar to us. Especially in the South, there are such close-knit circles based on established families, small towns, and football. Many times, the camaraderie around these networks is the very sense of closeness many Southerners feel when they consider the South, and the very same closeness they miss when they leave. But imagine if someone came to you who didn't know a thing about football and who wasn't related to anyone locally. What if the person had never lived in a small town where everyone knows everyone else by two or three degrees? What if he did not look like others in your community? That person may be warmly welcomed through general first-time meeting pleasantries, but for the person of color, many of these first-time pleasantries are laced with hurtful assumptions that are the opposite of warm and welcoming.

In these moments, the initial pleasantries, the everyday conversations, the meetings and greetings, we have an opportunity for micro-hospitality. While full-fledged hospitality can and should involve opening up one's home and offering a meal, micro-hospitality starts with the heart and moves to our mouths. This is hospitality on a smaller scale. Henri Nouwen puts it this way: "Hospitality means primarily the creation of free space where the stranger can enter and become a friend instead of an enemy."[2]

The creation of free space Nouwen refers to should not be limited to dining tables and coffee houses. Love of strangers begins with the heart and follows with our words, all before we open up our homes. In our everyday conversations with people of color, we have an opportunity to show micro-hospitality through shedding the false assumptions we have and humbly showing respect with our words. Jesus teaches us that out of the abundance of our hearts, our mouths speak (Matt. 12:34).

Christine Pohl, one of the leading scholars on hospitality, reminds us of Jesus' words in Matthew 25:35: "*I was a stranger and you welcomed me.*" Pohl argues Jesus was not referring to any particular physical location for hospitality. Instead, the verse "challenges us to examine our practices of welcome to strangers *in every setting*," and reminds us Jesus is more concerned about "relationships than with location—I was a stranger and you received me *into your group*" (emphasis mine).[3] Relational hospitality must begin with the attitudes of our hearts and requires a willingness to truly welcome people into our communities. This willingness to welcome must not be negated by faulty assumptions made in conversations, however unintentional they may be. It is time for intentionality. The type of hospitality Jesus calls his people to demands us to be intentional in our love, not neglectful and haphazard. We as the people of God must reexamine the assumptions we make about one another and strive for better.

We Need One Another

It's easy to say to someone, "Don't make incorrect assumptions about people," but it is much harder to do it. Many times, the assumptions we hold about those around us are extremely hard to see. It is vital for Christians to pray for the Holy Spirit to open our eyes to the false assumptions we hold dear, especially those that are culturally acceptable in our communities. It is also important for us to move toward people different from us with humility and a desire to learn. When the majority of our relationships revolve around those who are familiar to us, they tend to be one-dimensional. In his book *Befriend*, Scott Sauls says that these types of relationships "prioritize *sameness*, so views and convictions and practices are never challenged and blind spots are never uncovered."[4] We are in desperate need of outside perspectives to love us enough to show us our weaknesses and point us to Christ. We are in desperate need of the Holy Spirit to convict us of our love affair with our own comfort and give us opportunities to flourish amidst the beautiful diversity of the people of God. One-dimensional friendships "can't offer the natural, redemptive, character-forming tension that diversity brings to our lives."[5] Without people from other ethnic backgrounds in our lives, we miss out on one of the greatest tools God uses in our own sanctification. It is uncomfortable, yes, but it is worth it. God uses our differences to challenge each other and make us more like him.

Micro-Hospitality Verses Micro-Aggressions

In the academic world, what I refer to as the hurtful comments based on assumptions is sometimes known as micro0aggressions.[6] I have a love-hate relationship with this term. I love it because it embodies how I feel—people have been aggressive toward me and it hurts. I hate it because "aggression" seems to imply intent, and I know those who have incorrect assumptions don't intend to hurt me. Although the formal definition does leave room for the unintentional nature of micro-aggressions, the term itself can be misleading. For this reason, I have avoided using it until now. Regardless of what we call it, the slights made against people of color in the Church is a reality today. With an eye toward hospitality, even on a micro level, we can combat the micro-aggressions that plague the body of Christ and recover the biblical assumptions we are called to hold dear. It is my prayer that as awareness of these issues grows, the body of Christ would increasingly be a hospital for healing rather than a haunt for harm.

May the God of endurance and encouragement grant you to live in such harmony with one another, in accord with Christ Jesus, that together you may with one voice glorify the God and Father of our Lord Jesus Christ. Therefore welcome one another as Christ has welcomed you, for the glory of God. (Rom. 15:5–7)

---

1. Merriam-Webster, "assumption," https://www.merriam-webster.com/dictionary/assumption.
2. Henri J. M. Nouwen, *Reaching Out: The Three Movements of the Spiritual Life* (Colorado Springs: Image, 1986), 71.
3. Christine D. Pohl, *Making Room: Recovering Hospitality as a Christian Tradition* (Grand Rapids: Eerdmans, 1999), 151.
4. Scott Sauls, *Befriend: Create Belonging in an Age of Judgment, Isolation, and Fear* (Carol Stream, IL: Tyndale, 2016), 3.
5. Sauls, *Befriend*, 3.
6. See chapter 3 in *Heal Us, Emmanuel* for Dr. Alexander Jun's thoughts on this topic. Doug Serven, ed., *Heal Us, Emmanuel: A Call for Racial Reconciliation, Representation, and Unity in the Church* (Oklahoma City: White Blackbird Books, 2016).

SISTER, YOU'VE BEEN ON MY MIND
A PLEA FOR MORE WHITE, FEMALE ALLIES

ASHLEY WILLIAMS

Ashley Williams is a writer in Washington, DC. She serves on staff at Grace Mosaic. She has previously worked with Reformed University Fellowship (RUF) at Jackson State University, the first RUF chapter on an HBCU Campus. You can find her writing on Desiring God.

————

Out of curiosity, I recently did a Google search for "racial reconciliation" and scrolled through the results. Video thumbnails spanned a variety of evangelicals, with one group glaringly missing. Black men and women, joined by White pastors and teachers, spoke thoroughly and passionately about race and the Gospel. However, I rarely saw a White woman on the panel, engaging in the conversation. I mourned this, wondering if White women didn't care about these issues, or if, for some reason, they were not given the space to participate. I mourned for these sisters, but also for myself and other Black women because I know intimately the value of, and incredible need for, White, female allies, especially when people who look the way I do are few and far between.

I grew up surrounded by White Christians. It wasn't till seminary that I finally met other Black, Reformed young people. Granted, it was a whopping number of fewer than twenty of us, but the solidarity I experienced was as sweet as nectar! It was the first time I could experience all parts of myself in whole enjoyment.

I read works of Calvin, Frame, and Vos, and wrote theological papers to Kendrick Lamar's *To Pimp a Butterfly*. Once I left seminary to serve a church back home in Baton Rouge, I found myself in the all-White circles I had been in before. Yet this time I noticed my otherness more distinctly, and I felt Blacker than I ever had before. For how awoke I became in seminary, I was afraid that without Black friends in my life, I'd drift into sleep again.

Yet in that crisis, I met two White women who became those allies I had been missing and needed.

Katharine blows into rooms with long, brown hair and four flailing children behind her. Unassuming, without agenda, she puts herself in situations where she is the minority. For example, leaning into the liturgies of her family's life, she takes her children to the library in the part of town where others like her wouldn't dare go.

Kate, too, is an incredible force. Over many beers and burgers, I've talked through conflicting emotions about my race and faith while she has patiently listened and intellectually talked with me, having taken it upon herself to seek, to learn, and to surround herself with images of Black folk that contradict the narratives she's heard before. These friends, two among many, are not a rarity. They haven't tapped into some secret power that gives them an affinity toward Black people. They are two in a long line of rarely discussed, White women who have seen the implications of the *imago Dei* and have thrust themselves into the work of racial reconciliation.

Dr. Kimberly K. Little wrote a book heralding the few, but impactful, women who have cast off the cloak of White privilege in the name of equal rights and human dignity.[1] What is most striking about these women is that they were all wholly normal. Small decisions and gradual changes produced tangible fruit over time. Something as ordinary as a monthly luncheon became an active resistance against segregated restaurants in 1960s Memphis. Little writes, "This group of women, who named themselves the Saturday Luncheon Group, did not intend to turn the world upside down by marching on city hall or picketing local restaurants that refused to integrate. They merely aimed 'to remove some communication barriers by having lunch together monthly.'"[2]

Margaret Cherry, one of the founders of the group, did not rely only on the commentary and direction of Black men and women in her life, but became an ally, having been convinced "through reading and educating herself on African American history, that systemic White supremacy, not the inferiority of the Black race, crippled African American advancements in the United States."[3] There is not enough room to exhaust their stories and share my admiration of them and others carrying their torches. Like my friends, these women are not extraordinary. They simply understood that one cannot love God yet be indifferent toward his image bearers.

To understand the implications of the *imago Dei* and to fuel the desire for racial reconciliation requires action. Dr. Beverly Tatum's helpful illustration of a moving walkway at an airport paints this beautifully. To walk with the belt is to actively participate in a racist system. To stand still is to passively participate, ending up in the same place as the active participant, only slower. It's the one who actively walks against the belt that moves contrary to the system.[4]

I've been on a belt or two and I know how difficult this is. You move against what is natural and comfortable. But the Scriptures do not speak so kindly as to what comes natural to us. By nature, we are children of wrath and count the wisdom and goodness of God as foolishness.[5] So then, it'd be no surprise to us that the sweet promises of God for the coming Messiah, promises couched in language of the reconciliation of all people groups to one another, would seem foolish, impossible on this side of heaven, a waste of time and resources, and a liberal agenda item of identity politics not to be discussed in the pulpits of Reformed churches.

Maybe you've thought this before, my White sister. I, too, have counted the wisdom of God foolishness. I've often exchanged the goodness of God's Gospel with what was easier, prettier, and more comfortable. But I would invite you to run the good race against whatever belt would sweep you away with passivity and good intentions. White women have done it before and are doing it today. Your participation may look differently from mine or the myriad of women before you. Here are a few suggestions that may help you start:

Read Black Authors

Plenty has been said before about good books to start with for those who desire to learn and understand the experiences and perspectives of minorities, a practice integral in rewriting narratives and prejudices picked up over time.[6] This is not just for your sake, but also for Black women like me who grew up in majority-White environments. As amazingly as I was nurtured and trained in my home church growing up, had the leaders of that congregation put Black authors in my hands, I think I wouldn't have internalized for so long that to be Reformed and "right" was to be White.

Make Black Friends

This doesn't just happen. In a country where White flight is the legacy in many areas, Black people won't magically appear in your circles. But if you find yourself living and working in homogeneous spaces, prayerfully ask God to send diversity your way or move you toward it. Also, seek out those habits and liturgies in your life that, with one little twist or turn on a different street, can engage you and your family in the work of racial reconciliation.

Lean Into Commonality

Your Black coworker wants to live in a safe neighborhood and afford an education for their children as well. They probably like coffee, movies, and parks too. Think about how these basic commonalities can be bountiful bridges for new friendships and opportunities to share the Gospel.

———

These are only a few suggestions, but with them I offer one warning: Please do not get caught up in the language and attitudes of many others which says the doors to your churches and lives are open for Black people to enter if only they would. Imagine the Gospel story if God thought similarly. Thankfully, we have a Father who sees us in the distance and runs toward us; a God who tabernacled among his people to gather sinners to himself. The legacy of going into the mess is for all his children. As members of the majority-culture, you possess a certain influence in creating dialogue, not just with Black women like me, but with other White family members and friends who may not have the categories to engage with and learn from minorities.

And because of that influence, we need our White sisters. I would encourage you to lean into the legacy of women, encapsulated in the first name Eve, wrapped in life-giving giftedness. I'd wager this isn't just about childbearing, but about creating life and fostering relationships where none existed previously. You can do this. Join the women before you and see how your voice and your choices can provide a place and a seat at the table for others.

---

1. Kimberly K. Little, *You Must Be from the North: Southern White Women in the Memphis Civil Rights Movement* (Jackson: University Press of Mississippi, 2009). I encourage women to read this book as it includes numerous profiles of women who effected eventual change with limited power and influence. The language of privilege I used was inspired by Gail S. Murray's *Throwing Off the Cloak of Privilege: White Southern Women Activists in the Civil Rights Era* (Gainesville, FL: University Press of Florida, 2008), another book chronicling White women's roles in the Civil Rights Movement.
2. Little, *You Must Be from the North*, 17.
3. Little, *You Must Be from the North*, 21.
4. Beverly Tatum, *Why Are All the Black Kids Sitting Together in the Cafeteria* (New York: Basic Books, 1997), 11–12.
5. Eph. 2:3 and 1 Cor. 2:14.
6. "7 Books on the White-Black Racial Divide You Should Read," The Gospel Coalition, last modified September 22, 2016, https://www.thegospelcoalition.org/article/7-books-on-the-white-black-racial-divide-you-should-read/.

MANAGEABLE MANDATE

MICHAEL W. PHILLIBER

Michael W. Philliber is a twenty-year active duty Air Force veteran (1979–1999). After he retired from the military, he graduated from Reformed Theological Seminary and was ordained in 2001 in the Presbyterian Church in America. He has been Senior Pastor of Heritage Presbyterian Church (PCA) in Oklahoma City since 2016. Philliber is the author of Gnostic Trends in the Local Church *and* To You I Lift Up My Soul. *He has posted over 350 book reviews on his blog mphilliber.blogspot.com.*

———

If my two decades in the US Air Force and almost two decades in ministry have taught me anything, it's that most of us are not significant in the larger scheme of things. A good number of us will never be President, and the majority of us will never do anything world-changing. As I remind myself regularly, "I'm just God's third-string water carrier." This brings a liberating humility and a humble liberation.

How might this understanding apply to the racial tensions in our country and our churches? What could we possibly do?

The problems span centuries. They're widespread—coast to coast. It feels overwhelming.

The premise of this chapter is that God has given us a manageable mandate that is doable and accessible. In the first section, I will point out the biblical instruction that gives us our manageable mandate, and in the final portion I will relay some instances of how I and others have applied it.

Instruction

The manageable mandate is found in Galatians 6. The main point of that letter is to nail down for the Galatian churches the importance of justification and how it looks, for *"in Christ Jesus neither circumcision nor uncircumcision counts for anything, but only faith working through love"* (Gal. 5:6); and *"neither circumcision counts for anything, nor uncircumcision, but a new creation"* (6:15). In other words, what God declares of us, he makes true in us.

All this is the fulfillment of the promise made to Abraham:

> ...*in Christ Jesus you are all sons of God, through faith. For as many of you as were baptized into Christ have put on Christ. There is neither Jew nor Greek, there is neither slave nor free, there is no male and female, for you are all one in Christ Jesus. And if you are Christ's, then you are Abraham's offspring, heirs according to promise.* (Gal. 3:26–29)

Paul wraps up his point about justification describing the different ways it should affect our relationships within Christ's sacred society and the empowering role of the Holy Spirit. Then he comes to chapter 6. In this final chapter of the letter, he emphasizes that based on chapters one–five, we have every reason for resilient confidence. We should not grow weary nor give up on performing what is right. What God declares of us, he makes true in us!

And it's precisely at this juncture in chapter 6 that Paul gives his manageable mandate: *"So then, as we have opportunity, let us do good to everyone, and especially to those who are of the household of faith"* (6:10). Our doing good is shaped by opportunity, proximity, and fraternity.

Our carrying out what God tells us is good is for "everyone." Paul is referring to everyone in our proximity. Yet our main focus is on the fraternity: the household of faith, the brothers and sisters with whom we rub shoulders, with whom we share water, bread and wine, and those whom we may chance to meet in the market or on the way.

But Paul places a sensible, humble regulator on our doing good to everyone, especially to those of the sacred society. It's "as we have opportunity." That is the manageable mandate.

Paul's injunction "as we have opportunity" is a healthy and helpful thermostat on doing good. It keeps us from burning up or burning out with the heat of exuberant zeal, and from icing over with frigid heartlessness. "As we have opportunity" takes into account that the majority of us are most likely not going to change the world in this decade or in our generation. That's not ours to grasp for, but wholly up to God's doing and God's special gifting.

Our Spirit-enlivened responsibility is to do good as we have opportunity: in the moment in front of us, on this block, in this church, and with these people God has placed in our path. We don't need to be rebels out looking for a cause, change-agents stoking ideological fires, or caped crusaders hunting down social justice objectives. Because of Christ, we have been freed-up from pharisaical rigidities (Gal. 5:1) that demand national and international change this very instant. We have been freed-up by Christ so that as we have opportunity we do good to everyone, and especially to those who are of the household of faith.

Paul, in all of his uniquely hyperactive determination and divinely given vocation, hurried and scurried about hither, thither and yon. Nevertheless he counsels other disciples to have a slower, more patient perspective when he teaches "as we have opportunity." That's basically what he also told the young, newborn church in Thessalonica:

> But we urge you, brothers, to [love one another] more and more, and to aspire to live quietly, and to mind your own affairs, and to work with your hands, as we instructed you, so that you may walk properly before outsiders and be dependent on no one. (1 Thess. 4:10–12)

The muscle that gives strength to this "as we have opportunity" model is our confidence in God's sovereignty and his undefeatable eschatological end-game. But also, in a more down-to-earth way, our confidence is in the promise that "in due season we will reap, if we do not give up" (Gal. 6:9). We plod through the "as we have opportunity" manageable mandate confident that it is "God who gives the growth" (1 Cor. 3:6). It's not glamorous, glitzy, or glorious, but it does cultivate lifelong relationships, resilient communities, and durable disciples.

Obviously, this "as we have opportunity" model is far less ambitious than other agendas or possible strategies, and it is far more humble in its aim, but is most fitting for the majority of disciples of

Jesus. Many of the nation-sized and Christianity-sized racial problems and wrongs are well beyond my own puny, insignificant powers to straighten out or overcome. However, I can act on the opportunities God has dropped in my lap. I can work to notice those I encounter and seek their good. These are the people I'm most truly responsible for, and more likely to affect for good. And that seems to be why Paul counseled the Galatian churches and the body in Thessalonica to walk this way.

The following is a small sample of instances in which I and others have followed the manageable mandate. None of these are meant to say, "You have to do it this way, or you've failed!" They're simply illustrations that may hopefully encourage those who have done similar things, and stoke the imaginations and hearts of others as they look around.

Instances

After retiring from twenty years of active duty in the US Air Force, I became a stated supply (the regular student preacher) in a small-town church in middle Mississippi. It gave me room to practice pastoral ministry while I finished seminary, and in the end I was ordained at that church.

The congregation was located in a town of about 1325 people. Over the years the racial demographics had changed from exclusively White to only about 150 White folk. Everyone else was a Black resident: the city council was black, the police department, the mayor, almost all of the city employees, and half of the volunteer fire department.

When I first arrived at the tiny all-White Presbyterian Church in town, the elders sat me down and told me I was not allowed to invite any of the city's Black population to church. To say I was stunned would be an understatement!

I accepted the call thinking I could change the culture of the congregation, which never happened. Thankfully, one of my parishioners worked for city hall, the only White employee of the city. She encouraged me to meet the Black mayor because he was a Christian. She arranged a meeting.

After getting to know each other, I asked him if he ever had the opportunity to pray with his pastor on a regular basis, specifically as he sought to make good mayoral decisions. He told me that none of the Black pastors lived in town, and the only ministers in the city were the White ones.

Here was an opportunity, and it just landed in my lap! "Mayor, would you like for me to meet with you weekly? We can pray together about the city, and any of the issues you find significant. I don't want to come and talk politics, and I do not want to sway your decisions. I'm simply offering myself to come and pray with you, for you, and for your family."

He was shocked and asked, "You would do that?" I promised I sincerely wanted to, and he replied tearily, "I would really like that." We began a weekly friendship that spanned over three years. It was a growing friendship that crossed color lines and denominational boundaries. It was a manageable opportunity to do good, especially with a brother in Christ.

Another "as we have opportunity" moment concerns my friends Jon and Roy. Jon is an elderly, White, conservative, Evangelical Episcopal priest in another city. Several years before I met him he encountered a local Black Baptist minister, Roy, at the Ministerial Alliance. Jon and Roy became friends, and over time drew their congregations together, having a joint-VBS, working together on causes that were important to the city, and even having yearly combined worship services at Easter and other times (imagine that, crossing liturgical-racial-denominational-economic borders to worship the same King Jesus!).

The day came when Jon took a stance and led his Episcopal congregation out of the mainline denomination. Roy's Baptist church celebrated with them, gathered around them as they walked out of, and lost, their denominationally owned building, and helped them as their new church building was going up. The opportunities were right there before them and manageable, and their taking the opening in hand impacted far more than their own congregations.

In my life and the churches I've pastored, I've seen many other stories of ways "as we have opportunity" worked out cross-racially and cross-culturally. For instance, in Florida I preached once a month in a Black Baptist congregation for eighteen months. I have walked with other Black and White ministers in Juneteenth parades. I have baptized many adults and children from a large Latino family and watched as they were wholeheartedly embraced by my congregation.

My present congregation reaches out to the mixed-culture neighborhood next to our building, and we have started seeing results in our VBS and visitors to our church. Most recently, when I was being installed as the senior pastor of my present church, I was delighted to have a dear friend of mine, Ernest, a conservative, Black United Methodist pastor, preach at the service with the happy approval of our elders and congregation. There are numerous other episodes, and all of them are manageable "as we have opportunity" moments.

Most of us will not likely have the power, prestige, or proficiency to affect larger national or denominational changes in the area of racial and ethnic relations. Those troubles were made and deepened over numerous generations and will likely take many generations to completely remediate. But all of us—as individuals, as families, and congregations—have, and will continue to be afforded "as we have opportunity" openings and occasions that are accessible, and those are what we should look for and see.

As we do so we will possibly trip over cultural bumps and commit mistakes. But that shouldn't restrain us in fear. Instead when the "as we have opportunity" manageable moments open up before us, let us humbly walk into them knowing we are promised by the promise-keeping God, *"in due season we will reap, if we do not give up"* (Gal. 6:9).

GOSPEL NEIGHBORING

ALEXANDER JUN

Alexander Jun is a professor in the Department of Higher Education at Azusa Pacific University, where he teaches courses in advanced qualitative research methods, international comparative education, and diversity and social justice. He has degrees from the University of Southern California (BA, PhD) and California State University (MS). He is also a Ruling Elder and attends New Life Presbyterian Church of Orange County in Fullerton, California. He was the moderator for the 45th PCA General Assembly—the first Korean American with this honor. He serves on the permanent committee for Mission to the World. Alexander and his wife, Jeany, have three children.

———

[This chapter was adapted from Alexander's sermon as the outgoing Moderator at the opening worship service for the Presbyterian Church in America at its 46th General Assembly in Atlanta, Georgia, on June 2018.[1]]

———

Unless you've been living under a rock, you probably heard or saw a meeting between two leaders in the United States and the Democratic People's Republic of Korea (June 2018). This is a historic event. These two nations and its citizens fought one another, killing and being killed, over sixty years ago. Born in the United States, and being ethnically Korean, I grew up hearing stories from family and friends of suffering due to the atrocities during the Japanese occupation of a once united Korea, and then, later, horrific stories of a war that divided north and south. It's a sad history of the Korean people. This profound sadness, or *han* as we say in Korean, is often masked by the glitz and glamour and popularity of K-POP music, K-Dramas, and the meteoric economic prowess of South Korea... or the vilification and xenophobia when considering the North. Many parents and grandparents of Korean Americans I know still hold bitterness and hatred toward their Japanese colonizers, and perhaps with good reason. Some Koreans still refuse to purchase any Japanese products—a car or a TV.

As I get started, I want to note that we have a passage often referred to as "The Parable of the Good Samaritan" (Luke 10:25–37). Much can be made of the qualifier here: "Good" is the descriptor used to identify the Samaritan. I suppose if he were referred to merely as "The Samaritan," the knowing audience would rely on their prior knowledge of Samaritans and assume they were not good. This dialogue between the lawyer and our Savior captures the underlying tension between two people groups. Jews and Samaritans do not get along!

I am not sure why the two groups do not get along. Samaritans are recorded as being ethnic Jews (but only half Jews) who intermarried with other people groups. Samaritans also had different worship practices and they believed only in the Pentateuch. Perhaps the fact that you would leave your own ethnic group and marry outside of your kin was reason enough for the religiously righteous to despise the other and look down on them. I don't know.

The story reminds me that with the arrival of Jesus, change was coming. The way the religious leaders handled their day-to-day religious practices, including hate and disregard for other ethnic groups, was about to be disrupted. Now they were required to live and love in a radical new way.

Let me ask you beloved: Do you want to be more loving? Do you want to be more compassionate? Then this parable is for you because it shows how Gospel-love can cross any barrier or boundary. Sometimes our Gospel-compassion and love don't go across the other side of our bed, or across the dinner table, or across the street to our neighbor. Never mind across cultural, ethnic, and gender boundaries, and certainly not to our enemies as we see in the Good Samaritan.

I'd like us to consider how this kingdom parable illuminates and illustrates for us what kingdom-love and compassion look like and how we can grow in that very same love and compassion. There are many characters in this scene but I would like to talk about three specific characters mentioned in this passage: the lawyer, the Samaritan, and the victim.

The Lawyer

First, let's talk about the lawyer. The backdrop and context leading up to this exchange is fascinating, isn't it? Throughout Scripture Jesus confronts the misguided thinking of the religious leaders. They are zealous and pious leaders who think they are right in their theology. He also challenges these religious leaders along issues of ethnicity. Throughout Scripture we also see Jesus illustrating what the Kingdom of God is like, especially its nature and power. This parable has been used to teach about the need for social service, by Christians as well as secular friends engaged in social justice. And on some level that makes sense as this parable illustrates the nature of Kingdom-mercy and compassion—something the lawyer doesn't have and can't even begin to comprehend. But please know we must not separate the love of our neighbor from the love of our God, as our 46th General Assembly theme appropriately highlights. As John Stott once stated, "It is impossible to be truly converted to God without being thereby converted to our neighbor."[2] We notice in this passage between the lawyer and our Lord, that Jesus uses this parable to show the lawyer a deeper problem with his heart. In asking the question, *"What shall I do to inherit eternal life?"* (Luke 10:25), the lawyer reveals a fundamental flaw in his thinking and his approach to God, and our Lord offers this parable to begin "spiritual open heart surgery" with everyone watching.

"What shall I do to inherit eternal life?" There is much to deconstruct in this question. It is a strange question, is it not? Normally when you inherit something, you don't do something to get it. That's not the way inheritance works. The question, then, presupposes some fundamental misconceptions about inheritance. The lawyer is essentially a legalist whose whole life orients around performance—a works-based

approach to his faith. That's why he's asking, "what must I do" rather than asking, "how can I receive or believe?"

We see Jesus flipping the script and posing a question back to the lawyer when he asks him, well you know the law, you're the expert, what does the Old Testament say? The lawyer answers with a great response that summarizes the Decalogue in Exodus 20, along with Deuteronomy 6 with Leviticus 19. And this speaks to the heart of eternal life.

Again, a great response. It demonstrated his orthodoxy! But the lawyer wasn't really orthodox was he? The lawyer was a legalist, in fact he was quite unorthodox (not understanding the doctrines of grace). Perhaps sometimes we too struggle to know the difference. But Jesus knew the lawyer's heart. Even with all the orthodoxy in the world, the man was not able to reconcile preferential treatment against another person along ethnic lines. Jesus affirms the response. He says, you're right, but the lawyer continues to press the issue and asks, *"Who is my neighbor?"* Verse 29 is key here: *"desiring to justify himself."* You see, he tries to limit the overall number of people he has to love. He wants to hear the bare minimum standard requirement to love. He wants to compartmentalize his love.

He employs the *minimax* principle. Minimum investment; maximum return. Example: Have you ever had a person approach you with a question they already have an answer to? For example, I have often been asked, Elder Alex, do I tithe before or after taxes? Jesus responds and tells him this story. In the story he talks about the wounded traveler and the two people who passed him by: the priest and the Levite.

These examples of established religious professionals who, for whatever reason, chose to "walk on by" probably came as a shock to the listeners! Now, for the third person in this example, one might expect Jesus to give an example of a lay person Israelite, but no! Jesus then drops the final bomb. The one who shows mercy is a Samaritan.

There was long standing distrust, hatred, and broken fellowship between these two people groups. In offering this example, our Lord calls the listening Jewish audience on their blind spot. Sometimes it seems all the good orthodoxy in the world cannot save us from our cultural blind spots. Darrell Bock says it's quite possible that for the lawyer, a "neighbor" was only someone within Israel.[3] He never would have considered a neighbor to be outside the nation of Israel. So, let's talk about the Samaritan.

The Samaritan

Who is the Samaritan? A Samaritan is the last person you would expect. He is the worst enemy and the last person a Jewish man would want to help. And a Jewish person is the worst enemy and the last person a Samaritan would want to help.

The Samaritan is the hero of the parable. He meets basic human needs through deeds. Now I argue these deeds were costly, sacrificial, and audacious. What did the Samaritan *not* do:

- He didn't look upon the traveler and say, "My thoughts and prayers are with you."
- He did not argue for the spirituality of the church and the danger of the social gospel.
- He did not begin to rehash reasons these people ought to be despised.
- He did not blame the victim and question why he was there in the first place, wondering what he did or didn't do to bring this affliction upon himself.

No. The Samaritan had compassion. The Samaritan gives all he has—his time, money, bandages, oil, wine, and an animal. And his heart of compassion. There was a cost. Friends, there is always a cost. But let's turn to the topic of motivation. It begs the question: *why* did the Samaritan do what he did?

The Samaritan helps the Jew and enemy while under no obligation to do so. It is one thing to help someone who is your friend. It is entirely different when you help your enemy. Let me ask you this: What people group simply causes your stomach to turn at the mere mention of their names? For some people in the world, believe it or not, it's the Christian! I love how Scott Sauls described the Samaritan in *From Weakness to Strength*:

> But the Samaritan, the true neighbor who was labeled by every Jew not as a friend to be trusted but as an enemy to be avoided, risks his life to care for the man. You might say, based on the parable, that the Samaritan loves the Jewish poor better than the Jews love their own poor. Put another way, he loves his enemy even better than his enemies love each other. In a world where people of faith are sometimes treated as "the enemy" in secular society, are Christian

leaders in particular thinking like the Samaritan? If not, we should be.[4]

Perhaps *we* want to be recognized as the Samaritan, the one who shows mercy, being that good example the Lord uses to convict and rebuke others. I know I do. But the reality is I am the religious leader, saying the right things and knowing the right things, but filled with excuses about why I don't engage. But God is gracious to us, is he not? Despite our flaws and failings, he loves us.

Dear Christian, guilt cannot and must not be a reason for us to engage. So what is the motivation for us to pursue mercy for the stranger, for the enemy? Why did the Samaritan do what he did? The key is shown to us in verse 33: *"But a Samaritan, as he journeyed, came to where he was, and when he saw him, he had compassion."*

You see the word passion embedded in the word compassion. It means more than mere pity—your insides are all turned upside down; you are deeply moved. It's the same word the Bible uses to describe the kind of love God has for us. *Hesed* kindness. *Hesed* is God's covenant faithfulness to promises and plan for his people. It is self-giving and sacrificial. The Samaritan loved his neighbor with the very same love God has for us. We find *hesed* most clearly in Christ who is God's *hesed* to us on the cross.

In response to the question, "Who is my neighbor?," Your neighbor is *anyone* hurting right in front of you. Moreover, your neighbor is *anyone* you have characterized as your enemy. When your enemy is also hurting right in front of you—whoever is your moral, political and ideological enemy, God is calling you to love them. Love them locally, love them globally. Let's talk about global Gospel neighboring.

Perhaps we have prayed that the world will be evangelized with the Gospel. We pray for the lost, and pray Christ would be proclaimed to the ends of the earth. Harken back to my earlier example of the atrocities upon the Korean people by the Japanese. One viewed the other as pure evil. Perhaps you see images of North Korea and your American blood gets pumping! Perhaps cynicism sets in. You wonder what kind of media circus has led to this public display of false affection.

For me, I must confess, when I first saw the image I could not stop crying. Growing up I longed to see the day when the two countries would be reunited. Seeing the two leaders holding hands or embracing, even for that one moment, allowed me to dream of better days to come.

Perhaps those who came from broken families or children of divorce could relate. To see mom and dad holding hands and being civil, even if for that brief moment, gives you a glimpse of hope that what was once broken could possibly be restored. This broken relationship is a result of a fallen world, and even closer to home, our own broken fellowship with one another continues to reveal our fallen state.

I saw these events as perhaps an opportunity to see the Gospel enter into an otherwise closed nation. A few years ago I had a chance to visit South Korea and speak with several university colleagues and graduate students. They were all Christians, so I asked about reunification and how we'd see the Gospel preached in that region. I was quite surprised that the vast majority responded with doubt and fear concerning reunification—"it would devastate the economy" one said. "It would be a threat to national security" said another.

Here I thought fellow Christians would certainly see this as an opportunity for the Gospel to be preached. Perhaps the same is true here in the US as well. When you see leaders of the US and North Korea shaking hands, do you see hope of the Gospel or something else? Sometimes our confessional theology collides with our functional theology.

For example, we pray and pray to the Lord that he would use us to take the Gospel to reach the lost, like our Muslim friends. And our churches think about sending one unit to a Muslim community. "Hey, MTW has a one percent campaign, so why don't we send that one socially awkward person at our church to the mission field?" some might immediately think. Yet God answers our prayer with abundance and in his sovereignty. He brings Muslim friends to us, as strangers seeking refuge into our country, to our neighborhoods, into our lives, and how do we respond? "That's not what I meant when I prayed. I want them to be served *over there* not *over here*.

Brothers and sisters—we all hold dual citizenship. When our responses to opportunities for mercy are primarily as citizens of this nation rather than as citizens of heaven, we may need to seriously reevaluate our identities. We need to hold on to multiple realities. F. Scott Fitzgerald was quoted as saying the test of the first rate mind is the ability to hold on to two contradictory thoughts at the same time and still be able to function.[5] You can fundamentally disagree morally and ideologically with someone and still love them and see them in the *imago Dei*, the image of God. You can despise someone's politics and lifestyle yet still show mercy, charity, and grace. For some of us this simply means making it through Thanksgiving Dinner. Make no mistake: Our sound biblical theology toward God should lead to deep love of neighbor. Finally, let's turn our attention to the victim.

The Victim

So what do we know about the victim? The Bible doesn't say much about this person, and the commentaries do not go into great detail on the victim. I am reminded just how true this is for victims. Victims are usually voiceless aren't they? We see that time and again in our own spheres today. But what we do know about the victim is he is in dire straits. He is in desperate need of compassion. Friends, guess what? We are that dead traveler in need of saving. We are the ones in need of help; in need of a good Samaritan. We need a Samaritan not only to help us, and heal us, but ultimately to save us! Jesus found us, not half dead, but completely dead in our sin. We were not just some random person on the road. We were his enemy. And he loved us still. The Samaritan is a type of the Savior. And unlike the Samaritan, Jesus doesn't mount us on donkey, but he mounts us on his own back as he carries us to the cross.

The Samaritan is actually the one who tells us this parable. Jesus Christ is the ultimate Samaritan who paid a great cost. He gave up *everything* to save us.

Let's return to the original question: What can we do to inherit eternal life? Absolutely nothing. This parable says you inherit eternal life *not by what you can do*, but by embracing what Jesus *has already done!*

---

1. The author would like to thank his pastor, William Chang, for providing guidance.
2. John Stott and Christopher J. H. Wright, *Christian Mission in the Modern World* (Downers Grove: InterVarsity Press [1975] 2008) 93.
3. Darrell Bock, *Luke 9:51–24:53*, Baker Exegetical Commentary on the New Testament (Grand Rapids: Baker Academic, 1996).
4. Scott Sauls, *From Weakness to Strength: 8 Vulnerabilities That Can Bring Out the Best in Your Leadership* (Colorado Springs: David C. Cook, 2017), ch. 7.
5. F. Scott Fitzgerald, "The Crack Up," *Esquire Magazine* (1936): https://www.esquire.com/lifestyle/a4310/the-crack-up/.

DIVERSITY AND CULTURAL
NORMATIVITY

DUKE KWON

Duke Kwon is the pastor of Grace Meridian Hill, in Washington, DC. He has degrees from Brown University (AB) and Gordon-Conwell Theological Seminary (MDiv, ThM). Duke and his wife, Paula, have two children.

———

I stole from my dad. It was a half-used bottle of hair-tonic called Vitalis, which is a nasty brown stuff. But it was better than the alternative in his cabinet, which was Wildroot, a greasy lotion that was basically Soul Glo for middle-aged Asian men. But this Vitalis was critical for a twelve-year-old boy trying to do whatever he could to get his hair to look like Johnny Depp's.

Mind you, this wasn't washed-up, dog-smuggling Johnny Depp. This was *21 Jump Street* Johnny Depp. Who didn't want to look like *21 Jump Street* Johnny Depp?

But the thing that kept getting in between me and personal glory was my wiry, black, Korean hair. This hair was thick and unmanageable, not flowing and wavy like Johnny Depp's. After months of attempt after failed attempt, I had poured so much of that junk on my hair that it started bleaching, and I was forced to conclude that I must be biologically hair-impaired. I quietly despised the thick, black mop on top of my head, because I couldn't attain to those unarticulated standards of appearance and coolness and beauty that Johnny Depp embodied for me.

I didn't have the words or categories for it yet. But that was an early encounter with a force I'd bump into the rest of my life, something I've come to describe as "White Cultural Normativity."

Here's another encounter: That time in the tenth grade when Jenna, an athletic, blonde, 6' 2" tall friend told me, "Well, you're pretty good looking for an Asian guy." She wasn't trying to be mean. She was just putting words to White Cultural Normativity.

I understand these examples might seem petty. They might even sound like evidence of vanity. But they're worth noting, I think, for the same reasons that Rev. Dr. Kevin Cosby reminded us at Muhammad Ali's funeral: "Before James Brown said, 'I'm Black and I'm proud,' Ali said, 'I'm Black and I'm pretty.'"[1] With those words, Ali infused African Americans with "a sense of somebodiness." Because there's something profound, and profoundly disfiguring, about being unsure that your reflection in the mirror is the "right" one.

By normativity, I mean both what already is as well as what ought to be. I'm talking about assumed norms, standards of correctness. Normativity implies what's acceptable; it defines what's right. It's woven into the very fabric of our relationships, our practices, and our traditions. White Normativity is that set of unwritten cultural precepts that serve as a source of minority alienation in a majority-culture—yes, even in the Church.

Dismantling White Normativity

White Normativity is what my family and I recently encountered when visiting a church, where a friendly gentleman asked us where we were from. When we answered, "Washington, DC," he responded, "No, you're supposed to say China, or Japan, or South Korea"—and then enthusiastically invited us to their missions night to do a reading in the Korean language. You see, White Normativity isn't just racial insensitivity. It's seeing a non-White individual and only thinking about your global missions ministry.

White Normativity is defining ministry to certain communities and contexts with qualifiers— "*Ethnic* ministry," "*Urban* ministry," "*International* ministry," or "*Outreach* ministry"—while calling ministry to the majority-culture simply, "Ministry." It's savoring the doctrine of justification in Galatians—which we should do, yes—while overlooking the original context in which the Apostle Paul points to cross-cultural fellowship as one of *the* preeminent fruits—and proofs—of our justification. It's embedded in an ecclesiology that habitually warns against the dangers of emotionalism in worship, yet ignores entirely the spiritual dangers of joylessness. When was the last time you heard a workshop or read an article warning against intellectualism in worship?

White Normativity is moral silence on social issues that are ancillary to White communities but core concerns of Black and brown communities. It's dismissing as "political" what is in fact personal, pastoral, and practical theological for brothers and sisters of color.

White Normativity is desiring diversity without discomfort. It tries to add diversity without subtracting control. It's the preservation of dominant culture authority in the name of theological purity. It's what makes so many young seminarians of color nervous about entering certain denominations like my own, the PCA, as they all too often feel forced into a false choice between ethnic identity and theological fidelity.

Because what keeps folks of color out of our churches, friends, is not public racial hostility. And the greatest hindrance to racial harmony in the American church is not crass bigotry. It's our shared, institutional blindness to the exclusivity of a White Normativity protected by plausible deniability. Indeed, insofar as it devalues, subordinates, and excludes minority culture members—even against our best intentions—and as it *over* values, *supra*-ordinates, and preferentially *in*cludes majority-culture members, White Normativity is the passive racism of evangelical Christianity.

I invite you, dear friends, not simply to repent corporately for past, overt acts of racism, which we must do. I call you also to commit to the dismantling of White Cultural Normativity in the church. And I call you to the establishment of a new norm, a new vision for our churches that might be called "Multicultural Normativity."

Establishing Multicultural Normativity

Multicultural Normativity is when the church confesses racial integration as the biblical norm and the cross-cultural family of Christ as the way things ought to be. Multicultural Normativity means your congregation's worship, relationships, and ministries are so defined by the presence of ethnic minorities—so built from the ground up on a racially integrated foundation—that if your members of color were to leave one day, nothing about your church or denomination would ever be the same. It's seeking creative ways to express your cross-cultural convictions not just on Dr. Martin Luther King, Jr.'s birthday, but every Sunday. It's when everybody in the church is a little uncomfortable—Red and Yellow, Black and White—but everyone in the church is richly cared for.

Multicultural Normativity is when the church is a resurrection banquet hall more than a lecture hall—and, occasionally if you dare, maybe even a dance hall. Multicultural Normativity rejects racial reconciliation as a pursuit of interpersonal harmony unless it also seeks interracial equity and mutuality. Because it's about inclusion, not just diversity. It's placing men and women of color in positions of influence and leadership. It's inviting guest speakers of color to teach on prayer or systematic theology or marriage, rather than racial reconciliation alone. Because diversity is about who's on the team, but inclusion is about who gets to play.

Again, Multicultural Normativity is being deliberate and public about hiring staff members of color. Because it's time we begin to collectively recognize the ability to navigate multiple cultural contexts not as a "soft skill" but as a vital ministry competency. And it establishes these things without denying the value of the Black Church and Immigrant Church, because Multicultural Normativity never closes its eyes to our broken racial history.

For those who are tempted to be discouraged and daunted by what can feel like an impossible task, please remember this: The book of Acts is nothing less than the story of a church that itself was deeply entrenched in cultural normativity—Jewish normativity. And take a look at the churches in your neighborhood, across the nation, and around the world, and notice in the multicolored faces of your sisters and brothers the amazing work the Spirit of Jesus has since done.

What Can We Do?

So, what can be done? What can we do? Institutional change is slow and gradual, no doubt. But it must be punctuated with deliberate advances. So, let's suggest a few things we can do.

Priority

Are we convinced racial justice and cross-cultural harmony are Gospel priorities? I could remind you of the global purview of the Abrahamic Covenant, the pan-ethnic mission of the suffering servant, the counter-cultural cross-cultural ministry of Jesus, the grand drama of Gentile inclusion in Luke's early church narratives, the major theme of reconciliation found across the Pauline epistles, or the apocalyptic vision of the Lamb, forever adored by people who don't look the same, or talk the same, or sing the same (see Rev. 7:9–10).

But what's presently on my mind is Jesus' high priestly prayer in John 17. It is there Jesus prays for his followers, *"that they may all be perfectly one"* (my paraphrase of John 17:22).

Jesus is about to suffer the misery of hell itself. He has the cup of wrath already pressed up against his lips. Of all possible things, what is on his mind? Our unity! Of all possible things, what was Jesus' intercessory and missional priority? That *you*, Chinese sister, that *you*, Black brother, that *you*, White brother, that *you*, Indian sister, that *you*, Puerto Rican brother, that *we* might be *one*.

So here's the question: Will our churches reflect Jesus' priority of multicultural normativity? Some of us need to make our church's commitment to racial reconciliation explicit and public. We need to write it into our vision statements. List it as a core value. We should shepherd our people into a corporate re-prioritization of racial reconciliation and justice.

Liturgy

Our Sunday liturgies—whether formal or informal, historic or contemporary—also reflect our ecclesial priorities. Yes, our worship must be biblical. And it must also be culturally adaptable. Of course this relates to music. But it also includes our style of praying, manner of preaching, seasons of celebration and lamentation, the range of physical and emotional expressiveness permissible in our service. Some of us should give our worship liturgies a cultural audit. That might involve asking a leader of color to give their input on the accessibility of your service to someone from a subdominant culture. But are you, in the first place, willing to explore culturally flexible forms of worship as part of your commitment to Multicultural Normativity? What are you willing to give up for the sake of building a cross-cultural church? What are you not willing to give up?

Money

"Where your treasure is, there your heart will be also" (Matt. 6:21). That's true of individuals, and it's also true of local churches and denominations. Some of us need to meet with our leadership teams and together look for ways our commitment to racial reconciliation can be reflected in our operating budgets. We talk about the importance of minority leadership, but we know recruiting, training, and installing leaders costs money—lots of it. What would it look like to create new funds—locally, denominationally, nationally—for the financial support of minority church planters, for cross-cultural churches, for majority-minority campus ministries and campus leaders of color? What if we did this so that in ten years we could double the number of minority ministry leaders in predominantly White denominations and ministry networks?

Generosity

I want to invite you to commit to stewarding whatever privilege you have—to employ your every social asset toward our growth in denominational diversity. Some of you are already doing this. It might be through your musical gifts or your financial gifts; it might be through your teaching gifts or your tweeting gifts. For all of us, this can be done through the gift of relationships. You cannot navigate church ministry without knowing people; it's the nature of the relational character of ministry, for better or for worse. So, share your relationships with minority leaders around you. Introduce them to everyone you know, especially those in positions of influence.

I like to believe I'm a self-made ministry man, leaning on my own individual competence. But that's simply not true. Here's the truth: I wouldn't be writing this today, and you wouldn't be reading it, if others hadn't gone out of their way to introduce me to people they knew, who knew people who knew people. Be generous with your social assets, especially your ministry relationships. Let's draw women and men of color deeper into the heart of the church.

Party

We need to celebrate every victory. We need to throw a party every time someone repents of racial sin, every time someone forgives another, every time someone has a reconciliation ah-ha moment. We need to do this in order not to give in to cynicism, and to refuel our tanks for the long journey by eating the fruit of our patient labor.

Gratitude

Brothers and sisters, never stop sharing stories and testimonies of God's transforming work. Read the race awakening stories of this book (or its first volume, *Heal Us, Emmanuel*[2])—and give God praise for his transforming work. Never stop being surprised when God shows up! And *thank* each other constantly for their faithful labor.

I want to thank our Black brothers and sisters. I cannot tell you how much I admire your humility, your winsomeness, and your long-suffering spirits. Your servant-leadership, the way you have *made space* for people to repent and forgive, has been the moral catalyst for the historic transformation of my denomination and many ministry spaces around the country.

And I also want to thank our White allies in this struggle for Gospel reconciliation, whose tears of sorrow, sincerity of heart, and teachable spirit so often outpace my own. When you confess your personal racial sins, and when you humble yourself as a learner in the cause of racial justice, you don't always see it, but I find myself wiping tears from my eyes. You don't know how healing you have been to me and my weary and all too cynical and sinful heart. Your earnestness and your zeal to repent has been, quite simply, heroic.

For Jesus' Sake

I leave you with this final word: Fight for the dismantling of White Normativity. Labor for the establishment of Multicultural Normativity. Yes.

But, dear friends, do all this for Jesus' sake, ultimately.

As the story goes, two young Moravians heard of an island in the West Indies where a British slave owner had 3,000 slaves. Compelled to bring to them the Gospel of freedom in Christ, on October 8, 1732, the first two Moravian missionaries, a potter and a carpenter, sailed out of Copenhagen harbor, ready to sell themselves into slavery in order to preach the Gospel in the West Indies. And, as the ship slipped away, they linked arms and lifted up a cry: "May the Lamb that was slain receive the reward of his suffering!"

Don't you know, friends: *Jesus was slain to receive glory in our unity.* Isn't this the best of all motivations for this work? To know that in pursuing racial reconciliation, we are giving to Jesus the reward of his suffering. Hallelujah! Don't do this for your offender. He might not change. Don't do this for the offended, not ultimately. She might not thank you. Do it all ultimately for Jesus' sake.

That hard conversation you had about race? *That was for Jesus' sake.* That criticism you endured? *That was for Jesus' sake.* That testimony of repentance you shared? *That was for Jesus' sake.* It's *all* for Jesus' sake. Because Jesus died for this very moment in the history of American Christianity.

May the Lamb that was slain receive the reward of his suffering in you and in me.

Amen and amen.

---

1. BBC Newshour, June 10, 2016, https://www.bbc.co.uk/programmes/p03xyxr1.
2. Doug Serven, ed., *Heal Us, Emmanuel: A Call for Racial Reconciliation, Representation, and Unity in the Church* (Oklahoma City: White Blackbird Books, 2016).

CREATING A NEW MULTIETHNIC PCA CULTURE

EDWARD S. KOH

Eddie Koh has served as a pastor of Reunion Church and New City Church, both intentionally multiethnic works in Seattle, Washington. He previously served as the Associate Pastor of Hillcrest Presbyterian Church (PCA) in Seattle for eight years. He has degrees from the University of Illinois at Urbana-Champaign (BS), Trinity Evangelical Divinity School (MDiv), and Covenant Theological Seminary (DMin). For his doctoral work, Eddie researched and explored how Korean American and African American pastors overcome personal and systemic leadership challenges while serving in predominantly Anglo PCA congregations. He and his wife, Jennifer, have three children.

———

Although we won't have space in this chapter to expand on this, I assert that the Great Commission is a call to create a multi-ethnic culture by making disciples of people of every ethnicity and race. Acts shows us that this was a long, painstaking process of challenging the old wineskin of Judaism and its religious structures and replacing them with the new wineskin of Gospel-centered Christianity and its multi-ethnic culture-redeeming principles.

———

The caption of a recent CNN video read, "Racism without racists?"[1] It was meant to catch my attention, and it did. This two minute documentary-style video reported findings of a recent 2015 poll conducted by CNN and The Kaiser Family Foundation on race matters. Some of the snapshots include the following:

•Forty-nine percent of Americans say racism is a big problem.

•Research has shown we all subconsciously see the world through a racially biased lens.

•White NBA referees call more fouls on Black players, and Black referees call more fouls on White players.

•A study in Milwaukee showed 17 percent of Whites with prison records receive callbacks on job applications, while 14 percent of Blacks without prison records receive callbacks on job applications.

•In 2004, 5,000 fictitious resumes were sent in response to 1,300 help wanted ads. Some had traditional White names like "Brendan," and others had traditional Black names like "Jamal." Applicants with White sounding names were 50 percent more likely to get calls for interviews.

•"The main problem nowadays is not the folks with the hoods, but the folks dressed in suits."

This video succinctly captures a sobering reality of the current nature of race relations in America. Race is a complex, systemic problem embedded in ordinary daily life, and it no longer is simply a matter of intentional actions of mere individuals based on personal prejudice. Engineered by generations of powerful White men for the benefit of White men the system of racial inequality works as designed, invisibly and effectively, in the daily life of American society. Unless the system is reengineered and transformed, Whites will continue to benefit from it, and racial minorities will not.

Lamentably, as authors Michael Emerson and Christian Smith have concluded in their book *Divided By Faith*, the (White) evangelical Christian church has made the problem of racial segregation worse in America.[2] A vast majority of churches across all denominations chose racial comfort and financial security[3] over Christian unity and a Christ-like display of the new, unified humanity we find in Ephesians 2:14–16.

In a country torn apart by race, the only lasting institution with true power to bring racial justice and healing—the Church—has a serious credibility problem. Unlike the first-century church which brought meaningful healing to cities divided by ethnocentrism,[4] the

Christian church today lacks a visible witness and a prophetic voice in our racially segregated cities. American Christians easily forget that all of us, regardless of race or ethnicity, are minorities together as sojourners in this world (1 Pet. 2:9–12). Not surprisingly, the evangelical Christian church is arguably the most racially segregated institution in America.

John Frame reminds us, "Reformed churches in America must bear the burdens of the history of slavery, segregation, and discrimination."[5] For our part as Reformed Christians, the diverse voices of *Heal Us, Emmanuel* have begun to name and address some of our own failings and struggles as an "overwhelmingly White denomination."[6] The PCA has been too long silent and complicit in following the racialized patterns of the broader culture rather than obeying the Gospel mandate of racial unity in the church. As a natural consequence, the PCA has created a culture that is "just not hospitable to Reformed African Americans."[7] But worse, as I have discovered in my research of minority pastors in our denomination, the PCA has cultivated a racialized culture that presents unique personal struggles and systemic challenges for minority pastors.[8]

A Journey of Discovering a Racialized PCA Culture

My own journey as a minority pastor and my focused qualitative research of other minority pastors ministering in predominantly White PCA congregations validate the pervasive nature of racialization in everyday American life. I define "racialization" as the unconscious act of differentiating or evaluating people based on skin color. It often stems from the attitude of thinking less of others based on implicit racial prejudice.

I recognize that much has been written on the topic of church and race since I did my intensive study on this topic in 2012. But at the time of my research, I discovered only one Christian book that directly addressed the problem of leadership challenges for minority pastors on a denominational level.[9] In *Many Faces, One Church*, the authors explain the experiences of ethnic minority pastors in their United Methodist Church denomination. They report:

> Some minority and ethnic minority pastors are naïve about subtle racism in the church and among their colleagues since they have never been trained on how to deal with prejudice within the church. Even as

they feel the power of racism and experience its unpleasant effects, they find it hard to name and address it. Worst of all, they are often unable to identify the sources of their racial and non cooperation problems. In dealing with such problems, some ethnic-minorities are culturally passive. However, this passiveness should not be interpreted as having no feelings. Unfortunately, even in the light of years of pastoral experience, minority and ethnic minority pastors are asked repeatedly to prove their credibility in direct and indirect ways, both by denominational leadership and church members... often minority and ethnic-minority pastors suffer and grieve about racism in silence. In many cases, the only people they share their true feelings with are their spouses and children.... The central issue for a sizable number of ethnic-minority persons is *not* job or career success, but survival in a culture that is foreign to them.[10]

I didn't expect to get teary eyed when I read these words for the first time. But they captured my own journey of eight years as an associate pastor of a predominantly White congregation. It was comforting to know there were people who understood what I experienced. And it strengthened my resolve to find answers to why racialized patterns pervade Gospel-believing churches and Christ-exalting denominations like mine.

I often describe my process of finding answers through prayer, study, and interviews as an experience of the Lord giving me a scroll to eat. Initially it was sweet to my mouth as I began to learn about the history of racism and understand why racialization exists in the church. But in time it became bitter to my soul as I realized how complex and pervasive racialization truly is, and how effectively Satan uses it to undermine the power of the Gospel in the American Christian church.

Two resources, then, began to provide answers. Stuck in Seattle traffic, I listened to a conference talk by Carl Ellis. He masterfully explained the reality of human inequality that manifests itself in dominant versus subdominant power struggles as a result of our rebellion against God.[11] Instead of subduing and ruling over God's creation as equally privileged human beings made in God's image, people choose to rebel against God by subduing and ruling over *each other*.[12] This power dynamic between the dominant White majority and subdominant non-White minorities causes much of our ethnic-based suffering. It also explains the struggles of minority pastors in the PCA.

Then I came across a key journal article that began to crystallize the nature of leadership challenges for minority pastors in majority-culture congregations. According to Harry Waters, minority leaders face systemic leadership challenges of presumed incompetence and resistance to their leadership because of widespread acceptance of racial stereotypes, prejudice, and bias in majority-culture organizations.[13] And as minority leaders encounter these systemic leadership challenges and perceptions of being "weak" or "inadequate" as leaders, they also experience personal anxiety and feel the need to prove themselves.[14] This pattern of racialization in majority-culture organizations is also a reality for minority pastors in an overwhelmingly White denomination like the PCA.

Indeed, my in-depth interviews of African American and Korean American PCA pastors reveal racialized patterns in the church cannot be ignored or underestimated. They play a significant role in the leadership challenges of these minority pastors. Let's face it: two hundred years of dehumanizing slavery, one hundred years of oppressive Jim Crow laws, and fifty years of post-civil rights racial discrimination in our country have left an indelible mark on everyday life in American society and racialized patterns in our institutions.

Systems have been set to benefit the White majority. Minorities are not treated as equals within the existing racialized systems. Therefore, the dynamics inside the church are interrelated with and interdependent on racialized patterns outside the church that inevitably and systemically influence people's identities, views, assumptions, and practices.

In view of these complexities, minority pastors in the PCA experience personal and systemic leadership challenges. While there is a correlation between these two categories of challenges, basic distinctions are apparent. Minority pastors encounter personal leadership challenges in majority-culture congregations because of their cultural identity and misperceptions, and systemic leadership challenges because of dominant culture assumptions and tendencies.

Personal Struggles Rooted in Cultural Differences and Misperceptions

The interviews of minority pastors reveal that most of their personal leadership struggles stem from cultural differences and misperceptions by those in the PCA majority-culture who view these minority pastors as different—as inferior minorities. Their identity struggle is not about "Who am I?" but rather "Why am I here?" or "Why am I doing this?" They know they are pastors like all the other White pastors in the PCA. And yet, because they are treated as inferior to White pastors, or because they feel no one really understands them, they struggle with their identities.

One pastor confessed, "I remember saying over and over to people I felt like I was Clark Kent from the TV show *Smallville*. I felt like the lonely Kryptonian on earth. I still had friends at the church, people that I cared for deeply, and I felt like they cared for me. Yet there was that sense of cultural isolation where you definitely felt there was a part of you that was just utterly dormant that was just not being accessed by anybody."

When asked what leadership challenges he faces that a White pastor does not experience at his church, another pastor revealed, "When I get up on Sunday morning to preach or to lead an event, and it's predominantly White, I think, 'Why am I doing this?' I don't think there's ever been a Sunday I haven't gotten in the pulpit and had to go through an identity struggle when I stand up there."

Minority pastors in majority-culture congregations struggle with how to be true to themselves away from their own culture, and, in response, they feel pressure to prove themselves as leaders. One pastor shared, "Part of being an African American in America is that you always wonder, 'Will I be accepted by the majority-culture?' There's always that thought in your mind, 'I can lead Black people, but will White people follow me, or will I be perceived as someone who's not worthy of being followed?' That's crazy, but that's just what segregation and racism has done for us—the subtle inferiority."

This struggle often comes with a sense of aloneness and personal anxiety unique to minority pastors. A pastor revealed, "If I felt like I'd done something not as well as I'd hoped, I would notice I would definitely go through seasons of discouragement, depression, frustration, and wanting to be isolated." Different expressions of faith in musical styles, preaching styles, interactions of congregants during worship, as well as the casual mannerisms (for example, consistently being called by his first name while the White pastor's name is preceded by "Pastor") heightened their struggle with cultural identity and isolation.

Socialization also plays a key role in why minority pastors struggle with a sense of loneliness. My interviews revealed that, because most White Christians in majority-culture congregations of the PCA were not socialized under the leadership and teaching of minority pastors in a meaningful way, they treat minority pastors with less respect, view them as incompetent, and undermine their authority and expertise. These experiences, stemming from socialization in segregated congregations, also heightened a sense of loneliness for minority pastors in majority-culture congregations.

Systemic Challenges Rooted in Dominant Culture Assumptions and Tendencies

Minority pastors also encounter systemic leadership challenges because of the assumptions, practices, and perspectives of the dominant majority-culture. This issue is raised by Bob Burns when he emphasizes that it is necessary for White pastors who hope to lead effectively in a multicultural environment to "recognize dominant cultural perspectives and the tendency to assume that these are correct."[15] The assumption of "this is how we do things in the PCA" must be challenged to see whether its perspectives and practices are shaped by the culture or being redeemed by the Gospel.

My research reveals that dominant culture assumptions perpetuate two major problems for minority pastors and majority culture-congregations. First, dominant culture assumptions sustain inequality and discourage mutual submission. Dominant culture assumptions are a problem because they are the unchallengeable standard that measures other perspectives, values, or ways of life.

For instance, Julius Kim and Stephen Um observe that while Asian Americans "are emerging as leaders in their respective secular careers, they are not finding the same kind of opportunities for advancement and leadership within American churches that are predominantly led and populated by Caucasians."[16] What is the reason? They assert that Asian American leaders who "tend not to be as assertive, aggressive, and outspoken as their Caucasian counterparts" are measured against White leaders, and such "passivity" of

Asian Americans is "often misinterpreted to signify a lack of leadership qualities."[17]

Sure enough, some minority pastors were viewed as weak leaders because they didn't display the qualities of White, alpha-male leadership. In such an environment, their leadership style of deference was misperceived as weakness and thus de-legitimized. One pastor was even told by his White lead-pastor, "God doesn't want you to be a weenie." But far from being weak, the minority pastor explained, "I was also trying to exhibit real biblical leadership traits, deference, being soft-spoken, not necessarily being very opinionated, keeping things to myself, being slow to speak, quick to hear, as Proverbs says."

Thus, dominant culture assumptions and tendencies pose a serious problem by disregarding or devaluing the unique identities and qualities of minority pastors and by viewing minority pastors as inadequate, inappropriate, inferior, or wrong. Under this presumption of incompetence, minorities feel the burden to assimilate and prove themselves to be legitimate, qualified, competent leaders.

White pastors serving in majority-culture congregations may also face challenges of presumed incompetence. However, the color of their skin is not likely to be an issue. They don't have to prove themselves because of presumed incompetence based on race. It is a unique challenge for minorities.

Second, dominant culture assumptions perpetuate a lack of cultural intelligence[18] among White pastors and congregants. Because minorities are expected to assimilate into the dominant way of life, Whites are dissuaded from developing cultural intelligence by learning from minority cultures, perspectives, and values. For instance, the preaching styles of some minority pastors were deemed ineffective or inappropriate in their congregations because White pastors lacked the ability to understand, acknowledge, and appreciate current contextual forces and cultural differences. One pastor was told by his White lead-pastor that his style of preaching was ineffective, improper, and getting in the way of people hearing the Gospel in their predominantly White congregation. Sadly, minority pastors' efforts to explain their cultural points of view or biblical basis for their practices are also frustrated by the inability and unwillingness of White pastors to carefully discern biblical principles and cultural nuances.

Consequently, because minority pastors are presumed to be

incompetent through the lens of the dominant PCA culture, their authority is often undermined or resisted. One pastor reported, "When I talk [at a Presbytery meeting], no one's really listening if it's not about some racial issue." In other words, in a racialized church environment, White pastors seem willing to listen to minority pastors only when they talk about race-related topics, but not when minority pastors discuss broader theological matters.

Such experiences burden minority pastors to repeatedly prove themselves as competent pastors, while their fellow White pastors benefit from the opposite presumption of competence. Therefore unless dominant culture assumptions, attitudes, and practices in majority-culture congregations are challenged and redeemed by the Gospel, minority pastors will continue to face personal struggles and systemic leadership challenges.

There is, however, a reason to hope.

Creating a New Gospel-Displaying Multiethnic Culture

Reflecting on her in-depth analysis of interracial churches in America, Korie Edwards contends "interracial churches work to the extent that they are, first, comfortable places for Whites to attend... because Whites are accustomed to their cultural practices and ideologies being the norm and to being structurally dominant in nearly every social institution."[19] Thus, she concludes:

> If churches want to realize Dr. King's dream, they must first embrace a dream of racial justice and equality. Interracial churches must be places that all racial groups can call their own, where all racial groups have the power to influence the minor and major decisions of the church, where the culture and experiences of all racial groups are not just tolerated but appreciated. This demands a radical approach and is certainly a high calling. Whites and racial minorities will have to resist white normativity and structural dominance and fully embrace the cultures, ideas, and perspectives of all racial groups. Otherwise, the dream will remain elusive.[20]

My own research demonstrates this truth. For minority leaders to effectively lead organizations, the organizational culture must welcome, support, and submit to them, fostering a culture of mutual learning and appreciation. Indeed, majority-culture PCA congregations that cultivate an environment of equality and mutual submission give minority pastors opportunities to thrive. In fact, whether they merely survive or successfully thrive as minority pastors depends in large part on the cultures of the congregations. Congregations that deliberately act to minimize the "toxic and deadly"[21] forces of racial bias, prejudice, and stereotypes give the minority pastors an opportunity to thrive, and create a multiethnic environment.But congregations that merely expect their minority pastors to assimilate and perform traditional duties within the existing system of dominant culture assumptions and practices make it challenging for them to even survive. Thus, the cultivation of a multiethnic environment proves to be an indispensable factor in how minority pastors overcome leadership challenges in majority-culture congregations. It validates Mary Connerly and Paul Pedersen's claim: "In order to move toward cultural competence, organizations must alter the power relations to minimize structural discrimination. This may involve including minorities in decision-making positions and sharing power with them."[22]

Specifically, my interviews reveal that "intentional invitation"[23] is the key to creating a healthy environment for minority pastors. That is, in view of racialized patterns and structural barriers in the church, majority-culture congregations become healthy environments for minority pastors through purposeful acts of placing minority pastors in positions of authority and influence equal to White pastors. One congregation intentionally pursued an African American pastor to be a senior pastor. Two congregations deliberately called their minority pastors as "co-pastors" (in lieu of the traditional pastoral hierarchy). White leaders and congregants appreciated and willingly submitted to their leadership.

Such intentionality is crucial for two reasons. First, an intentional invitation is necessary to systematically change the dominant-culture-centric way of life in majority-culture congregations. Second, it reverses and remedies the inferior status of minority pastors and brings them from the margins to the center of influence.

These intentional invitations begin to undo the power dynamics of racial inequality and the culture of White privilege. Minority pastors who are not so fortunate as to work in such a healthy environment repeatedly report facing leadership challenges throughout their years. Therefore, for minority pastors to overcome leadership challenges and thrive in majority culture congregations, a multiethnic environment that minimizes systemic inequality and addresses race-centric preferences is absolutely essential.

The minority pastors who received intentional invitations readily gave credit to their White pastors and lay leadership for their success. These White pastors and elders who risked their reputations and had the courage to change the culture of their majority-culture congregations are the unsung heroes of my research. They made a tangible difference for the sake of the Gospel. They showed true biblical humility. One White pastor, viewing his African American friend as more significant, submitted himself to his leadership and willingly became an associate pastor. Two respected White pastors laid down their White privilege and equally shared their pulpits and ministries as co-pastors. Many White elders respect their minority pastors as they would respect their White pastors. In a racialized society, they model for their congregants what it looks like to integrate and value others for their God-given uniqueness. They are simply Christ-like.[24] Through their humble and courageous leadership, they change racialized patterns in the church to provide Gospel-displaying equality and unity in the body of Christ.

Hope of a Multiethnic PCA Culture

As my journey of discovery and research has shown, there is hope for lasting, meaningful change in the PCA. One pastor, who often felt alone as a minority pastor and struggled with a weekly identity crisis, celebrates the joy of seeing a generation of Black and White children learning and growing as Christians under his non-White leadership. He told me, "And they're going to look at their less diverse churches and say, 'What's wrong here?' Or if they go to all-White churches or all-Black churches, they're going to challenge some of the thinking." Such intentional work of undoing racialization and renewing socialization in the church will not only impact future minority pastors and congregations, but also the Christian witness in our racialized cities and in the broader American society torn apart by racial tensions.

Multiethnic churches do not just happen. They require Gospel-intentionality to undo the forces of racialization. Thankfully God calls pastors and congregations to pursue his plan to undo the forces and patterns of racialization in his Church by his power and through our hard humbling work. Accordingly, Carl Ellis prays, "May God give us the grace to disciple the nations by demonstrating the true meaning of ethnicity rather than imitating the world with ethnic power struggles, marginalization, and oppression."[25]

For the sake of our Lord Jesus and our demonstration of his eternal Gospel, let us all agree and pray, "Amen."

---

1. "Racism Without Racists?" *CNN.com*, 2015, http://www.cnn.com/videos/tv/2015/11/23/racism-without-racists-ts-orig.cnn/video/playlists/race-and-reality/.

2. Michael O. Emerson and Christian Smith, *Divided by Faith: Evangelical Religion and the Problem of Race in America* (New York: Oxford University Press, 2000), 170.

3. Emerson and Smith, *Divided by Faith*, 168.

4. Rodney Stark, *The Rise of Christianity: How the Obscure, Marginal Jesus Movement Became the Dominant Religious Force in the Western World in a Few Centuries* (New York: HarperCollins, 1997), 158–62. According to Stark, there were eighteen identifiable ethnic groups in Antioch, and the disciples were first called *Christians* in Antioch because, as Tim Keller suggests in his sermon on 1 John 3:10–18, of their never-seen-before barrier-breaking familial love among Jews and Gentiles.

5. John M. Frame, "Minorities and the Reformed Church," May 21, 2002, http://frame-poythress.org/minorities-and-the-reformed-church/.

6. Doug Serven, *Heal Us, Emmanuel: A Call for Racial Reconciliation, Representation, and Unity in the Church* (Oklahoma City: White Blackbird Books, 2016), xiii-xiv.

7. Sean Michael Lucas, "Telling the Truth," in *Heal Us, Emmanuel: A Call to Racial Reconciliation, Representation, and Unity in the Church*, ed. Doug Serven (Oklahoma City: White Blackbird Books, 2016), 180.

8. Edward S. Koh, "Overcoming Cultural and Systemic Barriers: Exploring How Minority Pastors Overcome Leadership Challenges In Majority Culture Congregations" (DMin diss., Covenant Theological Seminary, 2013).

9. Ernest S. Lyght, Glory E. Dharmaraj, and Jacob S. Dharmaraj, *Many Faces, One Church: A Manual for Cross-Racial and Cross-Cultural Ministry* (Nashville, TN: Abingdon Press, 2006).

10. Lyght, Dharmaraj, and Dharmaraj, *Many Faces*, 57.

11. Carl F. Ellis, "The Sovereignty of God and Ethnic-Based Suffering," in *Suffering and the Sovereignty of God*, eds. John Piper and Justin Taylor (Wheaton, IL: Crossway Books, 2006), 123–41.

12. Ellis, "Sovereignty of God," 124.

13. Harry Waters, "Minority Leadership Problems," *Journal of Education for Business 68*, no. 1 (1992).

14. Waters, "Minority Leadership Problems," 19.

15. Bob Burns, *Pastors Summit: Sustaining Fruitful Ministry* (St. Louis: Covenant Theological Seminary Magazine, 2010), 30.

16. John Starke, The Gospel Coalition, March, 25, 2011, http://thegospelcoalition.org/blogs/tgc/2011/03/25/identity-history-and-passivity-julius-kim-and-stephem-um-discuss-challenges-for-asian-americans/.

17. Julius Kim and Stephen Um, The Gospel Coalition, March, 25, 2011, http://thegospelcoalition.org/blogs/tgc/2011/03/25/identity-history-and-passivity-julius-kim-and-stephem-um-discuss-challenges-for-asian-americans/.

18. Burns, *Pastors Summit: Sustaining Fruitful Ministry*, 29. Burns defines *cultural intelligence* as "the ability to understand, acknowledge, and appreciate current contextual forces as well as the cultural background of oneself and others."

19. Korie L. Edwards, *The Elusive Dream: The Power of Race in Interracial Churches* (New York: Oxford University Press, 2008), 139.

20. Edwards, *The Elusive Dream*, 140.

21. Taylor Cox, *Creating the Multicultural Organization* (San Francisco: Jossey-Bass, 2001), 12.

22. Mary L. Connerley and Paul B. Pedersen, *Leadership in a Diverse and Multicultural Environment: Developing Awareness, Knowledge, and Skills* (Thousand Oaks, CA: Sage Publications, 2005), 84.

23. In view of American racialized patterns of marginalizing minorities while Caucasians remain in the center of influence and power, I define *intentional invitation* as a deliberate and purposeful act of placing minority pastors in positions of authority and influence equal to White pastors to biblically redeem and systematically change the dominant-culture-centric way of life in majority-culture congregations.

24. In a racialized PCA culture, these White pastors live out the Gospel-displaying principles laid out in Phil. 2:3–7.

25. Ellis, "The Sovereignty of God and Ethnic-Based Suffering," 141.

CAN WE REALLY MOVE PAST RACE?

LISA ROBINSON SPENCER

Lisa Robinson Spencer holds a ThM degree from Dallas Theological Seminary and BA in Economics from California State University-Northridge. She serves as Executive Director of Local Colors, a nonprofit organization that promotes multicultural awareness through events and education. She has two adult children and is married to Evan. They live in Roanoke, Virginia, where she is a member of Christ the King Presbyterian Church. She blogs at www.theothoughts.com and co-hosts the Family Discussion podcast at Reformed Margins.

———

I grew up in a middle-class, predominantly African American context. Though my family was from Chicago, my parents got the West Coast bug, and so, when I was five, we took off for Southern California. I stayed connected to my Chicago roots by spending summer and winter school breaks there with my grandparents.

Even though my Los Angeles, Inglewood, and Chicago neighborhoods were for the most part Black neighborhoods, and even though I attended primarily Black schools, I was also exposed to a great deal of diversity. As a very fair-skinned African American, I enjoyed both the cultural richness of my heritage and some relative ease in associating with other ethnic minorities, as well as Whites.

While I never experienced racism directly, I was always acutely mindful of its existence, especially from those who recounted their first-hand experiences. This juxtaposition lasted well into my adulthood, including during my fourteen years living in New England. Because I can comfortably move between different worlds (Black and White), it is not difficult for me to worship in various contexts. I believe in the Christian mandate to be unified.

I confess—I struggle with issues of race. By that, I mean I wrestle with how much attention should be given to address racial disparities within the church. Don't get me wrong. I know racism still exists in this country. I'm aware implicit bias is an underlying factor in various aspects of our society.

I also know how the lengthy legacy of White superiority has subjected non-Whites to acceptance based on the majority-culture's approval. I don't want to ignore any vestige of marginalization, especially in the church.

But on the flip side, I believe progress still needs to be made. I acknowledge there is a place where we need to move forward and keep in mind the primary identity we all have in Christ. With this chapter, I hope to draw you into my struggle—to lay out the underlying issues that cause the tension I feel in striving toward racial reconciliation. I suspect I'm not alone. But more importantly, I believe that often the tension we live in comes from both our blindness *and* our exuberance to make corrections.

Part of the reason I struggle is because I see how even the way the issue is approached can cause fractures, suspicion, and even hostility on both sides. These fractures occur because of differing opinions on how much we need, and the methods we should use, to confront racial issues in the Church. Christians take various positions that run the gamut. Some deny race is a factor at all. They contend we could thrive if we only focused on being one in Christ. Those on the other side protest even the slightest hint of racial disparities, exposing and addressing them in every corner they might exist.

Suspicion can easily take root. From what I've observed, it's not so much because Christians don't want to thrive together, but particularly because we do. A fair amount of tension exists between those who believe any focus on racial issues tends to divide, and those who believe there is much more work to be done to unify us.

I have a growing conviction that if we are truly going to heal and have reconciliation, we need to come to some kind of consensus not only about how race has played a role in the history of Christianity, but also how it continues to play a role in the Church—particularly for people of color. But we also must recognize the tension this creates for those who are less inclined to understand or appreciate the impact every instance of racial injustice has on people of color. We must guard against the bitterness and suspicion that comes with a heightened focus on race.

I had an odd moment a few years ago during our celebration of the Lord's Supper. For many years, I took a common posture of closing my eyes to focus on the sacrificial atonement of Christ and the meaning behind his command to *"do this in remembrance of me"* (Luke 22:19). But I've come to realize that in participation of this sacrament, his life, death, and resurrection had significance for not just our individual salvation, but the whole body of Christ. So recently, instead of closing my eyes, I've been looking around. With my eyes open, I see those I am in a covenant relationship with. It reminds me that union in Christ is not just about me and Jesus, but Jesus and his bride, the Church.

For the most part, I relish seeing those whose commitment to Jesus mirrors or even exceeds my own. My brothers and sisters in Christ are there for the same reasons I am. They have been chosen by God, called out of darkness into light. They were lost, just as I was; dead in their trespasses and sins. Regardless of whatever family experience, ethnic background, or personal history we have, we can join together in celebration. We have been transported out of the kingdom of darkness and into the marvelous light of life in Jesus. We are one body, united to Christ through one Spirit.

But a funny thing happens when I begin to notice our anthropological composition. As an African American in a predominantly White denomination, this observation takes on an added dimension. Yes, we are united in Christ through the Holy Spirit who baptizes us into one body. But we do come from a disparate group of people.

The fact that 80 percent of the PCA's membership is White has definitely been reflected in the PCA congregations I have been a part of. I love that I have seen a spattering of different ethnicities, especially in my former congregation in Richardson, Texas—Latinos, African immigrants, Asians and Middle Easterners. This definitely eases tensions of being only one of a few African-Americans and reminds me that Jesus is building a multi-ethnic church.

But a tension sometimes rises, especially when the mono-cultural aspect of the service seems to snuff out any considerations of the various ethnicities represented in our congregation. I struggle with how much the racial and ethnic composition should play a role. After all, we are there because of our union in Christ.

But when the fabric of liturgy and practice seems to marginalize or even dismiss others, it makes me wonder how valued we are, the non-Whites. I'm not implying any ill intention. I think people are often not aware of how a White, Euro-centric framework impacts people of color. After all, there is no such thing as a-cultural. That Presbyterian liturgy is a product of European decent becomes pretty obvious.

I think we do well to remember that the categorization of race as Black or White was devised to segregate and subjugate classes of people with darker skin. One drop was all it took to be Black. Throughout history, this false construct of race has done much to denigrate the image of God by elevating the false construct of White race to a superior status. But this contradicts Scripture's description that out of one person, God made people of many nations (Acts 17:26). There is no such thing as a superior race.

I was keenly reminded of this in a Christmas Eve service not too long ago at my former PCA church. The church has an affiliation with a refugee ministry, which recently became a budding church plant focused on refugees. The church is located in an area with a significant immigrant population. A number of refugees from the Congo were in attendance.

They delivered a Christmas hymn in their native tongue and style that they put together just for that night. It was an acute reminder that the Revelation 7:9 church embodies all tongues, tribes, peoples, and nations. I pondered what the new heaven and new earth will be like with an even more expansive array of diverse worship. I imagine no interpretation will be needed as it would be a perfect embodiment of Acts 2:5–6, which will be a complete reversal of the Tower of Babel. What a glorious picture! It can be modeled here on earth as a foretaste of what we'll get soon.

But I also struggle with the lack of attention given to the mounting concerns of people of color, especially in light of the presence of racial disparities persisting in our society. I do believe we can be too demanding in this regard. We can prioritize race so much that we hold the church hostage.

However, given the historical framework and the current grievances, I think we must acknowledge persistent infractions with a sober and fair eye on all factors involved. I don't want to be dismissive of our core identity in Christ. We also must consider how those infractions have played out in the history of the church.

Citizens of African descent in the US have endured enormous transgressions at the hands of White people. I can fully appreciate the efforts to ameliorate racial tensions by rightly pointing to race as a social construct designed to subjugate non-Whites to inferior status. However, we can't ignore how race played a factor for so long. We can't be naïve about it. These transgressions were based on the premise that non-White skin, particularly Black skin, relegated the bearers of that skin to an inferior status. They could not enjoy the full rights of citizenship or even be considered human beings. They should have been afforded *full* citizenship—same value and social acceptance. They weren't.

Surely this mentality inserted itself into the church for centuries. This is one reason I appreciated Dr. Lucas' book *For A Continuing Church*[1] and the efforts of the various overtures submitted to the General Assembly to rectify historical transgressions of the PCA.

Yes, it's true we've come a long way in this country. Slavery no longer exists. Forced segregation no longer exists. All kinds of laws and cultural supports, such as consideration in college admissions, have been put into place to ensure non-discrimination. A number of barriers are gone.

Because heightened attention to issues of race has fueled allegations of sustained oppression, I have intentionally been more observant about the presence of minorities, and especially African Americans, in various settings: places of business, retail establishments, institutions of various sorts, and just day to day life. For the most I see a freedom that did not exist for much of the history of this country.

I strive to be fair. As one who has extensive experience in grant writing for the nonprofit human service sector, I am drawn toward empirical evidence. With the proliferation of news and opinions, I've observed an ease in decrying every publicized incident without compiling all the facts. As a person who seeks to build bridges in communication, I am drawn to defining terms. I often find terms like "racist," "White supremacy," and "oppression" are ready responses that mask a more comprehensive investigation. I can appreciate the frustration of those who want issues to be considered fairly and soberly.But I think what gets missed is why this visceral response exists. There is a sense of PTSD because of the lengthy injustices perpetrated against Black people. With every instance of racial injustice comes a flood of historical remembrance, telling us perhaps things are still not right, and leaves the cry of how long, O Lord, how long? I love how Russ Whitfield summarized it in *Heal Us, Emmanuel*:

Please understand that every act of racial injustice, every episode of racism and raced-based treatment takes on a symbolic status that brings to mind an entire network of historic injustices, sufferings, and the dehumanization of African Americans and other people of color. In the minds of many Black people, each racialized event serves as a heart-rending cipher for chattel slavery, Jim Crow, historic church bombings, Klan terrorism, redlining, and many other wounds received personally, and by living family members of former generations. Each event reads like another chapter in America's running commentary on my Blackness—my worth, my status, my place in society—and it's not a hopeful picture.[2]

Some Christians reading that statement might quickly retort that we need to move on from the past. In some sense this is true, we do need to move forward. However, the ingrained and sustained nature of racial injustice creates substantial barriers to overcome. Albert Einstein had a keen awareness of how this legacy plays out long term. In a document entitled, *A Message to My Adopted Country*, he wrote:

Your ancestors dragged these black people from their homes by force, and in a white man's quest for wealth and an easy life they have been ruthlessly suppressed and exploited, degraded into slavery. The modern prejudice against Negroes is the result of the desire to maintain this unworthy condition... I do not believe there is a way in which this deeply entrenched evil can be healed.[3]

Though this was written in 1946, when conditions were far more oppressive than they are now, hear what he is saying. The precedent of this treatment of Black people does not easily go away. Each new incident opens wounds.

In the past few years especially, issues of race have risen to the forefront. Particularly since the advent of the Black Lives Matter movement, the emergence of Black consciousness has highlighted the plight of Blacks in this country. In my opinion, these incidences leverage the very long legacy of mistreatment and arguments and tend to build from that historical perspective. Activism and increased social media presence have fueled a prioritized attention that has captured the imagination of Christians who long for justice.

When it comes to our fellowship as a family of God, I have found the tension resides not so much between Black and White, or minority and non-minority, but depends on how much race plays a role in relationships.

In the first camp are those for whom race is not, or should not, be an issue when it comes to Christian faith and practice. These are not necessarily people who refuse to see the role race has played. They may, and most likely they will, acknowledge the atrocities of the past and the ongoing presence of racism in society. But, in a quest for Christian unity, the matter is of secondary importance. The important thing is to live as brothers and sisters based on our union with Christ in the interest of the church representing God's kingdom agenda, and subjecting the issue of race relations to a secondary or even non-existent status. There is a spectrum. This group will put more focus on the spiritual aspect of Christian faith and less emphasis on how that relates to how people view each other according to their ethnic identity (anthropology), and how people organize and view each other as a group (sociology). I have witnessed that some will go so far as to say that these factors (ethnic and social) don't really matter. Only how we live as Christian brothers and sisters matters.

I confess I strive to lean in this direction. I want to follow Paul's exhortation, *"if possible, so far as it depends on you, live peaceably with all"* (Rom. 12:18). I am keenly aware that whatever transgressions have occurred, our first priority is to the Kingdom of God and the mandate to love one another. I understand we must acknowledge the factors that play a role in both the past and present hurt. But I'm also becoming increasingly aware how the cries of racial injustice impact those who want to prioritize the spiritual aspect of our Christian fellowship.

The second camp sees the issue of race as a prominent concern in the body of Christ since infractions still exist, even in subtle form. This group, made up of Blacks and Whites, considers our earthly identity as equally important as our spiritual identity, and would say how we accept and reconcile the former is a fruit of the latter. In other words, living out the Gospel should result in correcting any vestiges of the sins of the past that resulted in devaluing and dehumanizing Black people as those made in the image of God.

Specifically in the church, it means acknowledging and proactively pursuing reconciliation with brothers and sisters in Christ based on our earthly/ethnic identity as a product of our spiritual identity. Hence, you have continual discussions about race and the persistent need to point out where White superiority and racism still has a stranglehold. This becomes even more prominent in consideration of the events transpiring in our world regarding race relations—disparities in the criminal justice system, police actions against Black people, and other inequalities. The second group is more compelled to address issues and achieve activism as a representation of Christian commitment. This can even result in spurning other Christians and churches that do not satisfy this requirement.

I think we know what happens when these two groups collide. I see it on a regular basis. The efforts of the second group seem like a nagging nuisance to the first group, at best, or a sinful, divisive preoccupation, at worst. For the second group, the silence or even spurning of the first group comes across as a lack of spiritual fruit of Christianity and a lack of concern of what happens with those who are created in the image of God. Suspicion and frustration mount. Is this not what we are seeing?

What Is the Solution?

I started out this essay indicating a struggle, and here is where it really takes root. I have this growing conviction that we must move forward with the intent of reconciliation. Given the vast range of thinking regarding ethnic and racial concerns and their legacy and impact, the greater question is: "How do we go about this?"

I find the pages of the New Testament instructive for us so that we can come together. Scripture must take supremacy in our line of thinking.

In light of such struggles, I'm often reminded of what Paul commends to the Philippians, *"Do nothing from selfish ambition or conceit, but in humility count others more significant than yourselves. Let each of you look not only to his own interests, but also to the interests of others"* (Phil. 2:3–4). Paul then launches into having the mind of Christ, who left his own glory and heavenly abode for our sake. This is a must for real reconciliation to happen. This requires us to see beyond our own agendas and our own discomfort. We're called to lay down our lives for the sake of our brothers and sisters. It's a sacrifice.

We can't ignore the fact that when it comes to sacrifice, the burden has historically been on non-Whites, which speaks to the dominance of the majority-White culture. Whites set the rules to which everyone else is expected to comply. I think this is instructive for those in the first camp, especially for those who get annoyed or irritated whenever the cries rise up that all is not right. But on the flip side, there is a call for the second camp to endure and to prioritize our mandate to live as those whose union with Christ brings his work and purpose to bear on earth, his power to unite the most disparate group of people.

To be sure, the early church experienced tensions between Jews and Gentiles. Jewish superiority and Gentile marginalization provoked hostilities. Paul's word in Ephesians 4:1 is a clarion call for the church to demonstrate the power of reconciliation, *"I therefore, a prisoner for the Lord, urge you to walk in a manner worthy of the calling to which you have been called."* This is an anchor verse especially in light of the Jew–Gentile hostilities of that day.

In chapter 1, Paul lays out the great promises to which every member of God's household has access through Christ. These benefits were planned from the foundations of the world and they were extended to those who held no rightful claim to them. In chapter two, he explains the problem, exclusion of the Gentiles by the Jews, and what Christ did to fix it: he *"has broken down in his flesh the dividing wall of hostility* (2:14) to *"reconcile us both to God in one body through the cross"* (2:16) so that together we grow as one body (2:22), built on the foundation of the Lord, and all received as a gift of grace through faith (2:8–9).

But the real kicker comes in chapter three. The grafting in of the Gentiles and both Jew and Gentile walking together as one reveals the richness of Christ and the purposes of God:

> So that through the church the manifold wisdom of God might now be made known to the rulers and authorities in the heavenly places. This was according to the eternal purpose that he has realized in Christ Jesus our Lord (Eph. 3:10–11).

Therefore his urging to *"walk in a manner worthy of the calling to which you have been called,"* (4:1) demands a serious reflection on what Christ has done that overshadows any previous (or current) hostility. This is a mandate for his Church more so than for individual believers. Making every effort to walk worthy of this call, *"with all humility and gentleness, with patience bearing with one another in love, eager to maintain the unity of the Spirit in the bond of peace"* (Eph. 4:2–3) indeed shows God's work through the Son to bring such disparate groups together—from the rulers in high places to the people in low places— for his purpose is greater than the darkness known before. Jesus breaks through.

The prominence of distinctions or the propensity to deny them beckons us at every turn. I am reminded in Galatians 3:28 that though distinctions pull us into a defense or a defiance of the consideration of one another, we are all baptized into Christ through the bonds of the Spirit, *"There is neither Jew nor Greek, there is neither slave nor free, there is no male and female, for you are all one in Christ."* (Gal. 3:28). It's not a call to ignore the differences. It's a command to a higher consideration whenever those tensions flare up. As the Westminster Confession of Faith informs us:

Saints, by profession, are bound to maintain a holy fellowship and communion in worship of God, and in performing such other spiritual services as tend to their mutual edification; as also in relieving each other in outward things, according to their several abilities and necessities. Which communion, as God offereth opportunity, is to be extended unto all those who in every place call upon the name of the Lord. [4]

So that brings me back to the question: can we really move beyond race?

I believe the answer is both yes and no.

The answer is yes in the sense that our primary identification is our union with Christ. The Church has a mandate to live above the boundaries and calls of our society which perpetually draws us to consider ourselves, our comfort, our own interests, and our racial and ethnic identities as superior. We cannot afford to walk in step with any cultural calls to hold the Church hostage to our demands for prominence, nor can we live as those who ignore the plights of our brothers and sisters in Christ. Somewhere in the middle is that place of discomfort where we all learn to lay down our lives for the other.

But the answer is no in the sense that we have to account for the ways in which disparate treatment has subjected non-Whites to centuries of marginalization. Even though we might look optimistically at progress and consider the persistent cries of injustice a troublesome nuisance, we would do well to remember these cries exist for a reason. We are called to weep with those who weep.

1. Sean Lucas, *For a Continuing Church: The Roots of the Presbyterian Church in America* (Phillipsburg, NJ: P&R Publishing, 2015).

2. Russ Whitfield, "Moving Forward" in *Heal Us Emmanuel*, ed. Doug Serven (Oklahoma City: White Blackbird Books, 2016), 281.

3. Albert Einstein, "The Negro Question," originally published in *Pageant Magazine*, January 1946, https://onbeing.org/blog/albert-einsteins-essay-on-racial-bias-in-1946/.

4. Westminster Confession of Faith, 26.2.

THE UNITY FUND
A GOSPEL INITIATIVE

SCOTT BRIDGES

Scott Bridges was on staff with Cru for four years at the University of Missis-
sippi. After graduating from Covenant Theological Seminary (MDiv), he served
as an assistant pastor at The Covenant Presbyterian Church in St. Louis. In
1996 Scott planted Christ Presbyterian Church in Santa Barbara, California,
and initiated getting the first Reformed University Fellowship on the West
Coast at UC Santa Barbara. In 2008 Scott went to Wallace Presbyterian
Church in College Park, Maryland, where he served for more than nine years. He
is now the Presbyterian Church in America's Unity Fund Development Coordi-
nator. Scott and his wife, Julie, have two adult children, Emily and Jack.

———

I am no expert. I have blind spots. I am very, very much a work in
progress. And I have a story. It is my hope that this story—only the
beginning chapters so far, really—will be encouraging and helpful as
you answer God's call to take up a Gospel initiative of repentance and
reconciliation.

A Story of Confession and Repentance

Late in 2015 I met with other pastors in my denomination, the Presbyterian Church in America (PCA). We were editing and preparing an
overture that we would take before our denomination's annual

governing meeting (called the General Assembly). It was an overture of confession and repentance for failings during the Civil Rights Movement of the '60s. It was to be brought before our annual General Assembly in 2016. As we were concluding our work, a discussion began about the need to put the words of the proposed overture into action. Fine words, but how to find tangible ways for our repentance to bear fruit? Thoughts were bandied about, and in the end, I volunteered to try to put some ideas together and report back to my colleagues.

The essential question to answer is "What to do?" This question prompted a torrent of other questions: "What *can* we do in light of a less than stellar track record?" "What can we do that would be recognized as a Gospel-based initiative, and not just a humanistic band-aid?" "What can we do that would be sincere, not patronizing, and actually helpful?" "What can we do that would recognize and honor fellow image bearers?" "What can we do that would truly welcome and love brothers and sisters in Christ?" And finally, "Where does one even begin?" Daunting questions. Daunting, because behind all of them is the goal of expressing a repentance that would bear the fruit of Gospel reconciliation.

A Fact Provides Focus

It was in the face of these questions that I recalled a previous conversation with a friend. Earlier that year, an African American colleague informed me that there were only forty-seven African American Teaching Elders (pastors) in the PCA. The first thing I did when I sat down to try and answer the question, "What to do?" was to look up the total number of Teaching Elders in the PCA. In 2015 we had 4,713. And only forty-seven of them were African American. This grieved me.

And it helped in two ways: First, it provided a place to start, a first step, an initial answer to the question *"What* to do?" Second, it provided an idea of *how* to address the magnitude of the question: What to do about having only just under 1 percent of our Teaching Elders being African American?

That statistic helped define *what* it was we needed to accomplish because it gave us a measure of the distance between where we are and where we want to be. Rather than assuming the popular cultural notion that we come into parity with current demographics in our country, we needed to be aspiring to come into parity with another realm's demographic. Revelation 7:9 is a beautiful portrait of the Church in her glory: *"After this I looked, and behold, a great multitude that no one could number, from every nation, from all tribes and peoples and languages, standing before the throne and before the Lamb, clothed in white robes, with palm branches in their hands..."* And our denomination had forty-seven African American Teaching Elders (TEs). In 2020 it's not much different. We have 4,882 Teaching Elders. 51 are African American; 37 are Hispanic/Latino; 474 are Korean/Korean American and we have one Native American pastor. It is difficult to get statistics on other ethnicities, but I suspect them to be even smaller. Needless to say, we are a far cry from looking like Revelation 7:9. But these facts provide focus about what to do *first*.

Then the second question arose: "How do we move toward Revelation 7:9?" That original statistic (forty-seven African American Pastors) also made the path clear because it is a fact about our denomination's spiritual leadership, not the denomination as a whole. That helped to further focus and define first steps. A phrase from that Overture we had edited and improved brought the answer. It called upon "... our church's commitment to develop minority leadership at the congregational, presbytery, and denomination levels; and encourage a denomination-wide vision for and commitment to a more racially and ethnically diverse church in obedience to the Great Commission...." Minority colleagues in our denomination have already led the way in reaching people all around us that the PCA had, historically, not been reaching. It is already working. We have a scripturally mandated need to diversify our spiritual leadership. We decided to pursue obedience to this mandate through the Unity Fund.

The Unity Fund

Two words are key to understanding the Unity Fund. "Repentance" is a dreaded term because it is often misunderstood. "Reconciliation" is a fraught term because it is often misused. Reconciliation is the fruit of the repentance our denomination declared in 2016.

In 2016 the General Assembly called for the creation of a fund that would renew "our church's commitment to develop minority leadership at the congregational, presbytery, and denomination levels; and encourage a denomination-wide vision for and commitment to a more racially and ethnically diverse church in obedience to the Great Commission...."

The vision of the Unity Fund is to see future generations of ethnic-minority, Reformed Teaching Elders, Ruling Elders, and missionaries raised up in the Presbyterian Church in America. It hopes to do this by subsidizing the training, mentoring, and development of minority leadership in the PCA through partnership with churches and presbyteries. Currently, the Unity Fund Board has prayerfully set an annual budget of $200,000 and a goal of establishing a $5,000,000 Endowment. In light of this vision and mission, Unity Fund objectives include:

• Provide Seminary tuition subsidies.

• Provide General Assembly expense subsidies for underrepresented minority Ruling and Teaching Elders and Licentiates.

• Provide compensation expense subsidies for minorities serving as an Assistant Pastor in a PCA church for the first two years of their ministry in churches.

• Provide historical research expense subsidies to explore the role that reformed minority scholars, theologians, and pastors have played in church history.

• Provide resources and support for minorities interested in pursuing missions with Mission to the World and college ministry with Reformed University Fellowship.

Repentance and Growth in Grace

Both repentance and growth in grace are tied to the Unity Fund because its purpose is to be a fruit of repentance and a means to grow in grace. Some people questioned the wording of the overture of repentance because they personally did not feel guilty of the sins named. Some questioned the wording because they weren't even born during this era. I can respect their points of view, but our shared responsibility with our covenant family, as expressed in our membership vows, does need to be considered. One thing is truly unavoidable —whatever liability we may or may not carry with us for things done/not done in the past, those things have brought us to our present condition. To fail to address our current condition will inevitably lead us to become complicit with the misdeeds of the past. And in the end, the degree of guilt or complicity is moot because of a more fundamental question: "Have any of us actually (or ever!) loved our neighbor as ourselves?" The Unity Fund was created to give us a new way to love our neighbors as ourselves. The Second Great Command must be the ethos that drives the Unity Fund.

Repentance is God's great gift to those of us who are living in this time between salvation and glorification, and it is our most needed gift. That's why Martin Luther told us that "all of life is repentance," and the Puritans talked of the need to practice "continual repentance." For even what we call "growth in grace" is a form of repentance because we're being connected to the Gospel in a new way. Let's quickly define and review the practice of repentance and growth in grace. We need the reminder because, as my friend Pastor Dick Kauffman has often said, "We need to because we leak." We need to replenish ourselves with the truth because we invariably tend to fall out of touch with the truth.

Repentance is reconnecting with the Gospel. Growth in grace is a facet of it because it is making a new connection to the Gospel. First John 1:9 contains three elements of how one practices repentance: *"If we confess our sins, he is faithful and just to forgive us our sins and to cleanse us from all unrighteousness."* First, we take responsibility not only for our sin but what motivated us to sin. To confess means "to agree with." In this case we are agreeing with God that our sin is an offense against him, not merely grieving over the consequences of our sin. We have grieved him.

Second, we exercise our faith in the perfection and totality of Jesus' cross-work in calling it forgiven. He is faithful to forgive because he paid for that sin, too. And he is just to forgive because he paid for it all the way.

And then, third, we call on God to change us, having no illusions about our own morality or self-determination in terms of actually changing us redemptively. We turn to his Holy Spirit to guide and direct our hearts and efforts (Phil. 2:13) in what Frances Schaeffer used to call "active passivity." It is a saving grace because it is more than having hatred and grief over our sin. It is a simultaneous apprehension of the mercy and love of God in Christ. It is not one or the other—they must both be there in order for it to be Gospel repentance. Where they are together, true change, joy, and peace result.

Growth in grace occurs when we find a new way to connect our lives to the Gospel. It is a form of repentance, because it is the Holy Spirit's ministry in us, to make us aware of a new way to be conformed to the likeness of Christ. The Unity Fund is a new way to love our neighbor, and a new means of obeying the Great Commission.

As the Unity Fund was being birthed, I discovered a new way. It was created not only to express our "commitment to develop minority leadership," which we need to do, but also as a way to deal with the perception of the PCA. That perception of minorities became clear to me after I drafted the Unity Fund's first iteration. I sent it to three African American friends for whom I have deep respect. One of them, a long-time member of the PCA, a well-educated woman of great sophistication and poise, gave me this response: "Well, if this works, it will take the 'Whites Only' sign off the front door of the PCA and lay out a welcome mat for the rest of us." I was shocked by the depth of feeling expressed in that perception, which was backed by statistics. And we need a Gospel initiative to deal with it.

Reconciliation

Reconciliation has become fraught with baggage in this polarized age, but the essence of reconciliation is the eradication of enmity—God's enmity toward us (Rom. 5:9), and ours toward God (Rom. 5:10). Further, it's the replacement of hostilities with peace (Rom. 5:1) and even rejoicing (Rom. 5:11). It is brought about by the sacrifice of Jesus (Rom. 5:8–11). And it's motivated entirely by his love for us (Rom. 5:8). Therefore reconciliation takes away hostility between God and us, replaces it with peace between us, and is motivated by God's love for us.

This pattern is repeated in the Bible and includes eradication of enmity between people (Eph. 2:11–22). Further, it's the replacement of hostilities with peace (Eph. 2:14, 17) and unity (Eph. 2:14–22). It is brought about by the sacrifice of Jesus (Ephesians 2:13–16). And it's motivated entirely by His love for us (Eph. 2:1–10). Therefore reconciliation takes away hostility that has always existed in various forms between us, replaces it with peace and unity between us, and is motivated by God's love for us.

The Unity Fund is an attempt by our denomination to focus on saying to others that we honor you as image bearers of God (Gen. 1:31); we welcome you as fellow members of God's house (Eph. 2:19); we need each other to be who God made us to be (Eph. 2:21–22, Rev. 7:9); and we love you (John 15:12–17).

At this point in the story of the Unity Fund, it became apparent that this immediate need to show forth the fruit of repentance was opening us up to something much larger than ourselves. It was placing us on the continuum of redemptive history, fulfilling a new aspect of the Great Commission (Matt. 28:18–20). Reconnecting through the Gospel through repentance leads us to our place in redemptive history, with a role of eternal significance.

And when this reconnects us to the Gospel, and to our Servant/Savior whom we love, then reading the compelling narrative of redemptive history in Isaiah 49:1–16 becomes *our* story. We are included. We have a place in it. We are given a role to play. In short, we not only have the only one who will ever love us the way we need to be loved; he has given us lives worth living, lives of eternal significance, right now, today at our place in redemptive history.

This reconnection/new connection to the Gospel is happening in the PCA today. Overtures 43 is a signpost of the work of God's Spirit. It is a formal declaration of changes of heart and new Gospel initiatives springing up throughout the denomination, and it is exciting to see parts of it from my own limited perspective. Permit me to give you one thread of what I see happening in our part of redemptive history.

Our campus ministries, Reformed University Fellowship (RUF), are not only growing in number, they are also growing in diversity. Young individuals from diverse backgrounds are being called into ministry as a result of these campus ministries. The Unity Fund was brought into being to help make that happen. Reformed seminaries are eager for the Unity Fund to come into its own to help raise up minority leaders for the PCA. As I go to people and churches who are called to give to the Unity Fund, I find they want to do more about reaching out to their neighbors, particularly their minority neighbors. Yet they are perplexed, and asking the question "What else can we do?" One of the Unity Fund Board members is Dr. Irwyn Ince, who accepted a call from the Grace DC Church Planting Network (PCA) to found the Institute for Cross Cultural Mission (ICCM). The ICCM's mission is to guide churches in how to take those next steps. So multiple connections to redemptive history are being made, and it is an exciting time to be alive.

In June 2018, though still in its infancy in fundraising, the Unity Fund Board activated the first plank of the Fund by awarding seminary scholarships. That year they awarded 41. In 2019, the board awarded 67 scholarships and opened funding plank 2, helping present minority Ruling and Teaching Elders to attend and serve at our denomination's General Assemblies.

The redemptive paradigm shift is beginning to happen! 2019 also was the first year the the Unity Fund met its Primary Annual Budget of $200k. Also, more than $135k has been donated to the Primary Annual Budget, and there is presently less than $136k in the $5M Endowment.

Given the incredible racial turmoil and protest we see in our streets across America, people are more perplexed than ever about "What can I do that would actually be helpful and—better yet —redemptive?"

The PCA Unity Fund is an answer to that very question. Please join me in praying that God will connect us to those he's calling to join us in this redemptive paradigm shift.

Check out the Unity Fund's web site at pcamna.org/unity-fund/. Please pray about giving to the Unity Fund.

ABOUT WHITE BLACKBIRD BOOKS

White blackbirds are extremely rare, but they are real. They are blackbirds that have turned white over the years as their feathers have come in and out over and over again. They are a redemptive picture of something you would never expect to see but that has slowly come into existence over time.

There is plenty of hurt and brokenness in the world. There is the hopelessness that comes in the midst of lost jobs, lost health, lost homes, lost marriages, lost children, lost parents, lost dreams, loss.

But there also are many white blackbirds. There are healed marriages, children who come home, friends who are reconciled. There are hurts healed, children fostered and adopted, communities restored. Some would call these events entirely natural, but really they are unexpected miracles.

The books in this series are not commentaries, nor are they meant to be the final word. Rather, they are a collage of biblical truth applied to current times and places. The authors share their poverty and trust the Lord to use their words to strengthen and encourage his people. Consider these books as entries into the discussion.

May this series help you in your quest to know Christ as he is found in the Gospel through the Scriptures. May you look for and even expect the rare white blackbirds of God's redemption through Christ in your midst. May you be thankful when you look down and see your feathers have turned. May you also rejoice when you see that others have been unexpectedly transformed by Jesus.

Made in the USA
Columbia, SC
05 August 2020